CARDINAL NGUYEN VAN THUAN

ÉLISABETH NGUYEN THI THU HONG
and FR. STEFAAN LECLEIR

Cardinal Nguyen Van Thuan

Man of Joy and Hope

With a Foreword by
Cardinal Peter Turkson

Translated by Cyprian Blamires

IGNATIUS PRESS   SAN FRANCISCO

Original text:
Kardinaal Franciscus-Xaverius Nguyễn Văn Thuận. Getuigenis
© Betsaida, 's-Hertogenbosch, 2021

Some of the photos were taken by the authors of this book; others come from the archives of the Cellitinnen sisters in Cologne. The sketches are by Vu Dinh Lam, and the calligraphy is the work of To Bao An (Joseph).

Cover photograph used with the permission of the family of Cardinal Nguyen Van Thuan

Cover design by Roxanne Mei Lum

© 2025 by Ignatius Press, San Francisco
All rights reserved
ISBN 978-1-62164-737-9 (PB)
ISBN 978-1-64229-321-0 (eBook)
Library of Congress Control Number 2024950904
Printed in the United States of America ∞

For I think that God has exhibited us apostles as last of all, like men sentenced to death; because we have become a spectacle to the world, to angels and to men.... We are weak, but you are strong. You are held in honor, but we in disrepute.... When reviled, we bless; when persecuted, we endure; when slandered, we try to conciliate.

— I Cor 4:9–13

The joys and the hopes, the griefs and the anxieties of the men of this age, especially those who are poor or in any way afflicted, these are the joys and hopes, the griefs and anxieties of the followers of Christ. Indeed, nothing genuinely human fails to raise an echo in their hearts.

—Second Vatican Council,
Pastoral Constitution on the Church
in the Modern World
Gaudium et Spes (December 7, 1965), no. I

CONTENTS

Part III: Historical Background

FOREWORD

Cardinal Francis-Xavier Nguyen Van Thuan was my predecessor in the Pontifical Council for Justice and Peace. An intelligent and cultured man who was especially sensitive to the aspirations of his people, he guided the Diocese of Nha Trang between 1967 and 1975 with great pastoral zeal. During this period, Vietnam, his country, was devastated by war. As a pastor, he became deeply aware of his people's thirst for peace and dignity, and this marked him for life.

An insatiable thirst for justice and peace ran through his life like a red thread. It arose not merely from his personal and family experience but also from the experiences of many persecuted Vietnamese, especially those who managed to resist the temptation to hatred and bitterness in the midst of the harshest trials. Coming from a Catholic family much involved in the life of the Church and society, Cardinal Thuan counted among his ancestors several victims of the persecution of Christians in Vietnam. His family suffered as much under the colonial regime as during the Second World War, the Indochina War, and the Vietnam War. Four of his uncles met with violent deaths. Although his family lost wealth and honors, his relatives found in their faith the strength to forgive. Cardinal Thuan himself never stopped talking about hope, even in the harshest of trials.

He took as his episcopal motto "Joy and Hope" (*Gaudium et Spes*). These words from Vatican II took on an even greater importance for him after 1975. A short time after his nomination as archbishop coadjutor of Saigon in April of that year, he was deprived of his freedom for thirteen long years. But isn't the Lord always there to comfort us in darker days? During the first months of his imprisonment, Bishop Thuan wrote 1,001 words of hope on the leaves of a calendar. Intended initially for the Christians of his diocese, these meditations became known more widely. Placed later in solitary confinement and then sent to a reeducation camp, Bishop Thuan managed to compose several works on hope. He followed in the footsteps of Saint Paul, who likewise wrote important letters while in prison for his Christian brothers in their trials.

When he was released from prison in 1988, his family found him transformed. Bishop Thuan had suffered terribly, not just in his body but also in his soul. The years he had spent in a spiritual dark night meant that hope had become more than a mere episcopal motto. In the darkness of his captivity and in his extreme poverty, he had united himself more deeply to Christ forsaken and crucified. In prison, in the greatest secrecy, he managed to celebrate the Eucharist. Proclaiming the Resurrection of Christ, he brought that divine life to other prisoners. Jesus, who kept him going through his trials, pressed him to reach out not just to his neighbors but also to his enemies, who were often touched by the sincerity of his friendship, by his serenity, and by his faith. While he was bishop of Nha Trang, Thuan was overloaded with work, but as a prisoner, he could say with Saint Paul: "I will all the more gladly boast of my weaknesses, that the power of Christ may rest upon me. For the sake of

Christ, then, I am content with weaknesses, insults, hardships, persecutions, and calamities" (2 Cor 12:9–10).

This book is based mainly on the numerous testimonies we have from his friends and his former pupils, as well as on the letters he wrote to his family during his captivity. People who knew him well, his younger sister, and even his jailers give us an idea of this exceptional man. Research conducted in Rome has yielded further information about his journey through life. In the prisons of Vietnam as much as in his work at the Vatican for Pope Saint John Paul II, Thuan never lost his deep sense of union with the Lord.

A son of the exceptional people of Vietnam, Cardinal Thuan inspires us and helps us know Christ more in our hearts, as he himself did through meditation on His Word. Our Lady of La Vang guided him toward his refugee brothers and, more broadly, toward every person seeking truth and love. His simplicity and his humility are a model for the evangelization of the modern world: they call us to greater charity and unity. At the end of his days, when he was already suffering greatly from the malady that would end his life, Cardinal Thuan found the strength and the joy to preach a retreat to fifty priests. One certitude fortified his hope on the threshold of eternal life: everyone who is baptized, without exception, is called to holiness.

In the person of the cardinal, the Dawn of the East comes to meet us, the epiphany of a new life. Let us bless the Lord, for He is ever sending us saints who, like Cardinal Francis-Xavier Nguyen Van Thuan, remind us that God is always greater than evil and that He is present, by our side, as Father of the poor and Prince of Peace. Let us give thanks for Cardinal Thuan, who never stopped proclaiming that joy and hope in Christ are not extinguished even in the throes of the worst trials.

> Christians are light in the darkness,
> Salt where life has no zest,
> And hope in the midst of a humanity which has lost
>   its hope.[1]

—Cardinal Peter K. A. Turkson, Rome

---

[1] Francis Xavier Nguyen Van Thuan, *The Road of Hope: A Gospel from Prison*, trans. John Peter Pham (North Palm Beach, Fla.: Wellspring, 2018), 199n950.

INTRODUCTION

This book is intended to present the impressive figure of Venerable Cardinal Nguyen Van Thuan (Francis-Xavier) to a wider public.[1]

Having had the joy of knowing Cardinal Thuan, I asked Madame Nguyen Thi Thu Hong (his youngest sister, Élisabeth) to give me some interviews on Radio Maria (NL) in 2014, so as to make more widely known the life and spirituality not just of the cardinal but also of other members of his family: his grandparents; his father, Am; his mother, Hiep; his brothers and sisters; his uncles and aunts. When presenting Élisabeth's testimony, I have used italics.

Madame Hong is mainly referred to here under her baptismal name of Élisabeth, a Christian name that I use very respectfully, for respect is something the Vietnamese people rate very highly. The cardinal will frequently be referred to as Thuan, the name that Élisabeth and her family used for him. The Vietnamese refer to him not as Cardinal Nguyen but as Cardinal Thuan.

The various testimonies are presented chronologically. I have supplemented them with helpful information that will make it easier for the reader to follow the trajectory

---

[1] A person who receives the title Venerable may be presented to Christians as an example but not as the object of public veneration. Congregation for the Causes of Saints, *Sanctorum Mater* (May 17, 2007), appendix, art. 7.

13

of Cardinal Thuan's life. They make up the first part of this book.

Thanks to Élisabeth, I got to know Thuan's family and discovered the exceptional character of his relatives. She will give us more details in the second part.

The third part contains information helpful for a better understanding of Vietnamese history and culture and of the individuals and places referred to in the testimonies.

The division of this work into three parts corresponds to the three stages in my journey into the discovery of Cardinal Thuan's rich personality. The book approaches him from a point of view that is important in Vietnamese culture: that of family and roots. Élisabeth tells us about Thuan's spiritual family and about how he became a brother or father to a great number of people.

Vietnamese spelling is used here for places and persons. The first part of the name of a person indicates the family or the clan; then comes what we think of as the middle name. In the case of women, the term *Thi* (meaning "woman of the clan of") would have been added in the past, but this is frequently omitted nowadays. In the last place comes the forename most often used. Christians follow the practice of writing their baptismal name before their family name. In this book, which also mentions non-Christians, the Christian names are put in parentheses.

This work is dedicated to those Vietnamese who have suffered for their faith, for their desire for independence, and for the preservation of the fundamental values of their culture. I met the cardinal and his sister through the Cellitinnen sisters in Cologne.[2] Their desire to make known

[2] Cellitinnen zur hl. Maria. See appendix 2.

this great figure of the Church, their encouragement, and their material support have made this publication possible. Élisabeth and I have both also benefited from the precious assistance of those persons in Cologne who maintain the archives of Cardinal Thuan in Germany, and we want to express our gratitude to them. Thanks as well to all who have been involved in transcribing recordings of interviews or in proofreading this text. I am most particularly grateful to all those Vietnamese whom I have had the opportunity to meet throughout my stay in their beautiful country. They gave me not only unique confirmation of the information I gathered elsewhere but also real insights into the impact of the cardinal on the local Church. I was particularly touched by the infectious joy and great charity of those who live by his spirituality.[3]

Élisabeth and I would like to dedicate this book especially to Dr. Vinh Thua (1953–2020), closely related to the cardinal. We have all been deeply touched by his solid faith, expressed in the immense help he provided to the needy during his life of giving. Élisabeth, who was very close to him, cherishes the memory of her dear cousin, known for his generosity and strong attachment to his Vietnamese roots. May he now share his Master's happiness (Mt 25:21).

As a priest, I put this book together out of admiration for the magnificent testimony of faith of those Vietnamese Christians whom I got to know through Cardinal Thuan;

---

[3] Certain persons I met in Vietnam asked not to have their names mentioned in this publication. I therefore did not name them here, but I want them to know how greatly I appreciate the warmth of their welcome, their often very moving testimony of faith and charity, and their commitment to the spirit of the cardinal. [The notes that are not in italics are by Stefaan Lecleir.]

they have touched me deeply. May this small volume touch your hearts likewise!

This English translation was produced by Dr. Cyprian Blamires. As a theologian, he knew the right terms to use. He was a volunteer, and he did this immense work with precision. Special thanks to him!

—Father Stefaan Lecleir

Part I

The Cardinal's Life and Message

1

Thuan's Early Life

Introduction

Thuan was born on April 17, 1928, in Phu Cam, a village near Hue, the imperial capital,[1] into a cultured milieu deeply attached to Vietnamese traditions.

The house where he was born was close to the cathedral and across the beautiful River of Perfumes from the palace. His maternal grandfather was a counselor and minister of the emperor. His forebears had been involved in the construction of the cathedral. In his childhood, Thuan was greatly influenced by those members of his family who played a crucial role in the history of Vietnam and in the life of the local Church. He learned when very young to

[1] Back then, Hue was both the geographical and political center of Vietnam. At the start of the twentieth century, Phu Cam was a hamlet with about a hundred houses, and almost all the inhabitants were Christians. Even though the village was not far from the palace, a center of persecutions, the faithful in it felt secure in their fervent and very close-knit community. Today the village has become part of the town of Hue. Almost all the old houses have been demolished. The family home has become a memorial. The area around the imperial palace is the old historical center, but the cathedral of Phu Cam lies on the other side of the river in the more modern part of the town. A modern building now stands on the site of the old cathedral.

Seeing Phu Cam firsthand helps us appreciate the
natural protection the wide river once afforded
against the cruelty of some emperors.

look on his family, his church community, and Vietnam
itself as a priceless treasure. Élisabeth gives us a very precious testimony on Thuan's earliest years.

Childhood

*A year after she married my father, Nguyen Van Am (Tadéo,
1901–1993), my mother, Ngo Dinh Thi Hiep (Élisabeth, 1903–
2005), gave birth to a son, Xuan, whose name means "spring".
While she was pregnant with her second child, Xuan fell victim to
cholera, which, at the time, was killing thousands of Vietnamese,
and my parents went through a period of great sadness.*

*The death of Xuan was the end of an era in my mother's life;
it was like the end of spring. Seven months after the death of*

The old cathedral

Xuan, my brother Thuan was born. His name means "according to the will [of God]". Thuan was my parents' second child, but as Xuan had died very young, Thuan took on the role of the eldest son. When he was born, my parents made a special offering of him to God. They had lost their first son and promised that the second would be devoted to the Lord. My mother never stopped telling him: "You are a gift from God. You must always keep that in mind. You must always live in His presence." Later, when he was languishing in prison, the memory of those words was an enormous help to him.

The loss of a child leaves a mark on the heart of a mother for the rest of her life.

Thuan was a boy just like any other. He loved to spend his holidays and his free time playing with his friends. Whenever the children of the family or of the village organized games involving mock battles between two sides, Thuan was often the last to be chosen as a team member because of his unwillingness to "kill". So he was given the job of military chaplain, and he would sometimes begin the games with a "Mass". To do this, he would make a chasuble out of paper sacks that had been used for building materials. Later, in prison, when the Masses were no longer a game, the materials used to celebrate the Eucharist were just as primitive.

Thuan and other youngsters his age would sometimes go swimming in the river. They did not have any swimsuits, but it was hot enough for them to swim in the light clothing they wore, as it dried so quickly. One day, a girl took her dress off unashamedly and jumped into the water. From then on, Thuan began to tease her by calling her Eve,[2] which shows that even as a youngster, he had quite an original sense of humor.

The family home was big, and it housed a chapel. Priests came to celebrate Mass and often stayed overnight. Whenever a priest stayed with us, the whole family enjoyed the fine meals served in his honor, but one of my brothers would have to make a small sacrifice: he had to give up his bed for the guest!

Throughout his life, my father was always regarded as the head of the family. Even when Thuan became a priest and then a bishop, he was still a son in the family, and Am continued to lead the family prayers. A very organized man, my father ran a flourishing construction business with a large staff, and he was away all day managing it. Although he was home only in the evenings and on Sundays, he always took full part in all family events, not just in happy times but also in dark ones. My father's devotion to Saint Joseph says much about his personality. Less by his words, and more by his work and by his attentive presence, he fully assumed his paternal responsibility for our education.

For some years, Thuan went to Sainte-Thérèse School, run by the Vietnamese congregation Sisters of Amantes de la Croix

---

[2] It was one of our cousins, Nguyen Thi Dong, who kept closely in touch with Thuan until the end of his life. [The notes in italics contain supplementary information supplied by Élisabeth.]

Chapel in the family home in Phu Cam

(Lovers of the Cross), before moving on to Pellerin School.[3] Our maternal uncle Diem,[4] who lived close to us, contributed directly to Thuan's education. Among other things, he taught him the Chinese language and letters and explained to him the position of our country in the international context. A man of very deep faith, Diem was customarily very guarded about his inner life, but he would open up to his nephew. The conversations between Diem

---

[3] This school was run by the Brothers of the Christian Schools (a congregation founded by Saint Jean-Baptiste de La Salle, 1651–1719). It was called Pellerin School in memory of Bishop François-Marie Pellerin (1813–1862), a French missionary of the Paris Foreign Missions Society.

[4] Diem's name will crop up many times in parts 2 and 3. This maternal uncle was a scholar and a man of prayer. He was also very involved in national politics.

and Thuan locked in the Christian education that my brother received at home and in the parish.

Almost every day, my mother would say to us: "When you are in lessons or playing on the playground, never forget that you live in the presence of God. Try to behave in a way that will please Him." On the day of their First Communion, Sister Maria, who had led the preparatory catechesis, asked the children: "You are going to receive Jesus today. What will you ask Him for?" Thuan replied: "I am going to pray to Him to help me live my life in a way that pleases Him. I want to stay under God's gaze all the time, but I don't know what His gaze is. I would like to see Him, but I don't know how." The Sister told my mother she was sure my brother was called to become a priest. Much later, Thuan was to tell me, with tears in his eyes: "I was crazy enough to want to see the Lord, but in prison, I saw Him in my enemy!" He was completely changed by his prison experience. To me, he was no longer just a brother or a bishop but a man profoundly touched by God.

Our mother took particular care over Thuan's education from his youngest days. She told him Bible stories every evening and spoke about the Vietnamese martyrs, some of whom were our ancestors. She also instilled in him a love for our country.

Jesus sets an example of love for one's enemies.

Our mother shared with Thuan her faith in the Eucharist, and, when still very young, he showed he had absorbed this by his limitless devotion to our aunt Giao, an impoverished widow. She suffered from tuberculosis, a disease that, at the time, was highly contagious and almost incurable, even with the help of medicines, which were very difficult to obtain in Vietnam. For fear of contagion, no choir boy wanted to accompany the parish priests on their visits to the sick. Thuan happily volunteered to help our *old parish priest and walked with him every day, before or after school, to our aunt's home to bring her the Body of Christ. He continued to support her affectionately up to the day of her death. "Why take such a risk?" people would ask him. His answer consistently reflected his faith: "We have the duty and the honor to take the Bread of Life to our brothers and sisters so that Christ can bring them strength and life."*

At the Minor Seminary (1941–1947)

When he was only thirteen years old, Thuan, already fired with faith, expressed the desire to go to the An Ninh Minor Seminary,[5] situated in the countryside north of Hue, more than sixty miles from the family home. This was in 1941,[6] when the Japanese had just invaded Vietnam with the complicity of the French administration. Thuan had heard about the An Ninh Minor Seminary from his uncle Thuc, who was a priest, and from his uncle Nhu, who had studied there for a while. Every vocation is different. Thuan's vocation was personal and courageous. The eldest son of the house had to go away for the entire school year.

At that time, our uncle Thuc often visited our family. This gave him the opportunity to help nurture my brother's vocation. Meanwhile, Diem taught Thuan that life choices are not to be

---

[5] A minor seminary is a secondary school for boys who are contemplating the priesthood. Both pupils and teachers are boarders and take part in prayers and religious ceremonies. In the West, the minor seminaries were converted into colleges in the 1960s.

[6] Some sources specify 1940, others 1941. He himself talked in a sermon in Puy-en-Velay (March 25, 1993) about a missionary he had known and greatly appreciated from the Le Puy area and said it was in 1941, the year when he left for the seminary.

based primarily on advice from others or on parents' wishes but must be personal decisions consciously made. Later, when Thuan himself had to assist seminarians, he would help them discern their vocation based on their relationship with God.

In the family, Thuan's departure for the minor seminary was met with joy and gratitude but also with sadness and, indeed, anguish. It was a real challenge to see this young boy leave his family just when war had broken out. On the eve of his departure, our grandmother said to him: "Thuan, tomorrow, when you leave with your dad, pick up your suitcase and don't look back. If you see me and your mother, the sadness might get to you, and you might be tempted to give up on your plan to follow God's call."

The next day, the two men quietly left the house. Thuan was not the only one leaving for An Ninh. There were other parents there waiting with their sons for the boat, and they whispered to one another about Thuan: "That little fellow will be back with his mum in two weeks; he won't be able to cope at the seminary." When Thuan heard this, he felt embarrassed. Nonetheless, he showed great determination, accepting without objection a simplicity of life and an austerity such as he had never experienced before. He did not know it then, but his efforts would prepare him for the trials to come and would later enable him to survive in prison.

Human dignity cannot be reduced to the level of intellectual formation.

Though our grandmother did spoil my brother a lot, she was and remained, first and foremost, a woman of prayer. She always carried her rosary with her. Every evening, we would eat together as a family, and then we all went to the chapel in our house. There was room for about twenty people. The servants joined the family for prayers in the evening. After prayer, our grandmother stayed in the chapel while the others went back to their various activities.

But whenever home, Thuan prayed the Rosary with her and stayed with her. After his ordination, he would often say: "There are people who can't read or write, but their faith and their devotion to the Rosary have produced vocations for our country." The Virgin played a crucial role throughout my brother's life. He lived his times of suffering as well as his times of freedom under the gaze of Mary.

The minor seminary was run by priests from the Paris Foreign Missions Society (MEP). Contact with these witnesses to the gospel gradually led Thuan to modify his earlier views regarding the French colonization policy, views that had ignored France's rich cultural heritage and the faith that inspired the country's missionaries. His encounter with the MEP priests taught Thuan a great deal about the evangelization of Vietnam. His horizons were broadened. Present in several Asian countries, including Burma (Myanmar), Cambodia, China, Korea, and Thailand, these priests, dedicating their lives to the missions, had built up a considerable knowledge of the various cultures and could share that knowledge with their students. Thuan was a naturally gifted student: he learned various languages and was outstanding in Latin and Chinese.[7] Latin would prove very useful to him when he studied canon law in Rome in the 1950s. Coming from an educated family, Thuan very much enjoyed reading and spent a great deal of time in the library. He loved to read the lives of saints, such as the Curé d'Ars (1786–1859) and Thérèse of Lisieux (1873–1897). He discovered the writings of Blessed Dom Marmion[8] and

---

[7] On one of my visits to the Pontifical Council for Justice and Peace in the late 1990s, Bishop Thuan took me out for a meal in a Chinese restaurant, where he chatted amicably with the staff in their language.

[8] An Irishman, Dom Marmion (1858–1923) was abbot of the Benedictine Abbey of Maredsous (Belgium).

the life of Théophane Vénard (MEP, 1829–1861), a young French priest martyred in Tonkin in the northern part of present-day Vietnam. Thuan was inspired by Théophane both as a spiritual friend of Saint Thérèse of Lisieux and as a young martyr who would later become a model for him in his experience of incarceration.

Thuan's fellow students used to say that he had a wicked sense of humor and was always up for a joke—for example, mimicking the voices of other students or professors or sisters who worked at the seminary. He was capable of perfectly reproducing the partic-

One of the fruits of hope is humor.

ular accent with which missionaries spoke Vietnamese.[9] But he could be quite serious when he had to be. In 1946, when three seminarians

drowned and only one of the bodies was recovered, Thuan volunteered to wash the body and pray all night at its bedside while preparations were made for the burial.

The Allies began bombarding Japanese positions in 1942, and the seminary organized a pilgrimage to La Vang, north of Hue, where the Virgin had appeared in 1798 to a group of persecuted Christians. This place is the most important Marian shrine in the country, and Thuan cherished a particular devotion to Our Lady of La Vang all his life.

Although the buildings of the minor seminary were not badly damaged during the hostilities, accommodation there was very rudimentary. The war situation did not make for an easy life for the residents. The Hue area was devastated, as Thuan could see when he went home for his vacations. Japanese occupation, supported

---

[9] The Vietnamese alphabet contains a great number of diacritical marks, which are aids for good pronunciation. The missionaries found it very difficult to acquire a mastery of the wealth of vowels as indicated by the marks.

by the Vichy regime,[10] was brutal. Life then was very difficult. In the North, the Communists were gaining ground. The country was bleeding from multiple wounds. Bombs were destroying our town, and many people were homeless. The seminary was hated by the nationalists, who linked Christians and especially French priests with the colonizers and the troubles that the country was going through. But Thuan always said that within the walls of the little seminary there was a peaceful atmosphere. For him, it was a place where God

Our Lady of La Vang

was present. He was not exaggerating when he claimed that several of the priests there were saints.

The example of Father Nguyen Van Thich (Joseph-Marie, 1891–1978) impressed him deeply. A Vietnamese priest and convert from Buddhism and a friend of Diem's, Father Thich always carried the Word of God over his heart to remind the students that this Word stands firm, even in the worst of storms. Thuan wrote later that Father Thich gave him his copy of the New Testament, which he then kept under his shirt throughout his priestly ministry. To him, it was a precious treasure, even though the book was very old and thumb-worn with use. When

---

[10] The Vichy regime was installed after the armistice was signed in June 1940 between the Third Reich and the Pétain government.

*he was asked why he was so attached to it, Thuan would tell
us about Father Thich and his teaching: "The Word of God is
the most precious thing we have, and we should always have it
with us wherever we go."*

There is nothing more precious than to see the power of the Word lived around you.

*Later on, he explained to us
how it was that priest's example in particular that was a
source of great inspiration to
him during his periods of isolation in captivity. "I held on*

*all those years", Thuan would say. "[His] word is a lamp to my
feet and a light to my path [Ps 119:105]." Unfortunately, this
precious New Testament has been lost.*[11]

*It was another priest, Father Marie-Georges Cressonnier,
who inspired his great devotion to the Eucharist and whose
example led him to risk his life for love of the Blessed Sacrament. Father Bui Quang Tich (André, 1895–1978), one of
his French teachers at An Ninh,*[12] *was a model of simplicity for
Thuan. As an educator, he showed a deep attachment to the
young people in his care; his method of discipline was based not
on corporal punishment but on charity, a charity that led him to
guide young people toward Jesus. A serious fault by one of the
students would sadden him greatly, but, as rector, he would not
act harshly but would prompt the offender to go to the chapel,*

---

[11] Well-informed Vietnamese who are familiar with the conditions of his
imprisonment have told me that Bishop Thuan wrote about three hundred
pages during his incarceration: they contained passages from the Word of God
that he remembered. These texts nourished his prayer life and served as an aid
in the often-clandestine celebrations of the Eucharist.

[12] Like all the Francophone priests, Father Bui Quang Tich taught French
to several classes. He was appointed head of the minor seminary from 1945 to
1953, while Thuan was a pupil there. At the end of his life, he joined the Cis-
tercians in Saigon.

where Jesus could touch the youngster's heart with His love and forgiveness.

Finally, a word about one of Thuan's fellow students: Tran Van Hoai (Philippe, 1929–2010). They remained in close touch throughout their lives. He, too, was ordained, and he became a teacher and then rector at the minor seminary. From the 1980s onward, he did great work in Vatican departments in behalf of Vietnamese refugees. He chaired the committee for the canonization of the martyrs of our country and took an active role in the dissemination of Thuan's writings.

The end of the Second World War was a period of great suffering for the Vietnamese population: famine, ultimate battles between Japanese and French troops, the imprisonment of MEP missionaries. Only after being served the two atomic bombs did the Japanese capitulate. Ignoring the longing of many Vietnamese for independence, the French set out to reclaim Indochina. Vietnam thus slid—almost seamlessly—from the Second World War into the Indochina War. Over the winter of 1946–1947, while Thuan was still at An Ninh, his family had to flee the Hue district.

At the Major Seminary (1947–1953)

Thuan's call to the priesthood remained strong. In 1947, he moved to the major seminary, in the parish of Kim Long, west of the imperial palace of Hue.[13] For a while, during his early years there, Thuan was thinking of becoming a Jesuit or a Benedictine.

---

[13] During this period, the missionaries were still in charge of the major seminary.

With our uncle Diem, he sometimes visited a monastery at Thien An, in the Hue Diocese.[14]

While he was at the minor seminary, Thuan could see his parents, brothers, and sisters only over the summer break. During his years of preparation for the priesthood, contact with family members was easier, especially with our sister Niem,[15] *who at that time was living in a Carmelite monastery at Kim Long, near the major seminary and Phu Cam. I was only a little girl at that time, and my older sisters did not usually take me with them when they went to play outside. Thuan enjoyed spending time with me, and I loved his calmness. He had a lot of patience. I was forever asking him innocent questions, but he never got tired of answering them.*

Actually, he was very attentive to all the children. My sister and I went to school in France, where we learned children's rhymes that we liked to sing as loudly as possible. My elder brother was the only one who could put up with our boisterous voices—and he often joined in. One of his hobbies was keeping pet birds and fish, which he would entrust to my care when he was away. When I talked to him about how ugly and dangerous snakes were, he would talk about the beauties of birds and nature. He wanted to make me learn to see the presence of God in His little creatures.

Our uncle Diem had become Thuan's "godfather" after the death in 1943 of Nguyen Van Le, his baptismal godfather and the husband of our aunt Hoang.[16] *Thuan could communicate only*

[14] Visitors to the monastery today will still find a fervent community and receive a joyful welcome. Much of their estate is devoted to agriculture. Close to the monastery lies one of the most beautiful areas in the region: hills and forests make the place a marvel of creation.

[15] For more details on the family members, see part 2, devoted to the cardinal's family background.

[16] Nguyen Van Le was a rich businessman. After his death, his widow continued to run the business and so was able to support several members of the family financially.

Diem liked to go for walks in the vicinity because he delighted in the peace and quiet he found there.

sporadically with Diem because our uncle often had to go into hiding during this turbulent period. After 1950, when the country was divided by the conflict between the French and the Communists, Diem, known for his anti-Communism and anti-colonialism, decided to emigrate.

Despite all the fighting in the Hue area, the Indochina War did not stop Thuan from devoting himself to his priestly training. He loved to read the letters of Saint Paul and managed to commit them to memory. He did the same with the Psalms. The Rosary and the Eucharist were fundamental parts of his life as a seminarian.

Father Hoa Nguyen Van Hien (Simon, 1906–1973), one of his teachers, was his spiritual director. Ordained bishop of Saigon (1955–1960) and then of Da Lat (1960–1973), Bishop Hien chose as his episcopal motto "We proclaim to the world Jesus Crucified." Thuan's writings from his time in prison often reflect the spirituality of Bishop Hien. They worked together in the 1970s in the formation of the faithful for the work of justice and reconciliation.

Always keen to learn, Thuan steeped himself in the works of Dom Columba Marmion and also in *The Imitation of Christ* and the lives of the saints—Don Bosco (1815–1888), among others. Later, as a teacher, he would apply the principles of this saint: for Don Bosco, better results in education are to be achieved by way of a stimulating example than by punishments. Thuan enjoyed studying the *Summa Theologica* of Thomas Aquinas, and he relaxed with *Don Camillo* by Giovanni Guareschi; he had a particular liking for the simple conversations that Don Camillo had with the crucified Christ.[17]

---

[17] André Nguyen Van Chau, *The Miracle of Hope: Francis Xavier Nguyen Van Thuan; Political Prisoner, Prophet of Peace* (Boston: Pauline Books and Media, 2003), 91–97.

Thuan was deeply moved by the life of the Jesuit father Blessed Miguel Pro (1891–1927), martyred under the dictatorship in Mexico, and it later helped him cope with the challenges that he himself was to face: Father Pro forgave his executioners as he died.

> Saint Thomas Aquinas calls us to love our country.

Thuan had other things in common with this martyr. Both in his time as a student and during his clandestine ministry in Mexico, Father Pro was a cheerful man, always keen to promote a happy atmosphere among the students. Although he wasn't as adept as Thuan at mimicking his teachers' voices, he did like to draw cartoons on the blackboard. Father Pro's sense of humor often enabled him to save himself from dangerous situations. He loved to slip little humorous asides into the middle of profoundly serious letters.[18] In Thuan's case, it was in conversation that he really sparkled!

[18] There is an interesting biography of Father Pro, written shortly after his death: Antonio Dragon, S.J., *Pour le Christ-Roi: Miguel-Augustin Pro de la Compagnie de Jésus* (Montreal: Imprimerie du Messager, 1928). It seems this is the work that Thuan read.

The cardinal practiced the virtues heroically. That is why we have chosen to adorn each chapter with the calligraphy of a virtue.

Tin
Faith

2

Thuan the Priest

Curate at Dong Hoi

On June 11, 1953, Thuan was ordained to the priesthood. The bishop of Hue sent him north, to a sixty-seven-year-old priest, Father Nguyen Van Tam (Simon), in the large parish of Tam Toa. This parish was in the town of Dong Hoi (in the Quang Binh Province), more than sixty miles north of Hue. Although located in a different province, that parish was under the jurisdiction of the Diocese of Hue. The priest already had three other curates, two of whom had been ordained a few years before Father Thuan. A French military chaplain—the Indochina War was coming to an end—also lived in the big presbytery. Father Thuan arrived in August. There, even more than at the seminary, he experienced the reality of war. He realized the extent to which the Communists had infiltrated the country, even though the French had arrested and imprisoned a great number of them.

At the time, Thuan was not in the best of health. "Good grief!" the Tam Toa parish priest said to him. "I asked the bishop for someone healthy, but you look rather frail to me, more like a young bamboo stick; I fear you won't last very long here." The priest assigned Thuan to lighter responsibilities. He had no sermons to prepare; his ministry consisted mainly of visiting prisoners, lepers, and other patients in the hospital. Our mother wanted to know how well he was doing in his ministry. At the time, there were a lot of Communists in the prisons, and my mother was afraid that they would attack him, but Thuan reassured her: "Mum, I went to see them to hear their sufferings, to show them love in their despair, and to remind each one of them that God loves him and is close to him, even if these wretches are hated by many.

Man is greater
than his actions
and his thoughts.

"I try to share their pains and their joys; I cry and sing with them. I try to be a witness to the love of God, for the Lord wants to be in their midst. I even share the Word of God with these Communists. Above all I remind them that God is ever forgiving and that He does not look at them in the same way as do those who condemn them."

Sickness and a Miracle

As the parish priest had foreseen, Father Thuan fell ill fairly quickly. Shortly after his arrival in Tam Toa, the town suffered serious flooding. Father Thuan joined forces with the scouts to help the victims. Cold, damp, and fatigue unquestionably weakened his health. In April 1954, he was diagnosed with tuberculosis and was referred to a hospital in Saigon.

A French priest had arranged for him to be admitted at the Grall Hospital,[1] in the South. According to the doctors, his

---

[1] The military barracks where French soldiers had been cared for in the early years of colonization have been transformed into a proper hospital. In 1925, the institution was named after the military doctor Charles Grall. By 1950, the

left lung was diseased, and they decided it would have to be removed. But first Thuan needed to recover from his fatigue and regain his strength. He was put on a nutritional diet with vitamins. Just before the operation, the doctors decided to perform yet another X-ray to check the condition of the other lung. Thuan waited long hours before they returned with the results. As it turned out, the doctors were bewildered: all trace of Christian compassion is charity. It is eternal. *tuberculosis had disappeared! Nobody could explain the cure. Thuan wrote to his mother: "There has been a miracle: my lung is clear. I am coming home."*

As a child, my brother had shown great compassion for our aunt Giao, who suffered from tuberculosis. Now he himself had been miraculously healed of that illness. Was this perhaps a kind of wink from God, hinting at His recognition that Thuan had acted well at the time of our aunt's illness?

Parish Priest in Hue

The Geneva Accords, signed in 1954, resulted in the division of Vietnam into two parts. My uncle Diem was called back to the country to form a government in the South. The departure of French troops and the government takeover by the Communists in the North led to the exodus of about a million North Vietnamese who sought refuge in the young republic in the South. During that unsettled period, Thuan was appointed parish priest of Saint-François-Xavier Church in Hue, where quite a few French lived. The church had been built between 1914 and

---

hospital had five hundred beds and was considered the finest medical institution in East Asia.

1918 by one of our paternal forebears. Thuan first assisted and later replaced French priest Father Pierre Richard (Father Co Phan).[2] *This missionary had been one of his teachers at the minor seminary and had taken care of Thuan during his illness. It is thanks to him that my brother was able to secure admission to the French hospital in Saigon.*

Thuan prepared to receive the influx of refugees in his parish— a very delicate task! He made great efforts to ensure that the gradually departing French and the new arrivals could live together in harmony. Although our family was committed to the struggle for the independence of Vietnam by peaceful means, we always appreciated French culture and maintained excellent relations with the missionaries.[3] *Everyone knew that reconstructing the country was going to be a monumental task. Aside from his duties as parish priest, Thuan was also appointed chaplain at the Pellerin School, at the main clinic in town, and at Thua Thien, a provincial prison camp.*

[2] Pierre Richard (1910–1993), born in Cornimont (Vosges), was ordained a priest in Saint-Dié on July 11, 1934, and joined the Foreign Missions Seminary in 1937. He went to the Hue mission on September 15, 1938. After studying the language in Phu Cam, he was appointed to a teaching post at the minor seminary in An Ninh, and in 1945, he was appointed in Hue to the parish of the French community. In 1955, Father Richard left Saint-François-Xavier parish and was replaced by Father Simon Nguyen Van Lap (1911–2001) after Thuan left for Rome. In 1956, Father Richard became military chaplain in Saigon (Gérard Moussay and Brigitte Appavou, *Répertoire des membres de la Société des Missions Étrangères (1659–2004): Ordre alphabétique suivi de l'ordre chronologique* [Paris: Archives des Missions Étrangères, 2004], no. 3599). In the living room of the present presbytery, where the parish priest gave me a warm welcome, you can see a great many photos of the old church, of the damage done by the battles that took place during the wars, and of its restoration. Portraits of all the priests who have served the parish hang around the room.

[3] Colonization was primarily a political undertaking, but Thuan's family had sufficient intellectual finesse to recognize the positive contributions made by French civilization.

Return to Studies

Thuan was sent to Rome from 1956 to 1959 to study at the Pontifical Urban University, where he earned a doctorate in canon law. His doctoral thesis was titled "The International Organization of Military Chaplaincies".⁴ In it, he dealt with the structure of chaplaincies, the pastoral support needed by young soldiers and military wives, and the services offered to children of the employees. He drew from his experience in Hue, where he had volunteered as chaplain to the armed forces, hospitals, prisons, and leper colonies. It was a brilliant thesis, and Thuan was awarded his doctorate summa cum laude.

While in Europe, he visited Fátima and Ireland, among other places.

On a pilgrimage to Lourdes, he had a premonition that he would be called to suffer for his country. During one of her apparitions at Lourdes, had the Virgin not said to Bernadette: "I do not promise you happiness in this world, but in the next"?⁵ The words that the Virgin had addressed to Bernadette about suffering seemed to be meant personally for him too. It was as if Mary were speaking straight to his heart, yet Thuan did not want to compare himself with Bernadette. Could it be his imagination going wild? He spoke only to my mother about this spiritual experience; he shared with her his absolute conviction that the Virgin had wanted to communicate an important message to him. She was scared. "What is going to happen?" she wondered. Later, when Thuan was enduring intense suffering, both he and my mother acquired a better understanding of this mystical intuition.

---

⁴ The Latin title is "Studium comparativum de organisatione capellanorum militum in mundo".

⁵ Bernadette was to experience very great suffering, even though her vocation as a religious was fulfilling.

Our Lady of Fátima

During his stay in Europe, he also decided to learn German over the summer. So it was that he spent several summer holidays in a convent of the Cellitinnen sisters: they had various houses in the Archdiocese of Cologne where he could easily offer his priestly services, since Mass, in those days, was celebrated in Latin. He remained in very close touch with the sisters until the end of his life, and they set up a little museum to commemorate his presence in Cologne.[6] The letters he wrote to the sisters indicate that he had become fluent in German.

[6] See appendix 2.

Professor and Rector

Upon returning from Rome, Thuan was assigned to a teach-
ing position at the minor seminary, which had been moved to
Hue because students and teachers had to flee An Ninh during
the Indochina War.[7] French missionary activity had waned over
time, and the missionaries' departure accelerated after the Geneva
Accords. In 1960, our uncle Thuc became archbishop of Hue. By
virtue of his new position, he was Thuan's immediate superior,
and in 1961, Thuan was appointed rector of the minor seminary.
As a teacher, Thuan displayed remarkable originality among his
colleagues: he decided to implement in the minor seminary the
pedagogy of Don Bosco, whom he admired very much.

Lu Giang (who eventually moved to California) and Le Thien
Si (who remained in Ho Chi Minh City), two students at Thuan's
minor seminary, gathered precious testimonies about Thuan's apos-
tolate within that institution, describing his work ethic when he
returned from Rome. Thuan was excellent at identifying the stu-
dents' true vocations: Were they really called to move on to the

[7] In the French colonial era, a major seminary was built in Hue, in the parish of Kim Long, near the Phu Xuan area. That is why people occasionally refer to it as the major seminary in Phu Xuan or in Kim Long. When the minor seminary was transferred to An Ninh, it was moved into the buildings of the major seminary in Kim Long, while the major seminary was itself tem-porarily moved to Saigon. Under Am's management and Thuan's supervision, the minor seminary was built to the south of the river, a few miles east of Phu Cam, and the Kim Long building was once again free to house the major sem-inary. During the construction of the new buildings, father and son were in close contact. The minor seminary was called Hoan Thien. *Hoan* signifies "we rejoice, we celebrate", and *Thien* is a reference to Tran Van Thien (Thomas). Born in 1820 and martyred in 1838, Thien was a virtuous and courageous seminarian. He was beatified in 1900 and canonized in 1988. The fact that the minor seminary was named after Thien reminded the students that one can become holy even at a young age. Various priests from the area have told me that Thuan also gave courses in canon law at the major seminary.

There is now a statue of Don Bosco in the garden of the family home.

major seminary and to proceed to the priestly life? Or was it rather their mission to serve God in the world? A great defender of freedom of conscience, Thuan always stressed to young persons the importance of following one's conscience, so necessary for the discovery of the will of God. "To become a priest is a beautiful vocation", he would say, "but you may also be called into the world. What you need to keep in mind, above all, is to avoid evil. Sinning is evil, but it is much worse to lose the idea of what sin is."

One of the pupils had discovered that he did not have a vocation to the priesthood, but he was afraid to tell his father, whose most cherished wish was to have a priest for a son. My brother called him into his office and said to him:

> *You know that there are many different trains you can take to get to town—express trains and trains with limited stops—but they all get to their destinations. Likewise, there are young people who come to the seminary and get ordained: that's a very straight route. There are others who stay with us for five or six years, then give up the idea of priesthood—but at least they will have spent those years with the Lord in a house of God. They make a stop, just as the train does, and they feel another vocation. In any event, all are called to be bearers of the Word of God wherever they live.*

When the seminarian asked my brother how he had guessed that he wanted to leave the minor seminary, Thuan simply replied: "The Lord has just as much need for engineers, for teachers, and for fathers. Children do come from families." He then suggested that the young man stay on a few days more at the seminary and spend time The Lord needs each one of us. *praying. The discussion with Thuan, followed by prayer, helped the man overcome his feeling of despair. He thought that he was not good enough for the Lord, not worthy enough, and that he would be rejected by God if he left the seminary. But Thuan was able to offer the young man—by his own testimony—a new opportunity: "He gave me another life, a second life." Thuan maintained contact with many of these students who had followed another vocation.*

Mr. Nguyen Ca was a pupil at the minor seminary from 1961 to 1967.[8] In a testimony dating from 2003, he described how the new rector eliminated the entrance exam:

> It was to encourage candidates coming from the countryside who had not had the opportunity to attend good schools. He also took great care over the quality of the teaching, which was much better than that of the public schools. Thuan was attentive to all, rich and poor alike. One day, when I was alone in a corridor in the seminary, he noticed me and kindly asked me how I was. I was delighted that he knew my Christian name. Throughout my life, I have retained happy memories of him, and they helped me get through difficult times in the reeducation camps. His courtesy and generosity were an example for me that I have cherished all my life. As rector, he would spend every evening teaching us about practical aspects of life. Sometimes he would speak about politeness in conversation

[8] He presently lives in Denver, Colorado.

*or good table manners or about how to love in a Christian manner
if we made the decision to marry. This was a great help to me
when I got married and started a family. At that time, we had
no Vietnamese missal, but while using a Latin missal, Thuan
proclaimed the Gospel in our mother tongue: he knew it by heart.
This gave me a great love for the Word of God.*

Scouting instills   *In 1964, Thuan introduced Scouting
a sense of   into the seminary. He taught the young
responsibility   people practical things: camping, first aid,
in its members.   how to make a canoe to sail on the River of
                      Perfumes, mountain climbing. Of course,*
*he also spoke to them about the motto of Scouting: do a good deed
each day.*

Mr. Nguyen Ca confirmed this:

*Scouting helped us learn a spirit of service, unity, and fraternity.
Thuan taught us to live in a healthy way and to think and
speak of others positively all the time. He organized pilgrimages
to La Vang to pray to the Virgin there. He often talked to us
about the difficult situation in our country and encouraged us
to get involved in the building of the nation and the Church.
When we made our Scouting promises, he asked us to love
God, to be faithful servants of our country, and to love our
neighbors.[9]*

[9] It was a great delight for me to be able to meet a large number of former
students at the minor seminary—both priests and laymen—when I visited the
country. Their generosity, their welcoming attitude, and the happy memories
they had of their former rector confirmed the testimony that Élisabeth had
passed on to me. They told me about the spirit of prayer and joy that filled
Thuan. He was often to be seen in the chapel, united with Christ, or praying
the Rosary during his walks. One of his former pupils told me that he and
about ten others were invited late in the evening of Ash Wednesday to a surprise midnight meal that Thuan organized, after the fast had been observed all
day. I was particularly touched meeting the Scouts in the Hue Diocese. They
adopted me as one of theirs, simply because I was interested in their founder.

Some teachers at the minor seminary thought that Thuan was overindulgent with the young people. When he was sent sweets, he would distribute them to the seminarians. One of his pupils, who later joined the army rather than the priesthood, emulated his generosity: he would sometimes offer a soldier a cigarette to boost his morale.

The sweets proved so attractive to the students that they often disappeared from Thuan's office. Once, before Mass, knowing that there had been little thieves at work, he said: "You know, there are a lot of mice around in my office. If by chance you meet one of them, you should take back the sweets they have stolen and return them to me." The students remembered words like these, and they would say to themselves: "Oh, he knows we have been pilfering, but he doesn't want to spell it out, so as not to humiliate us."

Thuan encouraged sports and music. The seminarians could also watch interesting films, such as Spartacus, Ben Hur, and The Longest Day. Later, after he had left the seminary for other assignments, Thuan came back to preach a retreat. One of the participants remembers what he said to them about experience: "It is about repeatedly making mistakes, because each mistake is different."

Vicar-General

In 1964, Nguyen Kim Dien (1921–1988) was appointed archbishop of Hue. Archbishop Dien lived a life of poverty in the service of the most deprived, in line with the spirituality of Blessed Charles de Foucauld.[10] He was a

[10] Archbishop Dien had earlier been in charge of the major seminary in Saigon. Later he would become a symbol of peaceful resistance to the Communist regime with the aim of acquiring more rights for the Vietnamese Church and society. In his apostolic letters, he spoke about the right to form seminarians

true father to the people of his diocese, supporting them tirelessly in those troubled times. He had the courage to choose as vicar-general Father Thuan, nephew of the assassinated president, while keeping him in his position as rector of the Hoan Thien Minor Seminary. The two of them were more or less of the same generation.

Thuan had the good fortune to be supported by this new arch-bishop, who had promoted him to a position of responsibility. Our family had suffered greatly: two of our maternal uncles, Diem and Nhu, had been killed at the end of 1963 by the military junta.

We often call the suffering of Christ His "Passion". Easter and the Passion are connected.

My uncle Can was arrested and executed one year later. Thuan was deeply saddened, and he also struggled with overwhelming anger. He was rarely able to sleep.

In the face of all these sufferings, he at first experienced much bitterness. Outwardly, though, he remained calm and was always ready to listen to people who came to talk to him at the diocesan offices. It is likely that his demanding work routine helped him overcome this deep heartache. But it was prayer, above all, that kept him sane. Without God's help, he would not have been able to forgive.[11] Our mother's moral strength was a great support to him during those tough times. Vietnam had become

---

freely (1979), the right to hold meetings without constraint (1981), and the right to freedom of thought and information (1986). The police made it extremely difficult for him to practice his ministry. A huge crowd of faithful attended his funeral, and many Vietnamese in exile remembered him as a hero, on account of his virtues and, more particularly, for his courage as a pastor. The Nguyen Kim Dien Association still exists.

[11] André Nguyen Van Chau, *The Miracle of Hope: Francis Xavier Nguyen Van Thuan; Political Prisoner, Prophet of Peace* (Boston: Pauline Books and Media, 2003), 99–109.

*engulfed in a new war. Mother was constantly encouraging us
to empathize with the soldiers' families, often poor people who,
when they lost a son in battle, were not even told where he had
been buried. It was perhaps during that period that Thuan became
radically united with the Passion of Christ. In some way, those
years were a kind of prelude to the life of suffering that he was
to experience after 1975—suffering that was also that of a whole
people. As episcopal vicar and later as bishop, he acquired the
ability in those troubled times to reach out to the enemy, to be a
peacemaker, and to work in behalf of refugees.*

Vatican II

From Vietnam, Father Thuan followed very closely the
changes proposed during the Second Vatican Council. One
has the impression that he had already foreseen the upcom-
ing changes. Was that due to his studies in Rome in the
late 1950s or to his great sympathy for Pope John XXIII,[12]
who, like Father Thuan, admired Don Bosco and had *The
Imitation of Christ* at his bedside? In any case, like several of
his teachers, he had chosen a pastoral life that aspired to be
completely free of any form of clericalism.

---

[12] Angelo Giuseppe Roncalli (1881–1963) was pope from 1958 to 1963.

Hy-Vong
Hope

3

Bishop Thuan

Episcopal Ordination

In 1967, while battles were raging between the Communists and the Americans, Thuan was appointed bishop of Nha Trang, a coastal town between Hue and Saigon. This diocese had been in existence for only ten years and covered the Khanh Hoa Province, with Nha Trang as its capital, and also the provinces of Binh Thuan, Binh Tuy, and Ninh

Thuan.[1] Thuan was consecrated bishop in Hue at the Hoan Thien Minor Seminary,[2] and he succeeded the first bishop of Nha Trang, the Frenchman Raymond Marcel Piquet (Co Loi, 1888–1966).[3] By the time he arrived in

[1] The geographical partition of these two latter provinces was modified several times over the second part of the last century.

[2] For practical reasons, Bishop Thuan was consecrated not in Nha Trang but on the premises of the minor seminary, where he had been rector.

[3] Gérard Moussay and Brigitte Appavou, *Répertoire des membres de la Société des Missions Étrangères (1659–2004): Ordre alphabétique suivi de l'ordre chronologique* (Paris: Archives des Missions Étrangères, 2004), no. 3141.

Vietnam in 1912, Father Piquet had exercised various ministries before taking over as the head of this new diocese and opening a seminary. A devout, virtuous, intelligent, and zealous man, he was appreciated by all in his flock.

While the theme of love is certainly present in his writings, Bishop Thuan is known above all as the Apostle of Hope in darkness.

For his motto, Thuan chose the first words of Vatican II's Pastoral Constitution, "Gaudium et Spes" (Joy and Hope)—just what a region at war needed! His coat of arms was composed of a white star representing the Virgin Mary; land and the sea in the center, depicting Vietnam; three mountains representing the three regions of the country—the North, the Center, and the South—and ten bamboo branches symbolizing the Ten Commandments.

Bamboo is a very important symbol in our country; it grows everywhere, and the branches bend easily but do not break. Thuan was convinced that through perseverance, courage, and prayer, a person acquires the qualities of bamboo: the storm outside us can force us to bow, but we do not break. Because the bamboo trunk is hollow, this plant symbolizes values that are Asian and also Catholic: if a person is filled with himself, he cannot make space for the Lord or for his neighbor.

Prayer helps us detach ourselves from our self-love, from our pride, and in this emptiness, in this self-effacement,

there is room for others and for God. The spirituality of our uncle Diem was also infused with this idea.

Help for Refugees

At the end of January 1968, the People's Army of Viet-nam (PAVN) and the National Liberation Front (NLF)[4] launched the Tet (Tet Mau Than) Offensive, a military campaign by the Communists against American positions: eighty thousand soldiers launched assaults on a hundred southern towns. These battles were a disaster for the local population.[5] In 1970, Cambodia, which was shelter-ing the NLF bases, came under mas-sive attack by the Americans: the latter dropped more than two million tons of bombs on the country. Four hundred thousand Vietnamese living there bore the brunt of the anger of the Cambodian population and were obliged to flee the country and take refuge back in Vietnam.

> Let us allow God to fill our emptiness.

The problems were immense, and my brother faced this human-itarian catastrophe courageously. With help from the government, he supplied moral and spiritual support to the thousands of per-sons in distress. In his work in behalf of the refugees, his goal was not so much to provide aid as to ensure that the disaster victims

---

[4] The PAVN (previously Viet Minh) and the NLF (Viet Cong) were the most important Communist military forces. The NLF acted within the South-ern republic.

[5] In Hue, the assault was particularly bloody. Thousands of civilians were murdered, especially young people—the future of the country—and intellec-tuals. The fact that the victims had taken refuge in the cathedral made no difference to the Communists.

could become independent and responsible for their own future as soon as possible. To this end, the Catholic Organization for the Reconstruction of Vietnam (COREV) was set up. Its headquarters was in Saigon, and Thuan was in charge. The hundreds of thousands of refugees could not be left to languish in camps: they needed decent accommodations and help in finding work. Thanks to his knowledge of various languages and his episcopal position, Thuan was able to establish contact with international organizations and obtain significant financial aid. In cooperation with Caritas,[6] he even went to Europe twice to intercede in behalf of the refugees. His experience of the world of migrants would prove very useful when, in 1992, he became a member of the International Catholic Migration Commission (ICMC).[7]

Other Roles

Bishop Thuan held various positions within the Vietnam Bishops' Conference: president of the Pontifical Council for Justice and Peace, president of the Communications Department—in which he collaborated in the foundation of Radio Veritas—and president of the Council for the Pastoral Care of Migrants and Itinerant People. For some years, he was also a consultant for several pontifical dicasteries: the Pontifical Council for the Laity, the Congregation for the Evangelization of Peoples, and the Congregation for

---

[6] Caritas Internationalis is an organization of the Catholic Church that fights poverty and strives for justice by restoring human dignity to the most vulnerable persons in society. See http://www.caritas.org.

[7] The ICMC is a nongovernmental organization established in 1951 that seeks to help refugees and those who are obliged to move within their country or to flee abroad as a result of war, natural catastrophes, or poverty. Pope Paul VI gave a great deal of encouragement to the ICMC.

Liturgy and the Sacraments. He belonged to the Pontifical Council for the Laity for the longest period—from 1971 to 1975—during which he had the opportunity to meet the archbishop of Kraków, the future Pope Saint John Paul II.[8] In November 1970, he was present, in the name of the Vietnamese Episcopate, at the meeting of the Federation of Asian Bishops' Conferences (FABC) in Manila.

[8] André Nguyen Van Chau, *The Miracle of Hope: Francis Xavier Nguyen Van Thuan; Political Prisoner, Prophet of Peace* (Boston: Pauline Books and Media, 2003), 175–76.

Bac Ai

Charity

4

Pastoral Commitments

Introduction

In the midst of the atrocious battles that were the daily context of his ministry in Nha Trang, Thuan gave priority to his pastoral work. Laypeople were invited to reflect on their role in the Church. My brother believed that we should not limit ourselves to our comfortable ways: the Word of God must permeate society. He wanted to strengthen family life and encourage a greater openness toward our neighbors, regardless of their religion, their social status, or their political beliefs. He gave high priority to interreligious dialogue and unity among all Vietnamese.

As bishop, Thuan visited New Zealand, where he took part in predominantly English-language Masses with a significant Maori component, the traditional language of the indigenous people. On his return to his diocese, he felt inspired by his experience in New Zealand: he said that you can evangelize people only if you respect them. In the Nha Trang region, there are still a large number of Raglai, an ethnic group close to the Cham. A minority in the country, they have a culture and a language that differs from mainstream Vietnamese. In 1968, Thuan set up a Cham Cultural Center and published a Bible and a dictionary in the Raglai language. He always displayed an independent mindset,

*as this concern for an ethnic minority ran counter to the prevalent
way of thinking at the time.*[1]

*Although he was a partisan of a national church, Thuan
looked for the full integration of the missionaries into the life of
the diocese. Those men were spiritual explorers who had often
lived heroically in the most difficult circumstances. He encouraged
religious and priestly vocations, organized continuing formation
for his priests, and exhorted Christians to commit more to parish
and social life. Both the major and the minor seminaries received
an influx of students.*

*By the late 1960s, well informed about the difficult life of the
Christians in the North, Thuan had already begun to prepare
the faithful for a Communist invasion of the South, which seemed
more and more likely to him. The future was looking extremely
bleak. During this period, his love for Christ and his loyalty to the
Church impelled him to build more Catholic schools and religious
institutions and to train lay groups in new evangelization projects
for the time when bishops, priests, and religious would be prevented
from working freely. Thuan never stopped reminding everyone of
the duty of every Christian: to sanctify daily life, to live the message of Christ in his home, his workplace, and even his sufferings.
He was already laying the foundation for the Hope Community
(Cong Doan Hy-Vong), which he established with the blessing of
Pope Paul VI. The mission of this movement, intended to reach
every corner of Vietnam—even the least accessible—is evangelization in daily life. It includes married persons, consecrated laypeople,
and priests. While living in society and exercising their various
professions, the consecrated integrate into their lives Ignatian spirituality and devotion to the Sacred Heart. Like other religious, they*

---

[1] During my visit to the south of Nha Trang, to Suoi Dau, I witnessed one
of the finest examples of charitable work to be found in the country: religious
sisters living a simple life among these minorities and continuing this work of
emancipation with heart and mind.

make promises, live celibate lives, pray the Liturgy of the Hours, and prioritize daily Mass and meditation.[2]

To reach as many of the faithful as possible, Thuan wrote numerous pastoral letters and delivered inspiring homilies to share his message of faith and his convictions with his flock. Many individuals all over the world still derive spiritual benefit from his writings. Much of his work has been published, but there remains a plethora of unpublished material: lectures and sermons that deserve to be better known.[3]

The Message of the Cross

We managed to send to the West drafts of the homilies that Thuan had written while in prison. Reading them makes it possible for us to learn the content of the teaching that Thuan had been imparting to his fellow believers. I would like to draw particular attention to those that speak of the Passion of Christ and His death on the cross.[4] *In those texts, Thuan was not afraid to deal openly with the difficult situation prevailing in our country.*

[2] When under house arrest at Cay Vong, Bishop Thuan wished to associate Hy-Vong with the secular Institute of the Priests of the Heart of Jesus, one of the branches of the Cor Unum spiritual family, and he wrote to Father Jean Canivez, head of the institute (January 16, 1976). The letter is kept in the archives of Giang Xa. Hy-Vong is now part of the Cor Unum Family, and Bishop Thuan is considered its cofounder (https://www.uspcj.org/the-cor-unum-family).

[3] The historical commission that is preparing for the beatification in Rome has gathered all of Cardinal Thuan's writings. Thanks to Élisabeth, I have been able to see copies of the most important.

[4] *In 2009, various homilies were sent clandestinely from Vietnam to the West. I sent a copy of these sermon notes, together with a provisional translation, to the Cologne archives. There are more than forty of these precious texts. I cite only a few passages from them (homilies 1 through 7). The sermons are not dated.* Individuals I met in Vietnam often told me that Thuan's preaching was special, different from the type of sermons they were used to. The faithful were particularly attentive, and many of them were marked for life by his clear, profound words.

Interior of the Cathedral of Nha Trang

He began one of his homilies by expressing his disgust at violence: "Never has human life been so cheap—and that is revolting to me. I can barely breathe, when I am forever hearing nothing but lie after lie and broken promises; I am losing the taste for life." Then the tone changed:

> *But ... God created me; He wanted me to live here and now. This is my time, and I look at the Cross. I am helpless and I have nothing more to give, like Christ in His nakedness on that cross. All that remains is His love. Jesus also invites us to love one another. It would be so easy for us to turn a deaf ear to the suffering of our brothers. It is even possible for us to side with the oppressors. But let us give glory to the crucified Christ, whose message is considered madness by the world (1 Cor 1:23)![5]*

Evoking in another homily the mystery of the Cross, he explained that those who choose to remain close to Jesus may lose their good name. They run the risk of being considered crazy, just like the Lord Himself:

> *I do not dare to say to Him, like Peter: "Lord, I am ready to die with You." I am all too aware of my weakness. But in moments like this, the Virgin is there to help me. I will not make any grand declarations, but, like her, I contemplate His face shining with love, and I try to remain by His side. Mary dared to be seen as the mother of a criminal. In the same way, I am the brother of that criminal; He is one of my family, and I am willing to unite myself with His fate. Mary, let me stay by your side. I will try to hang in there, courageously, close to this beloved criminal, because right now, Your cross, Jesus, is also mine.[6]*

---

[5] Extract from homily 1.
[6] Extract from homily 2.

I am convinced that such preaching on the Cross helped Thuan and his listeners cope with the torment that Vietnam endured over so many long years.

In another homily, he spoke of the skies that were full of black clouds, plunging the world into darkness:

> *In the midst of an uncertain future, I stand facing Golgotha: the image of the Cross enlightens me, and Jesus gives me the strength to focus on the problems of today. Even when I look beyond the present moment, I know that Jesus will be with me in suffering, and that allows me to retain my serenity and even my joy. Trust and hope live within me. If I give in to the temptation of fear, not only will I fall tomorrow, but I will already feel paralyzed today.[7]*

For Thuan, the "foolishness of the Cross" gave meaning to the life of suffering Christians: "The Cross, which I did not think I was able to carry, I do now, thanks to the presence of Jesus by my side. I have a better understanding of the logic of His suffering, and Jesus blesses me with His cross. That is how He saves the world and gives meaning to our lives. Let us never speak about Jesus without referring to His cross."[8]

Without the presence of Jesus, the cross loses its meaning.

The merciful Heart of Jesus is especially manifest in His agony. In one of his homilies, Thuan reminded us that Jesus opened the gates of paradise to the criminal crucified next to Him: "His love is eternal." He added: "I put my trust wholly in His Heart, and I feel myself called to become merciful like Him. He was merciful toward the woman caught in adultery, and He is merciful toward me. I must treat my neighbor as Jesus treated Peter and the Samaritan woman. My heart must grow

[7] Extract from homily 3.
[8] Extract from homily 4.

Statue of the Sacred Heart in the chapel of the family home

to the stature of this immense love. Jesus has an open Heart and loves without counting."⁹

Showing no sign of obsession with pain or any hint of sentimentality, Thuan dared to speak of the Cross as the supreme means of saving the world:

> To be crucified is to suffer; although that seems like a hard truth, suffering is part of the work of our redemption. The Cross raises each one of us, as it raises the whole of humanity. The world is united to God. All that is ephemeral disappears. To be raised is painful, for it means that I must free myself from all those ties

⁹ Extract from homily 6.

that keep me down. The two arms of Jesus are not made of steel, like those cables that prevent me from breaking free. The Lord embraces me in my struggle, and I am no longer afraid of being held by Him. Lord, lift me up toward You![10]

These short extracts give us only a very partial idea of the richness of Thuan's homilies, which are a testimony to the way he lived. My family inherited a great number of souvenirs of Thuan, and many of them are exhibited in the little museum in Cologne that is dedicated to his memory.[11] The cross he made during his imprisonment, and which he wore for the rest of his life as a pectoral cross, is one of those precious objects. I still have the crucifix that hung on the wall across from his hospital bed and that he stared at virtually all the time in the last weeks of his life. For Thuan, the Cross was a sign of hope. The sculptor Vu Dinh Lam[12] made a statue that sums up the message of Thuan. Two hands hold up a cross, a sign of hope—like the bronze serpent that was a source of life for the Hebrews in the desert.[13]

Prayer

When he was bishop of Nha Trang, Thuan published six pastoral letters.[14] Since they have been translated only into Italian, I feel it is important to share their main themes.

---

[10] Extract from homily 7.

[11] See appendix 2.

[12] *He left our country at fifteen years old as a refugee, and he greatly appreciates my brother's writing.*

[13] *Other symbols can be discerned in the sculpture: bamboo and my brother's coat of arms. But the cross as a sign of hope is the central element in this magnificent piece of work.*

[14] François-Xavier Nguyen Van Thuan, *Lettere Pastorali sulle orme del Concilio Vaticano II* (Vatican City: Libreria Editrice Vaticana, 2013).

Dated 1968, the first letter ad-dressed the theme of vigilance, espe-cially in prayer. In this letter, Thuan linked the suffering of Christ to that of the Vietnamese people. "Like the apostles", he wrote, "we, too, are in danger of falling asleep in the face of suffering. Parents are mainly the ones who should be giving the example: watch and pray. Prayer will help them listen to their children and share their problems. Parents are true guardians when they control their children's  access to films and pictures. Parents who stay close to their sons and daughters can more easily steer them toward the Lord."

Thuan then referred to the war—which, by that time, had been raging for more than twenty years. To refer solely to the kingdom of heaven in the midst of these difficulties was not suf-ficient: "We are also citizens of this world, and we must pay attention to the political situation." Watching and praying also meant "feeling responsible". But, my brother added, "the Church is not to be identified with any political system: she wants justice and love to prevail."

For him, charity was not an abstract concept. He wanted to open the eyes of the faithful to the devastating effects of armed con-flict: famine, physical suffering, abandonment of farming, and an exodus to the big cities. Moral points of reference disappear. "Peo-ple get too quickly inured to the exploitation of their neighbor, to lies and terror. The import, sometimes clandestinely, of luxury products lays the ground for moral depravation, entices the indi-vidual to gambling and delinquency, fornication, thievery, and exploitation of others." Thuan recalled the courage of those ances-tors who forfeited their wealth and their social position for the sake of remaining faithful to their Catholic faith. He urged his readers to listen to the voice of their consciences, to live according to their faith, and to have faith in Divine Providence. But, he immediately added, to grow their faith, they need to know it. Ignorance of the teachings of the Catechism, among other things, weakens Christians, who are called to spiritual combat. Thuan stressed that, at the time, the Church was going through the gravest crisis she had had to face in all of her history. The doctrine of atheistic Communism was spreading throughout the world, throwing society into confusion and fomenting conflicts, condemnations, and mass killings, from Russia to China, from Mexico to Poland, from North Korea to North Vietnam.

Members of the Church, called upon to be the light of the world, must be born again out of prayer: "The Church was born from prayer. The Church achieved victory thanks to prayer. The Church lives thanks to prayer. Before each important stage in the foundation of the Church, Jesus prayed. The world puts its faith in nuclear weapons, in compromises, and in treaties. In Fátima, the Virgin asked us to pray the Rosary every day and to trust in her heart, while doing penance regularly. It is the remedy for spiritual tepidity, materialism, religious illiteracy, and moral decadence."

Thuan forcefully emphasized the link between life and prayer: "To pray means to be at one with the environment in which we live, with the world and its multitude of problems. To pray is to unite with God and to bring God to humanity so that we fulfill His will on this earth. If we do not pray, we exclude God from the reality of our lives."

Moved at the sight of the commitment of many of the faithful, religious, and priests in the difficult war situation, Thuan ended this long pastoral letter with an expression of compassion toward those who lived in poverty, fear, and insecurity because of the fighting. Finally—given so many urgent issues that he addressed, one could almost forget that he wrote this letter close to Easter—he ended by turning to the Lord Himself: "I pray the Lord to grant our hearts the grace of the Resurrection and peace to our land." [15]

Family and Communism

In a second pastoral letter, Thuan united himself to Pope Paul VI, who had declared 1968 a year of faith. On this occasion, he reflected on the marvelous vocation of man and his dignity: [16] *"Created in the image of God, man is capable of knowing and loving God, His Creator. Man possesses an immortal soul." Thuan stressed the universal right to life, to private ownership, to freedom of association, and to freedom of conscience and religion. He had particularly strong words about the family, as he forcefully denounced Marxist ideology and the misdeeds of Communism:*

- *The refusal to recognize any sacred spiritual character to human life leads to the disappearance of the family.*
- *For Marxists, family and marriage are merely civil institutions, and purely artificial. There exists no matrimonial bond of a judicial or moral nature. All that is involved is the well-being of individuals and the collectivity.*

[15] The letter can be read in its entirety in Nguyen Van Thuan, *Lettere Pastorali*, 16–34.

[16] To reduce the thinking of Bishop Thuan to his battle with Marxism would be to ignore all his work at the Roman Curia aimed at promoting justice and peace in the world. He was a great defender of the social dimension of the Church, he defended the dignity of every human being, and he offered his friendship to each person, regardless of that person's political or religious allegiance. His love for freedom led him to warn about the dangers of totalitarianism. Perhaps that is why, when he was in prison, he wrote a biography of Father Maximilian Kolbe, a victim of Nazi barbarism.

- *This ideology denies parents the right to educate their children. They can care for them only in the name of the collectivity, as mandated by the party.*

In the face of the huge threats to family values at the time, Thuan was forceful in his denunciations: "According to Marxist doctrine, society is a collectivity organized with a single goal in mind: the production of material goods, which can be achieved only by means of collective labor. Karl Marx and his disciples seem to believe only in the state and its political power. Marxists advocate a new civilization, a new era, and a new society. But all this is done without God: humanity is only the product of blind evolution, and God is no longer the Creator."

In this pastoral letter, Thuan also deplored the fact that, in order to defeat Communism, some relied on weapons rather than on the transformation of men by grace. Others, refusing to see the dangers of Communism, were silent and made themselves complicit in these attacks on the faith.[17]

Justice for the Poor

In 1970, Bishop Thuan was invited to Manila to give a speech at the Federation of Asian Bishops' Conferences (FABC), on the occasion of Pope Paul VI's visit to the Philippines (November 27–29, 1970).[18] He described the situation of

[17] Nguyen Van Thuan, *Lettere Pastorali*, 37–62. Given the sheer length of this letter, the reader will appreciate that only a part of the text is reproduced here. The rest of it is devoted to a clarification of Bishop Thuan's anti-Communist position. I do not know whether the Communists, who imprisoned Thuan in 1975, were aware of these writings.

[18] Francis Xavier Nguyen Van Thuan, *Political Problems of Asia and Their Solutions*, November 24, 1970, handwritten document.

this immense continent, at the time largely under Communist rule. Even if Christians were a minority—less than
3 percent of the population—they represented a great hope
for so many men and women living in inhumane conditions. The Church's social doctrine asks Christians to relieve
suffering and reject all forms of oppression.

Bishop Thuan urged the bishops, his confreres, but also
all Catholics to engage in "a noble fight for the emancipation
of all the disadvantaged". He cited the conciliar document
Gaudium et Spes, which recalls that God created the earth
for every human being. International aid to poor countries
is a question not primarily of charity but of justice, which
the Asian continent is entitled to, "in all honesty".[19]

Out of concern for the poorest, by educating the young,
the Church can "today, now, improve the destiny of Asia"
and bring her hope. Later, when the bishop of Nha Trang
joined the Pontifical Council for Justice and Peace, he
developed the proposals already formulated in 1970.[20]

Commitment and Missionary Zeal

Right from the beginning of evangelization of the country, the missionaries had been forced to hide to avoid
being killed. Propagation of the faith was for a long
time the responsibility of committed laypeople, fervently

[19] Second Vatican Council, Pastoral Constitution on the Church in the
Modern World *Gaudium et Spes* (December 7, 1965), no. 85.

[20] Francis Xavier Nguyen Van Thuan, *Jesus Christ the Savior and the Mission of
Love and Service of the Church in Asia: A Reflection in View of the Synod of Bishops
for Asia*, handwritten document; Francis Xavier Nguyen Van Thuan, *The Church
and Social Justice in the Next Millennium: New Directions and the Pope's Call*, handwritten document, Embassy of the Philippines to the Holy See, April 21, 1999.

determined to proclaim the gospel, even if it meant risking their lives.[21]

Whenever the threat of persecution appeared to be receding, religious fervor showed a tendency to flag. That is why the bishop of Nha Trang wanted each Christian to commit himself in the name of the gospel. The faith once displayed by persecuted Christians, which marked the advent of the Church in Asia, notably in Vietnam, called for a reawakening. It was as if the bishop saw a parallel between the long period of persecution that the Church in Vietnam had already experienced and the forthcoming Communist occupation that would drive out of their parishes a great number of foreign as well as native priests. As in the early days of evangelization, laypeople were going to be called to play a prominent part in the life of the Church. Those concerns of his formed the guidelines in two other pastoral letters.

Thuan was rightly appreciative of the work of priests and religious, but he wanted the spirit of Christ to permeate the daily lives of all Christians. "The Church must be incarnate", he wrote. "And especially you, faithful laypeople, you can live with the Spirit of Christ in your daily work. That is how you will bring the Church to the modern world."

While the teaching in schools may well have reflected the gospel message, many young people were beginning to get distracted by

---

[21] For centuries, Christians were persecuted in Vietnam. Pastoral activities were conducted clandestinely for a long time. In the eighteenth and nineteenth centuries, the Christians of Europe—especially in France—were familiar with publications covering the lives of Vietnamese and French victims over this long period of persecution. Although the canonization of the Martyrs of Vietnam took place relatively recently (1988), many of our contemporaries know nothing about these episodes in the life of the Vietnamese Church. This is why the present work provides some details on this situation of suffering, very much present in the memory of Cardinal Thuan and those close to him.

television. Thuan also noted that divorce was becoming common-place and that more and more children were being born through illegitimate unions. Delinquency was increasing. Self-interest rather than friendship was becoming the bond between people. Material wealth, if not used for the common good, is likely to lead to moral and spiritual decay.

Faced with this situation, Thuan called on every Christian to commit: "You must live among the people and share their sufferings and their humiliations to be able to help them regain their dignity and their capacity to construct a more human world. By so doing, we shall break free from a situation of spiritual and social atrophy. Justice is predicated on mutual respect. It requires that each party puts himself in the other's shoes. We can attain perfect justice only through mutual understanding and friendship."[22]

In another letter, dated 1971,[23] Thuan recalled the commitment of the missionaries who, in spite of persecution in the seventeenth century, performed their work of evangelization with courage and patience.[24] On the occasion of the three hundredth anniversary of the evangelization of the country, he inaugurated a missionary year in order to nurture the spirit that had inspired the first carriers of the good news.

Reconciliation

Up to the end of his ministry in Nha Trang, Thuan was filled with this apostolic zeal. In 1973, when the Vietnam War was drawing to a close and an invasion of the South by the

[22] The whole text may be found in Nguyen Van Thuan, *Lettere Pastorali*, 84–98.

[23] Ibid., 99–113.

[24] The letter contains a short account of this evangelization.

Communists in the North was imminent, he turned his attention to the universal Church and, in particular, to the announcement by Pope Paul VI of a holy year for 1975. The theme for it had been announced: "Renewal and Reconciliation". Thuan was convinced that a deep relationship with God will bring home to us the need to live at peace with all, in charity and justice— not simply with fellow members of the ecclesial community but also within society and between various political factions, and all this in a spirit of ecumenism and peace. According to him, reconciliation signifies "bringing man back to God and God to the world".

Within his diocese, he proposed concrete measures: the promotion of a better understanding of the meaning of the liturgy, for instance the Penitential Rite at the beginning of Mass. He also wanted to promote pilgrimages in order to encourage spiritual development in an atmosphere of prayer, examination of conscience, and openness to renewal. He wanted Catholics in his diocese to deepen their faith. He took other initiatives as well: the publication of a weekly newspaper, Dan Than *(Commitment), and the offering of guidelines specific to the laity. He also planned to publish a catechism with better distribution of information regarding the teaching of the Council.*[25]

Serving and Not Being Served

Thuan's pastoral tasks did not amount simply to a series of initiatives. Service was the mainspring of his activities. Thuan thought of himself as a humble servant, even in small things.

[25] The full text of the letter in which these topics are discussed can be found in Nguyen Van Thuan, *Lettere Pastorali*, 117–26.

One example among others: after meals, he, the bishop, would clear the table, take the dishes to the kitchen, thank the sisters who worked there, take an interest in the jobs they were doing, and ensure that they were not overworked.

He never lost this spirit of service. At the end of his life, when he was spending a few days in the United States with a fellow cardinal, three sisters who worked in the house in which the cardinals were staying shared with Thuan the fact that their lives were very much like those of servants.

The American cardinal wanted to organize a meeting with several bishops, and the occasion began with a celebratory meal. At various times, the cardinal would ring a bell, and Thuan noticed that as soon as the sisters heard the bell, they would come immediately to the table to serve. So he told the following story to the other bishops:

> One day, some sisters died. When they came to the gate of paradise, they met Saint Peter, who told them he was about to take a nap. Nonetheless he took the time to show them the way to the kitchen so they could find something to eat. Shortly afterward, some pilgrims knocked at the gate of paradise. Saint Peter, still enjoying his nap, said to them: "Ask the sisters in the kitchen to make you some food." Next to come was a priest. Saint Peter emerged from his nap and asked the sisters to make him a nice meal. A few hours later, two bishops knocked at the gate of paradise, and the apostle shouted to the sisters: "Quick, quick! Get a nice meal ready, make sure the food is good, and don't forget to put out a fine tablecloth!" Then a cardinal died, and Saint Peter ordered a cow to be slaughtered, for, he said, "it doesn't often happen that a cardinal gets to the gate of paradise."

I do not know whether the bishops and the cardinal appreciated my brother's sense of humor. At any rate, the gathering continued, and when the cardinal took up the bell again to have the *table cleared, Thuan said: "Perhaps it isn't necessary to ring the bell this time? We could clear up the dishes ourselves."*

Although this episode took place when Thuan himself had become a cardinal, it is indicative of the spirit in which, as a bishop, he had already chosen to live his ministry. He valued the commitment of Christians and viewed his own vocation, above all, as a gift to his diocese. Like Christ, he was there to serve and not to be served.

Than Trong

Prudence

5

Archbishop and Prisoner

Arrest

In 1973, American troops left the country. Many guessed that South Vietnam would soon lose its freedom and very quickly succumb to a Communist invasion. By 1975, troops from the North occupied the whole country. The refugee situation turned catastrophic. Thuan's parents and other members of his family were able to flee to Australia, where one of his sisters was already living. Remaining in the country, Thuan was muzzled. Just before the Communists came to Nha Trang, he had ordained to the priesthood a great number of seminarians, thanks to a dispensation issued by Archbishop Henri Lemaître (1921–2003), the apostolic delegate to Vietnam from 1969 to 1975.[1] Thuan was now bishop under a Communist regime, a prelate known for his condemnation of Marxism, his friendly

[1] In fact, these were the last public ordinations. I was given this information when I visited Vietnam. I found out some more details: the bishop of Nha Trang ordained only those seminarians who were at the end of their formation. Others were clandestinely ordained a little later. I was especially impressed by the large number of priests who had to wait a long time for their ordination, some more than ten years, during which they underwent periods of imprisonment or forced labor.

relationships with American military chaplains, and his cooperation with the international community on account of his work for refugees. He was, above all, well-known as the nephew of President Diem.[2]

The archbishop of Saigon, Nguyen Van Binh (Paul, 1910–1995), had, on several occasions, expressed a desire to retire.[3] On April 23, 1975, at the suggestion of Archbishop Lemaître, Pope Paul VI appointed Thuan coadjutor archbishop. On April 30, the Communists entered the town. Paradoxically, it was not only the new regime that viewed the appointment of Thuan with displeasure. There was adverse reaction to it even within the Church in Saigon.

There were various demonstrations by patriotic priests opposed to Thuan's appointment to Saigon.[4] This hostility toward him

[2] André Nguyen Van Chau, *The Miracle of Hope: Francis Xavier Nguyen Van Thuan; Political Prisoner, Prophet of Peace* (Boston: Pauline Books and Media, 2003), 191–95.

[3] Bishop Binh was ordained a priest in 1937 and studied in Rome. Appointed bishop in 1955, he became archbishop of Saigon in 1960. He regularly expressed a desire to retire but remained archbishop until his death in 1995, since the Communist regime refused to accept the appointment of the candidate put forward by the Vatican (i.e., Bishop Thuan). He adopted a pragmatic policy in the face of the new regime (see Felix Corley, "Obituary: Archbishop Paul Nguyen Van Binh", *Independent*, July 26, 1995, http://www.independent.co.uk/news/people/obituary-archbishop-paul-nguyen-van-binh-1593410.html). In Saigon, I questioned various individuals about Archbishop Binh's "desire" to retire. They told me that although he would have preferred to remain in his post, he was a realist: he saw that a different type of bishop was needed to cope with the situation in the country. In the end, enjoying good health and still only sixty-five, he retained his role as archbishop for a long time. Rumors suggesting that Bishop Thuan was imposed on him seem to have been false: in fact, the appointment of a coadjutor is done in collaboration with the apostolic nuncio.

[4] Some priests were delighted to see the departure of all foreigners from Vietnamese territory. They do not seem to have grasped what was at stake in the changes: in their view, the seizure of power by the Communists would mean independence for the country. It is true that the battle against Communism had been one of the main reasons for the continuation of the French—and

was not simply due to the fact that he was Diem's nephew but also that he was the bishop who, in the ranks of the Vietnamese episcopate, had the most contacts with Western countries. COREV, of which he was president, received a great deal of financial support from the West. Archbishop Binh, however, was a staunch defender of the choice made by Pope Paul VI. In a pastoral letter, he asked Christians to respect the decree of the Holy See. He also invoked the freedom of religion with regard to political life.

Thuan was then a young, dynamic bishop, and everyone was aware of his great intelligence. Despite the efforts of Archbishop Binh, some priests and laypeople thought that this new "anti-Communist" archbishop represented a danger for the local Church and for the Vietnamese people, an obstacle to the establishment of good relations between Catholics and the Communist occupier. They saw in his appointment an ambush set up by the West. There was so much opposition that he could not stay with Binh at the archbishop's house, and he took refuge for several months in the major seminary in Saigon. Protesters even removed the Vatican flag from Archbishop Lemaître's office.

---

then the American—military presence. Those who opposed the appointment of Bishop Thuan, however, had not understood that he came from a family that rejected both Marxist ideology and colonialism. Élisabeth mentioned two patriotic priests who later regretted their behavior at this time. *Their names were Huynh Cong Minh and Thanh Lang. On November 28, 1988, shortly before he died, the latter wrote a letter asking for forgiveness, first from God and the Church, then from Vietnam and especially from Thuan. As for Father Minh, he asked to take part in the closing ceremony of Thuan's beatification process. My brother had himself, long before, already turned the page on the past. He saw everything with the eyes of God.* Father Minh reconfirmed to me personally what Élisabeth had said. With great humility, he explained to me that he had even been a member of a local political committee, but he then realized very quickly that the powers of this so-called parliament were nonexistent. Father Minh had the courage to apologize publicly for the way he had acted in 1975 in relation to Cardinal Thuan. He gave me a most gracious welcome, and he made no secret of his great admiration for the cardinal.

In July 1975, the Communist government sent the new coadjutor a letter ordering him to return to Nha Trang, but Thuan stayed on in Saigon. On August 15, the Communist government organized a priests' conference at the opera house in town.[5] While it was underway, Thuan was taken to the Independence Palace to be questioned, and he was arrested that same day. The course of history had changed! But what struck Thuan was the fact that the day of his arrest happened to be a feast day of the Virgin Mary.

Thuan was never put on trial. His thesis on military chaplaincy, which he had written in Rome, was one of the fallacious arguments advanced as a reason for suspicion: he had allegedly collaborated with the capitalist enemy. At the time, the reasons the Communists gave for his arrest were these, among others:

1. *His post as director of Caritas Vietnam, an organization they accused of collusion with the American CIA*
2. *His membership in COREV, seen as a tool of the great capitalist powers*
3. *His founding of the lay movement Hope Community, considered illegal*
4. *His appointment as archbishop of Saigon, which de facto placed him squarely in the ranks of the "reactionaries"*

Thus began his pilgrimage to holiness, a pilgrimage that would subject both his faith and his hope to the harshest of tests.

The Communists were infuriated by the fact that the Vatican had appointed in this important city a man known

---

[5] In Saigon, I expressed my amazement at this move. Why did the "victors" take all this trouble, knowing in advance that they were going to set aside the coadjutor? The reply from connoisseurs of the regime was simple: "A person whose conscience troubles him is always afraid."

for his moral stature. Having fought previously against his uncle Diem, they now found themselves facing a bishop who might well reveal a strong spirit of defiance and who, during interrogations, spoke of Diem as a patriot assassinated because of his refusal to be beholden to anyone.

Residence under Surveillance at Cay Vong

Escorted by two policemen, Thuan was taken to the town of Nha Trang and told to remain under surveillance in the Cay Vong presbytery on the edge of that town.[6] Father Phung Van Nhu, an elderly priest there, had twelve hundred parishioners under his pastoral supervision. He was deeply touched by the fate of his former bishop. Officially, this priest was not permitted to address a single word to him, but he provided him with considerable material assistance and made sure he had plenty to eat. He also helped him send and receive letters clandestinely. He personally wrote to his own acquaintances to ask them to send Thuan toiletry essentials.

In the beginning, Thuan was content enough: he had a lot of time to pray, but fairly soon he was tempted by a spirit of rebellion, and he bitterly reminded himself how unfair it was that he should be deprived of his freedom. This inner struggle was the first of many in his long captivity. He came out of it purified. Following the example of Saint Paul, whose letters he had learned by

---

[6] There are a few more people living in the area nowadays, but it has retained its rural character. The presbytery has become one of the memorials to the cardinal. Unfortunately, the architecture of the church and the layout of the presbytery do not convey much of an impression of the life of Archbishop Thuan during that period. Some parishioners still remember the time their former bishop stayed there.

The parish church in Cay Vong

heart at the major seminary, he grasped that his captivity marked the beginning of his mission "outside the walls".[7]

In his book *Five Loaves and Two Fish*, Thuan recalls his captivity.[8] Day and night, he would think about his people, whom he loved so much: his flock was without a shepherd. Christian books were no longer available, and the regime had closed down Catholic schools. Teaching sisters were forced to work in the rice fields. The day came when Thuan realized that he must not remain idle but rather must live in the present. Whatever the circumstances, it must always be possible to practice charity. But how?

One night, it suddenly dawned on him that he could always emulate Saint Paul and, like him, write letters from captivity. He

[7] Nguyen Van Chau, *The Miracle of Hope*, 196–98.

[8] Francis Xavier Nguyen Van Thuan, *Five Loaves and Two Fish* (Boston: Pauline Books and Media, 2003), 5–14.

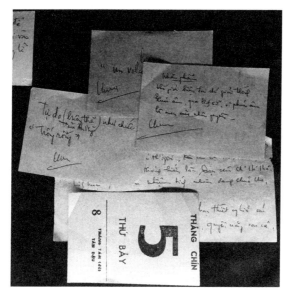

Diocesan archives, Hanoi

enlisted the help of Quang, a seven-year-old boy who passed the presbytery every day, to take notes secretly to his family.[9]

Cooperation between shepherd and lamb in the service of evangelization! God had to remain the focus when everything was collapsing around the Christians. These thoughts, scribbled down on calendar leaflets, were then copied by various families and communities.[10] These words of hope reached into prisons, where they

[9] Despite the fact that there are photos of the bishop and the parish priest surrounded by nuns, taken at the entrance to the Cay Vong presbytery, and although he received clandestine visits, Bishop Thuan chose this youngster as his "postman" so as not to cause any problems for the parish priest he was living with—since he was also being closely watched—or the visitors who came to see him secretly.

[10] I was able to see these calendar pages—much smaller than I had imagined—in the archives of the Hanoi Diocesan Center.

provided inmates with some relief from their distress, and the notes were also smuggled out of Vietnam by the Boat People. They would form the basis of the book The Road of Hope. *Thuan's message was made up of short reflections, somewhat akin to the book* The Imitation of Christ. *Thuan praised the Lord often; he saw the Holy Spirit at work: from his prison, the good news spread and reached other persecuted individuals. One of my sisters, Ham Tieu (Anne), translated these notes into English with the help of an Australian friend, Peter Bookallil. The first edition was offered to Pope John Paul II.*

Solitary Confinement in Phu Khanh

At 8:00 A.M. on March 19, 1976, the police arrived at the Cay Vong presbytery. The Communists had gotten wind of the messages of hope that had already been widely distributed. Prisons had been built in each province to eliminate all pockets of resistance against the occupation of the country, and Thuan was taken to the one in Phu Khanh, not far from Nha Trang Cathedral.[11] The parishioners and the parish priest of Cay Vong were deeply saddened at his departure. In spite of the fact that Thuan could not have any official contact with the community, his presence bore eloquent testimony to the parish at a time when Christians were becoming aware that the regime was going to muzzle the voice of the Church.[12] The government accused

---

[11] The prison—still a police building but now modernized—is close to the bishop's palace. The archbishop could hear the bells of the cathedral, as he had previously been able to hear the beautiful sound of bells from a dozen churches in the neighborhood of Cay Vong (information given to me by my guide).

[12] When I met people who were longstanding parishioners in Cay Vong, I became more aware of the importance of Archbishop Thuan's stay among them. A silent presence is sometimes more eloquent than a great number of encounters.

the archbishop of "rebellious acts", without defining what they actually were. Archbishop Thuan remained more than eight months in solitary confinement in Phu Khanh. This was one of the most painful periods in his life.

His imprisonment was a form of permanent torture. Physical conditions in the isolation cell were extremely harsh. Thuan related later that his cell and his mattress were very damp. Mushrooms grew on his mattress. When it rained, the water level rose, and insects, frogs, earthworms, and centipedes were all over his cell. He lost the will to kill them.[13] Outside air, which came in through gaps in the door, carried with it the stench of the latrines across from his cell. He spent long days lying on the ground because he had discovered at the bottom of the wall a hole for water to drain away. He stuck his nose close to it to inhale fresh air. He tried always to stay in good shape, and he exercised by walking from wall to wall inside his cell. In the summer, the cell became a real oven. Because of the great heat and humidity, his clothes quickly turned soggy, dripping with sweat.[14] Sometimes he lost all sense of day and night.

He was constantly under pressure to sign a document confessing to having collaborated with the CIA and conspired against the Communists, in connivance with the Vatican. He was also made to write an account of his life. This document was meant to serve as proof that he was guilty of having fomented a conspiracy against the Communists. Thuan composed a very short text that implied no admission of guilt. His captors kept making him rewrite his life story. He was careful not to deviate from his original text. He repeated the same exercise for many long years, up to the day when his jailers realized that it was a pointless

---

[13] François-Xavier Nguyen Van Thuan, *J'ai suivi Jésus . . . Un évêque témoigne* (Paris: Médiaspaul, 1997), 23.

[14] Nguyen Van Chau, *The Miracle of Hope*, 202–5.

undertaking, since he always wrote the same things. "He is stubborn; it runs in the family."[15]

And then there were the interrogations; brutal as they were, they at least brought him into contact with other people. Faced with his tormentors, he discovered that he had retained his capacity for sound reasoning. Thuan remained very lucid in spite of the torture of solitary confinement.[16] He realized that he had to remain vigilant, and his resilience during the interrogations surprised the people who were trying to break him physically and mentally.[17] Thuan never admitted that he had been tortured. But it would be very surprising if he had been an exception among the Communists' prisoners, especially those from whom they would like to extract signed confessions. Later, speaking to former detainees who had experienced torture, he referred to Galatians 6:14–17: "Far be it from me to glory except in the cross of our Lord Jesus Christ. . . . For I bear on my body the marks of Jesus." Thuan finished by saying pointedly: "I know what I am talking about."

Praying became difficult; his memory began to lapse. Even reciting an Our Father or a Hail Mary became impossible, and he was afraid he was losing his mind. He was hungry and thirsty all the time, and his body ached all over on account of the dampness. He tried not to eat or drink too much because he was rarely

---

[15] André Nguyen Van Chau, *A Lifetime in the Eye of the Storm: Ngo Dinh Thi Hiep, a Younger Sister of Late President Ngo Dinh Diem*, 2nd ed. (Canyon Lake, Tex.: Erin Go Bragh Publishing, 2015), 635–36.

[16] Nguyen Van Chau, *The Miracle of Hope*, 202–77. Chau's account of this period is full of empathy.

[17] Some individuals spoke to me about moments of weakness that Archbishop Thuan experienced during his imprisonment: he is said to have revealed "secrets" about the Church in Nha Trang. But well-informed witnesses confirmed to me that he was invariably lucid. He was sometimes kept awake for forty-eight hours at a time. Despite this torture, the archbishop "revealed" to his torturers only things that could not hurt anyone, such as the code for the empty safe in the bishop's residence in Nha Trang. Although the Congregation for the Cause of Saints has not had access to the reports of these interrogations, it has confirmed his heroic virtue.

allowed to go to the toilet, and that exacerbated his physical suffering. All that he managed to remember were very short prayers. He would simply repeat:

> Father, forgive them.
> Into Your hands.
> Mary, I am here.
> Hail.
> That they may be one.
> Have mercy on me, a sinner.
> Remember me when You come into Your Kingdom.
> Magnificat.[18]

His cell was surrounded by hatred. For many long months, his only contact was with boorish wardens whose main desire was to break him morally. Sometimes he was left for several days in total darkness and complete silence, and nobody spoke when they passed him his food. The Communist government and the spirit of evil sought to humiliate him. When we lose our human dignity, we lose everything. This dignity is born out of the fact that each person is a child of God. In solitary confinement, Thuan felt the urge to despair. Any person placed in such a situation is bound to feel worthless, and there is always the danger of forgetting that it is God who created us. In such moments, Thuan thought of Adam, who wanted to flee from the gaze of God, and he remembered that as a child he had wanted to see the Lord. But who was he, then, even to dare express such a wish? He felt abandoned by God.

The spirit of evil that inhabits people who want to take our dignity away was very much in evidence in the humiliating treatment Thuan received. They gave him very salty food. This made him horribly thirsty, with a constant need to drink, and for many

---

[18] François-Xavier Nguyen Van Thuan, *Témoins de l'espérance: Retraite au Vatican*, trans. Sylvie Garoche (Paris: Nouvelle Cité, 2000), 153–54.

consecutive days, they would not open the door of his cell, which he ended up using as his toilet too. Then they sent a cleaning woman who sneered contemptuously at him: "They say you are a bishop, but you look more like an animal. Look at the mess you've created around yourself."

"When slandered, we try to conciliate" (1 Cor 4:13).

She would demean him and drench him with water, wetting the floor around him. On such occasions, he would be held under this uncultured woman's glare. How could he, in such a humiliating situation, be expected to follow his mother's advice: "We must always live under the gaze of God"?

Hatred threatened to grip him. In our culture, a person's dignity is closely reflected in the way he behaves toward others. For weeks, he felt shame for himself, a bishop being so humiliated by a cleaning woman. He failed to see the image of God in his neighbor. He gradually became aware that he was on the verge of hating this woman who took such pleasure in taunting him. He shared with our family—though never with the wider public—that one day he felt so mortified by the filth in which he was placed that he got down on his knees and asked God for the strength to cope with the way this woman was lording it over him. She found him in this posture when she came in. All of a sudden, he felt bold enough to look her in the eye and say: "Miss, there's no quarrel between you and me. You are just doing your duty, and I did not choose to be here, in this revolting filth. I am just a prisoner, and you, on the other hand, have a job you need to do. For my part, I do not hate you, and I am sure that you have nothing against me either." The moment he finished talking, he felt a bright light bathing him and, at the same time, shrouding the woman, and he said to himself: "God must be here." From that moment on, the woman looked at him differently. He did not receive any more overly salty meals, he was treated with more respect, and *he no longer had to defile his cell. Thuan was surprised not only that this intense light had found its way into his dark and dingy cell but, even more so, that it had enveloped the woman, and he understood then that the Lord was present in his enemy too.*

When he told us this story, many years after his liberation, my sister and I were going through a period of worries, commiserating over the sad situation in our country. We asked ourselves: "How are we to understand that the Lord is love when He allows all this to happen?" That is when Thuan shared with us this experience. I asked him: "What was that light like?" He replied: "It was a very intense light, a light that warmed me inside and brought me such peace that I felt completely fulfilled. I have always wished to see God, but it is not possible. It is only in my enemy, who becomes a friend, that I must see Him."

This spiritual victory was followed by another. Imprisoned and isolated, Thuan was filled with great anguish: he suffered enormously from being separated from his flock. But while he was overcome by anxiety and crushed by a feeling of pastoral impotence, he heard a comforting voice in the depths of his heart: "Why do you torment yourself like this? All that you have accomplished up to now is good, but it only represents My will. If such be My desire, you will complete the task that I have entrusted to you; otherwise it is up to Me to decide who will do it in your place. You must distinguish between the work of God and God Himself." This revelation triggered a renewal of his spiritual forces, a grace for difficult moments. Peace was never going to leave him again. From that time, he surrendered himself completely to God and learned not to dread solitude anymore.

This experience and this spiritual discovery were crucial turning points in his life and helped him enormously during the thirteen years of his arbitrary imprisonment.

In the retreat that he preached at the Vatican, he referred to this revelation, stating that it had taken place at night during his incarceration in the prison at Phu Khanh.[19] *It seems that later he was able to relive this first experience, for, in another book, he wrote: "When the Communists put me into the hold of the*

Suddenly, Thuan saw things differently.

ship ... with another 1,500 starving and desperate prisoners, ... I shared their suffering, but immediately the voice called out to me

again: 'Choose God and not the works of God,' and I thought: In truth, Lord, here is my cathedral and here are the people of God you have given me to take care of."[20]

It is not easy to determine where these spiritual experiences took place. Thuan was deprived of his freedom for thirteen years, locked up in different prisons or sent to reeducation camps.[21] *When he was held in solitary confinement, he said to the Lord: "You are with me; You want me to live here with You. I have talked a lot in my life. Here, in my cell, I remain quiet. It's up to You now, Jesus, to talk to me." Recalling the lives of various saints and certain aspects of their existence—Thérèse of Lisieux in her cell in the convent, Théophane Vénard in his prison in Vietnam, Francis Xavier in his missionary solitude—and praying to them also brought him great comfort.*[22]

Transfer to the North

On November 29, 1976, Thuan was removed from Phu Khanh prison and taken, along with a great number of other prisoners,

---

[19] Nguyen Van Thuan, *Témoins de l'espérance*, 63.

[20] Nguyen Van Thuan, *Five Loaves*, 20.

[21] When the cardinal talked about his experiences, he did not always provide precise information as to the places and the contexts of the main events he was speaking about. What mattered the most for him was the spiritual aspect of his suffering.

[22] Nguyen Van Chau, *The Miracle of Hope*, 207.

to the transit camp at Thu Duc, near Saigon.[23] *All the prisoners were being relocated by boat to the north. Although the conditions were still very harsh, Thuan was happy to find himself in contact with other prisoners after his long period of solitude.*

Nguyen Thanh Giau, a high-ranking Hoa Hao Buddhist,[24] *was one of those in the convoy. He gave me some precious information about the transfer. He had recognized among the other detainees a captain and a village leader, but my brother suddenly caught his attention. Thuan was dressed like the other prisoners, but Giau realized immediately that he was in the presence of someone larger than life. He recalled:*

I found out that this intelligent-looking man was the bishop of Nha Trang. A great number of Christian prisoners gathered around to talk to him. In the few days I spent at Thu Duc, I noticed his pleasant disposition, his righteousness, and his generosity. My respect for him grew by the day. When it was time to leave camp, there was great confusion among the detainees. They all wondered where they were going to be sent next. To the island of Phu Quoc[25] *or to Con Son?*[26] *Only one person seemed to know our destination: it was Thuan. How he had figured out*

---

[23] Thu Duc is about twenty-five miles east of the center of Ho Chi Minh City (Saigon).

[24] This is a Buddhism devoid of pagodas and rites, a branch of Vietnamese Buddhism. The main initiator, Huynh Phu So, who came from the village of Hoa Hao, in the south of the country, drew a great number of peasants after him. So dreamed of a "religion of the heart", in which laypeople could be involved with teaching. Nationalist in its political tendency, this branch of Buddhism was persecuted by the French and by the Communists. So was killed by the Viet Minh in 1947.

[25] This island is in the Gulf of Thailand, south of Cambodia. Today it is a little tourist paradise. The prison, which can be visited, was built by the French in the 1950s; it was used during the Vietnam War and later by the Communists.

[26] This is one of the largest islands to the south of Vietnam. The French built a prison there in 1861, and it was used during the Vietnam War. Today the place is a tourist island destination.

*that we were to leave by boat, I do not know. To calm the other
detainees, he began to tell them about the journey he once made
by boat from Saigon to Marseilles and to make suggestions about
how to avoid seasickness.[27]*

On December 1, 1976, the prisoners did indeed embark on
a boat going north. As Thuan did not have a bag to carry his
belongings in, he improvised by tying a knot at the end of each
leg of a pair of trousers, which he then filled and carried around
his neck.

Buu Te (Jean-Baptiste), a member of our family on the paternal side and also a prisoner, related later that the boat did not
leave until after sunset, for they were waiting for the arrival of a
particularly dangerous criminal. When my brother appeared, Buu
Te realized that the criminal in question was none other than his
nephew Thuan!

Thuan wrote in one of his books that the prisoners were chained
in pairs.[28] "A short trip brought us to Tân Cảng (Newport),[29]
a new military port opened by the Americans a few years before.
Ahead of us we saw a ship, but it was well camouflaged so as to
prevent anyone from guessing what was happening. We boarded
it and headed north—a voyage of 1,700 kilometers."[30] Thuan
related that he was sent with other prisoners in the boat's cargo
hold, where the coal was stored. Mr. Giau, who was detained
in the same part of the boat, reported that the prisoners were all

[27] From an unpublished testimony.

[28] Francis Xavier Nguyen Van Thuan, *Testimony of Hope: The Spiritual Exercises of Pope John Paul II* (Boston: Pauline Books and Media, 2000), 75.

[29] Today it is the main port for shipments on their way to Ho Chi Minh
City. It continues to function as a military port. Located on one of the main
rivers (Dong Nai) in the country, the port, known also by the name of Cat Lai,
connects the city to the sea.

[30] Nguyen Van Thuan, *Testimony of Hope*, 75.

completely covered with grime from the coal usually stored in the cargo hold. "The archbishop told us that we must try to avoid getting sick, and he did all he could to help us avoid succumbing to despair."[31]

Hope in the Darkness

Their only source of light came from an oil lamp; otherwise, they were in complete darkness. Thuan was very upset. Until then he had been in prison, but at least it was in the heart of his diocese! Now he was entering unknown territory. He meditated on the words of Saint Paul: "Behold, I am going to Jerusalem, bound in the Spirit, not knowing what shall befall me there; except that the Holy Spirit testifies to me in every city that imprisonment and afflictions await me" (Acts 20:22–23). He spent that first night in a state of terrible anguish. The following morning, a little sunlight filtered into the hold, and he was able to make out the despair-filled faces of the prisoners around him. Some of them called him over because a man had tried to hang himself with a metal cable. Thuan spoke to him, and the distressed prisoner opened up to him, taking his advice. Later, at an interfaith meeting, Thuan met the man again.[32] Thrilled to see him again, the man went up to Thuan, thanked him earnestly, and told those present about the incident, showing them the scars around his neck left by the cable.

Once they realized that Archbishop Nguyen Van Thuan was among them, many prisoners approached him to share their distress with him. He spent time listening to the horde of sufferers,

[31] Ibid., 78–79.
[32] This man, who now lives in California, practices Hoa Hao Buddhism, which is widespread in that part of the United States.

comforting them as best he could. "The second night," he said, "in the cold of a December in the Pacific Ocean, I began to understand that my vocation was taking a new turn. I spent that three-day journey tending to my fellow prisoners and meditating on the passion of Jesus. . . . Now it looks as if I will be going with Him to die extra muros, 'outside the sacred wall'."[33]

"To the present hour we hunger and thirst, we are poorly clothed and buffeted and homeless, and we labor, working with our own hands" (1 Cor 4:11–12).

During this journey to Hai Phong, on December 3, the feast of Saint Francis Xavier, Thuan celebrated his holy patron in the quiet of his heart.

At Vinh Quang Camp, Vinh Phu

On their arrival at the port of Hai Phong, the prisoners were divided into three groups and taken to one of three camps: Hoang Lien Sơn, Vinh Quang, or Thanh Cam. Thuan was sent to Vinh Quang, at the foot of Mount Tam Dao, in the Vinh Phu Province. More than two thousand prisoners were kept there, and Thuan would share their hunger, exhausting labor, humiliations, and injustice.

Mr. Giau described life in the camp:

They divided us into three groups. Within the groups, teams were given various tasks. As the authorities forbade us from using religious or honorific titles, we called Archbishop Thuan "old man". We didn't want him to have to do anything physical,

---

[33] Nguyen Van Thuan, Testimony of Hope, 76.

and as we were somewhat free to allocate tasks within our group, we gave him the housekeeper assignment. He was to oversee the maintenance of the buildings and prepare meals, but he tried to turn down these lighter tasks, saying: "I am honored to be with you, but please let me do my share of work, just like the rest of you." One of Thuan's chores was to fetch coal that was kept in heavy sacks outside. One very cold day, the archbishop stumbled several times under the crushing weight, but each time, he got up again and sat down to catch his breath before finally succeeding on his own.

Sometimes the prisoners were gathered in a big hall in order to write their "confessions". For hours, we had to sit and draw up our own indictments. But during breaks, a lot of prisoners would gather around the archbishop to listen to him. They were not all Christians. Some were Cao Dai[34] *followers or Hoa Hao Buddhists. I myself belonged to the latter group at the time, and I did not see the archbishop as a Catholic dignitary but rather as a holy man, a respectable priest.*[35]

It was during this time that the archbishop made a wooden cross that he later wore as a pectoral cross for the rest of his life: it is still preserved as a precious relic. Because possession of religious objects was illegal in the camp, Archbishop Thuan often used to hide it in a bar of soap. That was how he was able to hang on to it and wear it openly when he was set free.

The fact that he was so popular among other prisoners did not endear

---

[34] This modern form of Buddhism integrates the values of Western thought. The movement was anti-colonialist and anti-Communist.

[35] Testimony of Nguyen Thanh Giau at a memorial service in California.

him to the authorities. On February 5, 1977, two months after his arrival, he was taken to Hanoi and put in the Thanh Liet prison camp.[36]

Prisoner in Thanh Liet, Near Hanoi

Thanh Liet camp was in the Thanh Tri district, south of Hanoi. Nowadays its site is part of the town suburbs. From the outside, passersby could not guess that prisoners were held behind the main front door and the solid walls sixteen feet high. In each section (A, B, C, D, etc.), there were eight cells, twenty-six feet long and eight feet wide, their walls covered with the names of American prisoners who had been held there before 1973. My brother shared cell 7D with a former Viet Cong colonel, a certain Thuyen, accused of corruption but imprisoned in the same cell with Thuan so as to spy on him.[37] This former colonel came from the Hue area, and very soon the two prisoners in cell 7D were talking openly to each other. When he was freed, Thuyen promised to go and "pray" for Thuan at La Vang. This meant visiting the ruins of the chapel, which had been destroyed during the war. Though not a Catholic himself, Thuyen promised Thuan that he would go and tell the Virgin that Thuan needed her help.

Six years later, when he was being held in solitary confinement, Thuan received a letter from Thuyen, who wrote: "Dear friend, I promised you that I would go to pray for you at the shrine of Our

---

[36] Nguyen Van Chau, *The Miracle of Hope*, 213.

[37] Among the political prisoners, Bishop Thuan mentioned the Reverend Tran Huu Thanh, a Redemptorist father known for his opposition to the Communists. He was held in cell 5D, while Nguyen Tu Thai, a nationalist and an anti-Communist, was in 3D. Father Tran Huu Thanh died in Hanoi in October 2007, in Bach Mai Hospital. I had difficulty finding out more information about these prisoners.

The ruins of the former basilica in La Vang

Lady of La Vang. I do so every Sunday, if it isn't raining. I ride my bicycle there. I pray for you like this: "Madonna, I am not a Christian; I do not know how to pray; but I ask you to give Mr. Thuan what he desires.' "[38]

Thuan was very touched by the gesture of friendship from this Communist, who reminded him of the power of prayer! He remembered that his vocation was, above all, to listen to the Word, which was much more important than any work of charity. I have kept a poem that he wrote at this time:

> *Prison is a cathedral.*
> *The sound of the door keys*
> *Replaces the church bells.*
> *But it still proclaims*
> *The sacred time of the Eucharist*
> *Celebrated in union with the universal Church.*

[38] Nguyen Van Thuan, *Five Loaves*, 30–31.

The rest of the poem speaks of the viciousness of the "teachers": the jailers, who demand submissiveness of the prisoners, but the "head" is still the Holy Spirit, and divine grace is felt at every moment.[39]

At Thanh Liet camp, the meals were frugal. My brother was under constant surveillance, obliged to put up with the electric light that was on all the time in his cell. Over the course of the fifteen months he spent in Thanh Liet, he was frequently interrogated by officers of the Ministry of the Interior. They wanted to know everything about the Church in Vietnam, about its priests and their involvement in society. The officers, however, were also coming under pressure from international opposition to Thuan's arbitrary detention. The authorities therefore decided to send him to live in a presbytery. This meant that in response to organizations such as Amnesty International, the Communists could claim that Thuan was no longer in prison but could still keep him under surveillance! In these difficult situations, Thuan kept his faith. As at Vinh Quang, the prisoners helped and protected one another. In the camp, Thuan received help from a prison guard, illegally fashioning a chain on which to wear his pectoral cross.

"Despite the fact that we are hated and despised, I have found a homeland: God is within me."

---

[39] It is difficult to translate poems without being unfaithful to the original language! Mrs. Thu Hong has in her possession a large number of poems written by her brother in the various places where he was imprisoned. Some were composed at the time of the Lunar New Year; in some poems, he compares his celebrations of the Eucharist in prison with those at which he presided in his cathedral. On that occasion, he wrote that, as a bishop, he preferred to die in a prison rather than in a bishop's palace. In other poems, he expressed his faith in God and His providence. Along with texts by the cardinal that have already been published, there exists a great treasure: writings that, happily, have been preserved and that merit—quite apart from this present book—being offered to the public.

Prisoner in Giang Xa Parish

On Saturday, May 13, 1978, the chief of the secret police informed Thuan that he was being released. In reality, thirteen days later, on May 26, Thuan was taken to Giang Xa, in the Hoai Duc district, about twelve miles from Hanoi. He was to live there under surveillance in the abandoned presbytery, in the middle of a small community of 350 who were running their parish with the help of a local council. One small consolation for Thuan was that the church building had been modeled on the La Vang shrine.[40] He was not authorized to perform pastoral activities. The instructions were clear: no public celebrations or preaching. The locals were advised to keep their distance from Thuan, branded as a dangerous criminal who needed to be kept under constant surveillance. But his mild demeanor toward his prison guard[41]—who soon allowed him more freedom—and toward the council and the parishioners convinced them that he was far from being a dangerous man.

He gradually won everyone over. Every day, he got up very early and began his day by cleaning the church gate; then he would scrub the floor. Passersby whose curiosity was aroused began to ask him questions. Thuan asked for more brushes and mops, and more and more helpful individuals gradually joined in; many who had looked on him with suspicion began to help him and became his friends. The guard, who shared his bedroom in the presbytery, made it easier for priests, nuns, and others to visit

---

[40] Both the church and the presbytery are open to all who want to get to know the life of Cardinal Thuan better. It is quite possible to meet individuals there who knew him well.

[41] At the time of the archbishop's residence there under surveillance, one of his neighbors, Nguyen Ngoc Dien, secretly organized meetings of priests and religious with him.

The parish church in Giang Xa

*him. They sometimes came long distances—as far as 185 miles—
and they chatted with Thuan at night. Having grown up in the
North, they did not know much about what was happening in
the Church worldwide, not to mention Vatican II. Thuan even
managed to ordain seminarians clandestinely. Those ordinations
lasted "a very long time", he said, since they began at about
11:30 in the evening and did not finish till 1:00 the following
morning. During the night, he also visited the sick and admin-
istered the sacraments to them. Every day, about one hundred
people attended the Mass that he celebrated at dawn. He was
surprised that the Holy Spirit was using him this way.*

*In Giang Xa, despite the fact that he was officially a prisoner,
he learned by daily experience that love can conquer all. The*

Communists had agents in every village. Thuan managed to win their friendship. These spies reconciled with the Church and even collaborated with the guard to protect the archbishop whenever there were celebrations organized by the villagers or when he had visitors. His prison guard had to draw up a report on the prisoner each month, but after a while, he ran out of inspiration! Thuan decided to write the reports himself, fearing that if the man failed to perform his duty, he would be replaced by another guard who would be less forgiving toward him. The police even congratulated the guard for "his excellent reports"![42]

During his captivity, Thuan was visited by foreign observers. There were always "translators" present, although he did not need them. In the presence of those spies, he would sometimes give quirky replies to questions put to him about his well-being. Without openly defying the Communists, he could subtly make it understood that the fundamental rights of prisoners were not respected. When asked if he was well treated, he would reply: "The government always takes very good care of me. I was very ill recently, and a doctor came to see me after three weeks." Another time, he said without blinking: "The government takes a great interest in me: they always keep a very close eye on me."

A life of hope is made up of brief minutes of hope.

He was permitted to take long walks and had a great deal of free time. He was thus able to write two books in 1979 and 1980: Pilgrims on the Road of Hope *and* The Road of Hope in the Light of the Word of God and the Council. *The manuscripts were smuggled south to be distributed. In a book that he wrote specifically for young people, he said that we must always use the present moment to do good; we must not wait for tomorrow*

---

[42] For further information, see Nguyen Van Chau, *The Miracle of Hope*, 219.

but must fill today with love. Like Mother Teresa of Calcutta, he said: "The main thing is not the number of acts that we do but the intensity of the love we put into each gesture."

Here are some extracts from a prayer that he composed:

> *Jesus, I will not wait.*
> *I will live the present moment,*
> *filling it to the brim with love. . . .*
> *My life . . . is made of millions of seconds*
> *united to each other. . . .*
> *If I live every minute perfectly*
> *my life will be holy. . . .*
> *Jesus, I love you,*
> *and my life is always "a new and eternal covenant" with you.*
> *Every minute I want to sing with your Church.*[43]

Some texts that Thuan composed have not been published. For instance, he wrote a little book called The Message of Father Maximilian Kolbe. *It was not just because Maximilian Kolbe is a canonized saint that Thuan pondered the life of this victim of Nazi barbarism. The charity of this Franciscan who died in Auschwitz touched him deeply: the gift of his own life to save that of a father was the culmination of a long journey into holiness, a road that was very Marian and that influenced the spirituality of Pope John Paul II. Thuan's own life can be compared with that of this martyr of faith: one and the same love for God and others, one and the same influence in captivity.*[44]

We have also kept several dozen postcards that my brother managed to send to Sydney to my parents and my sister Anne.

---

[43] Nguyen Van Thuan, *Five Loaves*, 13–14.

[44] This unpublished text dates from October 1982. The English translation that Élisabeth gave me is eighty-nine pages long. It is worth noting that at the end of this work, Archbishop Thuan cites seven French books on Father Kolbe for further reading.

Most of them were written between 1979 and 1982, toward the end of his imprisonment in Giang Xa. He often responded to family news, giving thanks for signs of life received from the outside. During that period, it was easier for him to receive presents and medication. He was particularly happy to get family photos. He even received a New Year's present from the police! He was always very careful to be optimistic. "I am well", he would often write. There was no guarantee that these letters remained private; they were most likely vetted by the security police. How humiliating that these letters, expected to be treated as confidential, were open to inspection by the Communists! But the little positive comments in these letters do not seem to have been written solely to reassure the family or to make sure that the mail got past the censors. It seemed to be encouragement to himself as well: "Don't worry too much" or "My health has improved." He often made references to nature, the harvests, the succulent lychees, the plants that he was growing in his garden. He mentioned how the village folk were planting potatoes and growing other vegetables, such as tomatoes and beans; he admired their resiliency when they had to cope with floods or insect infestations. In a message sent around the end of his stay, he announced that he was going to make apricot juice and plant a dozen coconut trees. His hope of one day harvesting and tasting the fruits he had grown did not materialize.

Two important subjects kept coming up in these letters: alongside family and friends, prayer was theme number one. Thuan wrote about his brother Thanh (Michel), also imprisoned.[45] He

---

[45] See appendix 1. This message must have been written when he was in Cay Vong, since it is dated January 14, 1976. It says: "Thanh is still alive, but he has not yet returned from the reeducation camp." Archbishop Thuan sent his brother's address so that the family could send him some food. And he added: "The number of individuals sent to camps is very large, and some of them are quite elderly." Later, around 1980 (?), he referred again to his brother, imprisoned in a very isolated camp in the Than Hoa Province, between the

never forgot to send birthday greetings, and he repeatedly asked Anne to take good care of our parents. He urged us to pray fervently to the Virgin, especially in the month of May. He kept reiterating this last recommendation. He invoked Saint Joseph and Saint Anne, my sister's patron saint. He promised to pray for each of us and asked us to pray for the sick as well as for him. Amazingly, he had no qualms about mentioning the people he had been able to meet. In 1980, for example, he was visited by eight Vietnamese bishops.[46] He was extremely diplomatic about it: he wrote that he was thankful to the Vietnamese government for this favor! The messages on the cards tell us that, at the time of the New Year in 1982, he was able to visit about thirty families in Giang Xa. In the spring of 1982, Bishop Cuong and Archbishop Binh[47] came to greet him. He also mentioned that he was able to visit the new cardinal, Trinh Van Can (Joseph-Marie, 1921–1990).[48] He talked about his concerns over the health of

North and the center of Vietnam. This district, which is close to the sea to the east and which extends westward as well, is a long way from anywhere and close to the mountains. Archbishop Thuan indicated that there were forty-one priests in this prison and that malaria was rampant. We also learn that the family was sending large quantities of rice, which Thanh was sharing with his fellow prisoners. Archbishop Thuan put forward the hypothesis that the government might set these prisoners free since there was no longer any threat of rebellion. He asked that an appeal be made to the United Nations Refugee Agency (UNHCR), which works to save the lives of refugees and to protect their rights.

[46] At this time, there was a meeting of about thirty bishops in Hanoi, and they apparently sent a delegation to see Archbishop Thuan.

[47] Archbishop Thuan was still Binh's coadjutor. It seems that the two prelates in question visited Russia and took part in a demonstration against nuclear weapons. Their "freedom" of movement was therefore connected to their support for the policies of the Communist bloc.

[48] He was archbishop from 1978 to 1990, so he was able to welcome Archbishop Thuan after his release. It is difficult to know exactly when particular messages were sent, as, it seems, the police sometimes put stamps over dates or over text. Thanks to another card, we know that Archbishop Thuan visited this cardinal at the end of August 1982 in Hanoi.

At Giang Xa presbytery

people he was able to meet: he mentioned the passing of Uncle Ba in the autumn of 1981,[49] the hospitalization of Bishop Hoa, Father Bang's poor health, Uncle Danh's cancer, and the illness of Father Huynh, a friend of Am.[50]

The information in the cards gives the impression that Thuan enjoyed a certain degree of freedom in Giang Xa. In April 1981, he was even able to take part in the elections! It was only a relative degree of freedom, though, as his correspondence was censored. But every sign of life was precious to us, and we were inspired by the faith and charity expressed in the cards he was able to get to us. In 1982, things changed, however, and he was again placed in solitary confinement.

[49] According to a card of May 7, 1980, this uncle was then celebrating his diamond jubilee of priesthood.

[50] In September, Archbishop Thuan wrote that Huynh had received the sacrament of anointing. On January 15, 1982, he said that this father had died and had promised to pray for them once he reached paradise. The persons mentioned were well-known to his parents and perhaps also to his sister Anne. Time has passed, and it has become difficult to find any information about these individuals who played a part in his life and whom he carried in his heart.

Can Truong
Courage

6

The Power of Faith

Solitary Confinement in Hanoi under the Security Police

While Archbishop Thuan was in Giang Xa, the Communist regime was growing increasingly fidgety. Relations with China were becoming problematic: both Vietnam and China longed to dominate Cambodia. At the same time, Vietnam's most faithful ally, Russia, was facing problems of its own in Poland. The election of Pope John Paul II on October 16, 1978, was about to create shock waves in the Communist world: "Be not afraid" was his battle cry at the start of his pontificate. The Vietnamese Communists began to worry about the pope's growing surge of popularity among Catholics, who had had the courage to face up to the regime in Poland. They wondered about the odds of Thuan's becoming a Vietnamese Lech Wałesa.[1]

---

[1] As a trade-union leader, Lech Wałesa managed to unite the Poles against the Communist government. In the long term, this "Polish revolution" influenced other countries, especially East Germany. In the end, the Berlin Wall fell in 1989. Wałesa became the first non-Communist president of his country (1990–1995).

On November 5, 1982, the archbishop was taken from Giang Xa to Hanoi so that he could be kept under closer observation. Thuan was going to experience another long period of solitary confinement.[2] Transported in an armored vehicle, the archbishop had no idea where the police were taking him. In fact, this second, longer period of solitary confinement took place in various secret-police premises. The Communists no longer cared about interrogating him: all they wanted to do was put him away. He was moved from one place to another, kept in isolation in a succession of cells, and largely deprived of contact with the outside world.[3]

Those nine years were, for the most part, an unending period of solitude and deep boredom. Thuan had nothing to do. He felt

---

[2] André Nguyen Van Chau, *The Miracle of Hope: Francis Xavier Nguyen Van Thuan; Political Prisoner, Prophet of Peace* (Boston: Pauline Books and Media, 2003), 225–26.

[3] Prison conditions varied depending on where Archbishop Thuan was being held. At the beginning, he seems to have been kept under very close surveillance; he was later allowed more freedom, so that, once again, he had a chance to write to family and friends, and the authorities even allowed him to give language courses to his guards. Although the Communist authorities were once hell-bent on keeping him cut off from the world, they let him have an easier life than he had in 1976. Bishop Thuan wrote a vast amount during his imprisonment in Hanoi. Many of his writings are preserved in the archives of the diocesan center of this archdiocese: notes on the pastoral care of young people, on how to run a retreat, and on liberation theology, along with dictionaries that he composed. The bonds of friendship that he gradually established with his jailers could explain how he was able to smuggle his writings out of the prison. One would be surprised to see the number of people, in Vietnam itself and in diaspora, who have copies of these dictionaries. The meticulous care involved in their composition shows how fluent Bishop Thuan was in different languages and, above all, how he loved to share his knowledge with others. Writing them was also a useful way to combat boredom. Although toward the end of his time in prison, the conditions in which he was held were more relaxed, the bishop was still kept in solitary confinement for lengthy periods, often without anything to do, and when he was eventually released, he was ill.

empty. In one of his testimonies, he wrote: "Time passes slowly in prison, particularly in solitary confinement. Imagine a week, a month, two months of silence.... They are terribly long, but when they become years, it is an eternity. There is a Vietnamese proverb that says: 'One day in prison is like one thousand autumns in freedom.' There were days when I was so worn out by exhaustion and illness that I could not manage to say a single prayer!"[4]

To keep arthritis at bay, he would walk around his cell for hours on end, back and forth by the side of his bed, or do physical exercises while praying or singing the Miserere, the Te Deum, or the Veni Creator. God was speaking to his heart again: he must give up everything to the hands of the Lord, have confidence in Him, and look for Him, not for what He did but just for Himself. It was "Prayer is the hour when the heart speaks." *a conviction that became the center of Thuan's reflection over this period of solitary confinement. He put it in writing and integrated it in prayers that were published for the first time in 1995.*

"Your times of prayer are moments of intimacy with God, who is your father."[5] *"It was not laziness that made Mary sit quietly at the Lord's feet. Mary chose the better part: to listen to the Lord and allow His words to permeate her heart and soul and—working in and with her—to effect a change. What could be more active than inner renewal and transformation?"*[6]

For Thuan, to pray was to contemplate the Lord, to adore Him, to have faith in His love, to offer Him everything we have: our lives, our desires, the people who are dear to us, our sufferings.

---

[4] Francis Xavier Nguyen Van Thuan, *Five Loaves and Two Fish* (Boston: Pauline Books and Media, 2003), 25–26, ellipses in original.

[5] Francis Xavier Nguyen Van Thuan, *The Road of Hope: A Gospel from Prison*, trans. John Peter Pham (Boston: Pauline Books and Media, 2001), 31.

[6] Ibid., 32.

In the beginning, the jailers hardly spoke to him, merely answering his questions with a blunt yes or no. His attempts at civility and courtesy were completely ignored. No conversation, even the most innocuous, was possible. But once again, he became aware that he owned a treasure within himself. He said to himself: "You carry the love of Christ in your heart; love them the way Jesus has loved you", and he began to love the Christ in them.

The softening attitude of the USSR—a regime that had been historically an ally of the Vietnamese Communists—toward religion made things difficult for the Communist Party, in power in a deeply religious country. The Vietnamese bishops' request to the Roman Curia in 1985 to canonize their martyrs also unsettled the government.[7]

Numerous celebrations took place all over Vietnam in June 1988 on the occasion of this canonization. But the archbishop of the largest diocese in the country celebrated it on his own. He sang a Te Deum of thanksgiving. He knew that his fate was intrinsically connected with that of the suffering Church of earlier times.[8]

Cardinal Thuan did not always specify exactly where he stayed in which year, but thanks to outside witnesses, it appears that he moved to a secret-police house, an old two-story colonial house in the center of Hanoi, during the last years of his imprisonment.

The prison authorities decided to assign two wardens to his cell, one for the day and one for the night, to keep him

---

[7] Certain individuals in Vietnam told me that Archbishop Thuan may have given the bishops—especially the bishop of Hanoi—"a key" that could help the government understand that this canonization in no way constituted an attempt to disrupt the existing regime. He apparently said: "The Church is my mother, and Vietnam is my homeland. I see no contradiction between the two."

[8] Nguyen Van Chau, *The Miracle of Hope*, 229–30.

under continuous surveillance. Élisabeth heard an account of what happened from one of the guards.

Mr. Pham Van Cong was given the job of watching my brother. He spent two years with him, in 1987 and 1988, toward the end of his imprisonment. In an account he gave in 2008, he recalled that he had been very close to Thuan, since he had to eat and sleep in the same room. In Europe, we often assume that it is always hot in Vietnam. But in January, the temperature in Hanoi often remains below fifty degrees. Unlike in the Phu Khanh prison, which was like an oven, both prisoner and guard here shivered from the cold. Thuan's family was able to send him a blanket, but though very thick, it was too short and did not cover his whole body. For his part, a blanket Cong received from his boss was longer but thin. Each struggled on his own with the cold, which infiltrated the room through the window, especially at night. Thuan made a suggestion: "We can sleep side by side, and then we can both make the most of the two blankets. The thick one will cover our upper bodies; the other will cover the rest." It was not just Thuan's common sense that sparked Cong's admiration but, even more so, the trust that he showed in a guard who was officially his enemy. He came up with little ways of cultivating friendships with those who should have been his enemies. In spite of his difficult situation, he always found the strength to love. Around that time, Cong began to think there must be a special deity infusing a spirit of love in Thuan, since everything in his demeanor seemed beyond what we could possibly achieve by ourselves. Cong added: "Later, I thought to myself: Jesus Christ must exist; otherwise, there couldn't be anyone like the archbishop. Besides, Thuan himself often said that he wanted to imitate Christ."

The endless time that Cong spent around Thuan enabled him to discover who that prisoner, so thoughtful toward others, really was: a sincere, highly intelligent man, full of optimism and a great sense of humor. Although, before being imprisoned, he had occupied very high positions, he remained unpretentious and eager to make peace. During his years of detention, Thuan was able to celebrate the Eucharist. He did it before breakfast, usually at around four or five o'clock in the morning. Could it be that he was revisiting the time when his teacher at the minor seminary, Father Bui Quang Tich (André) used to celebrate Mass?

The building where Thuan was kept at the time had a garden. My brother suggested raising some chickens there to improve their meals. He kept about twenty of them, feeding them rice that he put aside from his own rations. On feast days, chicken was on the menu.

Meals and blankets were not the only things Cong and Thuan shared. At the request of Cong's bosses, my brother held foreign language classes for him and two other guards. He enjoyed performing this task, as he said it gave him the opportunity to improve his own language skills. Cong learned Latin and Italian, and the other two learned English. Thuan had the charisma to motivate his "students". He managed to inspire them to love their studies. Once, Cong missed his homework. Instead of telling him off openly, my brother teased him in Latin, saying, "Hodie non cras", *which means "Today's work is not to be done tomorrow." He made the lessons exciting, and he was adept at incorporating words of proverbial wisdom into his teaching. For example, he taught the guards this fine expression:* "Ubi amatur non laboratur, et si laboratur, etiam labor amatur": *"Where there is love, there is no hard labor, for where there is hardship, the labor is loved." He also asked them to translate into Latin sayings such as these: "Love does not fear struggle" and "Love accepts a challenge and welcomes the hurdles with joy." He would sometimes make humorous references to Roman culture. Smiling, he would*

joke about the abbreviation SPQR, an inscription found all over
*Rome. It refers to the Roman senate and people (*Senatus Pop-
ulusque Romanus*—"This belongs to the Roman senate and*
people"), but Thuan gave Cong a more amusing interpretation:
"Sanctus Pater Quare Rides? Sum Pontifex Quia Rideo"*—*
"Holy Father, why are you laughing? I am laughing because I
am the pope." Thuan's commitment to lesson preparation was so
meticulous that he often went to bed very late, which was yet
another sign, Cong said, that he was thinking of others first and
was always ready to dedicate himself to acts of charity. To moti-
vate his students, he also taught them a Benedictine adage: "Lab-
orare est orare"*—"To work is to pray."*

One of the benefits Thuan reaped from having the class was
access to the Vatican paper, L'Osservatore Romano, which
Cong brought regularly. It enabled him to follow world and
Church news. Once he was amazed to read an article about him-
self in that paper: "1985, Arcivesco Coadiutore di Ho Chi
Minh; attuamente non si trova in questa citta"*—"Bishop*
Coadjutor of Ho Chi Minh City is presently out of town." He
was upset by the little notice, but Cong cheered him up, saying:
"What does it matter where you are, as long as you are in Vietnam! If the Vatican asks me where you are, I can tell them." And
they both found themselves laughing.

Mr. Cong particularly enjoyed their conversations, which
embraced all kinds of topics. Thuan talked about his travels, his
family in Australia, and the Church of Rome. He would say:
"Mr. Cong, one day I would love to be your guide in Italy,
especially in Venice, which is a magnificent city. I will intro-
duce you to Italian spaghetti, and we will finish the meal with a
good cappuccino." He also gave the guard a little picture of the
Virgin, along with a photo of a Vietnamese convent in Rome,
precious souvenirs that Cong has kept. How did Thuan manage

to remain so serene in such trying circumstances? According to Cong, the secret lay in a Latin adage: "Portatur leviter quod portat quisque libenter"—"What someone carries willingly he carries easily."

Conversion and a Miracle

In the summer of 2011, Mr. Nguyen Hoai Duc (Paul) sent me a long testimony in which he recalled how meeting my brother changed his life.[9] His initial training propelled him to a senior position in the Security Department of the Ministry of the Interior, to be engaged in the fight against "anti-revolutionary" activities. Around 1986, he was appointed to a post in the "Religion" Department of Counterrevolutionary Activities. Soon he heard about the man he now respectfully calls Bishop Thuan. He learned that this prisoner was a man of great talent, spoke eight foreign languages, was kind to everyone, and maintained an unwavering

[9] When I went to Hanoi, I was able to have a long conversation with another of his former guards, someone who must have been very young at the time. He explained to me that he had had to keep an eye on the archbishop during the last period of his imprisonment. According to him, eight guards lived with Archbishop Thuan during his imprisonment in Hanoi. Thanks to the information this guard gave me, I was able to visit the area where the building was and in which the archbishop spent his last years in prison. My informant described the layout of the upper floor, with one area reserved for the prisoner and the other for the guard. Although he remained an atheist and a Communist, this man had fond memories of the archbishop. The same was true of his wife. In fact, after he had been set free, Archbishop Thuan maintained contact with his former prison guard and encouraged him to marry his fiancée. This is how I found out that while he was in prison, some of the young policemen who were assigned to his watch would ask his advice about their girlfriends. The girl would stand in the street below the windows of the building, and Archbishop Thuan would give his opinion! This anecdote shows how these young people had come to regard him as an elder to be consulted for advice, someone they could thoroughly trust.

optimism, despite his long incarceration. Checking his file, Duc saw a photo that impressed him deeply: Thuan, dressed in white, on the beach at Nha Trang with two hundred religious and young people. What could his crime possibly be? His greatest offense, according to his file, was to have founded the Hope Community and to be a member of the family of Ngo Dinh Diem, a family regarded as hostile to the Communist Party.

Duc discovered that Thuan was being held in an old two-story colonial house, at 23 Hoa Ma Street in Hanoi. He was not allowed out. There were two police officers permanently posted to prevent him from making any contact with the outside.[10] He cooked and worked on the first floor; his bedroom was on the second. Having previously studied English and French as a student, Mr. Duc, thought well of by his bosses, asked his department chief, Colonel Nguyen Hong Lam, whether he could use the imprisoned bishop as a teacher to help him improve his French. The request was granted; at the same time, Mr. Duc was warned about the risk of "radicalization" he would run if he got too close to Thuan! Thereafter, he spent two afternoons a week with my brother. That was in 1987, shortly before his release. Right away, Duc was very happy to meet his new teacher. He immediately sensed how eager he was to communicate with someone from the outside.

Despite his long captivity, Thuan remained a very pleasant, gentle, and optimistic person. He was always happy to sing liturgical hymns and to tell funny stories. All who heard him talk were impressed by his intelligence and his deep faith. Thuan's kindness toward everyone, including his "enemies", triggered Duc's sympathy for him. Although Duc obeyed orders and never revealed to

---

[10] *Mr. Duc was not the only member of the secret police who came to this house, but his testimony does not specify whether the others came to work or to interrogate Thuan.*

him where he was being held, he very quickly realized that Thuan was no fool and was perfectly aware of the exact location.

To ward off the sense of isolation he had experienced for so many long years, Thuan composed various works for the purpose of helping language learners. During those lessons, he and his pupils—the various guards and Duc, the outside visitor—were free to talk about different topics. They chatted about the political and religious situation. While Duc approached such topics in the context of security affairs, Thuan never resorted to any subterfuge and always conversed openly and candidly with his students— for example, expressing his delight if, from his window, he saw women wearing traditional dresses going to Mass on a Sunday morning. As a member of the "Religion" Department of Counterrevolutionary Activities, Mr. Duc had the responsibility of studying religious documents, such as the Gospel or Buddhist texts, and he reached the conclusion that Jesus used simple words, while the Buddha expressed himself like a philosopher. Thuan and Duc tackled this subject, and my brother calmly offered him the following explanation:

> Buddha spoke like a scholar studying questions of philosophy and metaphysics, while Jesus speaks a very simple language because He is the Creator of this universe. He is above us all, and He presents the truth to us in such a way that we can understand it. His Word is the life of this universe. He created everything, and He knows all that He has created. Buddha tries to understand and analyze the universe—all that he sees, understands, and feels—with his intellect, and that is why he explains it in his way.

Duc still remembers this direct and crystal-clear reply. Thuan had really won him over.

A high level of mutual trust developed between them. The more Duc saw Thuan, the more Duc changed: he became more generous. To explain this turnaround, Duc used a philosopher's expression: "A rock placed in a particular place can change the direction of a stream." Duc wrote to me to tell me that his meeting with my brother had been the most important event in his life. He described Thuan as the most merciful and intelligent man he had ever met. And he added: "He is like a grain of wheat that germinated in my life and gave birth to an unshakable faith. Now I know that God is the most powerful force in me; God is the greatest victory of my life."

Thuan trusted Duc so much that he shared family memories with him. He liked to talk to Duc about his family, especially his parents and his desire to see them again while they were still alive. He was as happy as a kid when he showed off a pair of shoes that he had received from his relatives. "I will wear them when I am free", he would say. When Duc showed astonishment at the happiness he found in such a simple thing, Thuan added: "It's important to derive joy and delight in the smallest things."

They celebrated the Vietnamese New Year together. To make this possible, Duc had suggested to the police that he would keep Thuan under surveillance for them so that they could celebrate at home with their families. To enable Thuan to share in the joy of being with those close to him over these festive days, Duc brought his son along, and all three enjoyed a celebration undisturbed. Duc even helped Thuan draw up a letter in which he asked for his freedom: as a member of the Communist Party, he knew better than anyone the most appropriate format to expedite the request. When Thuan was freed from prison at the end of November 1988, he did not forget Duc: he visited him on several occasions before going into exile.

Duc's encounter with Thuan led him to seriously question the relevance of his work, which consisted in fighting all forms

*of religion. How could the regime justify the arbitrary impris-
onment of a man who was as peaceable as this? No tribunal
had ever passed sentence on him! The bloody repression of the
protest marchers in Tiananmen Square in Beijing[11] was the last
straw for Duc: he quit his job and found work with an oil company for a while before becoming a writer. The grain of wheat
that Thuan had sown in Duc's heart had begun to germinate!
Over his years of self-examination, Duc contracted a serious
illness that affected his nervous sys-
tem. His body was contorted and his
legs paralyzed. As the Bible tells us,
God sometimes speaks to us through
dreams. Duc remembers a dream in
which he went into a bathroom and
turned on the faucet, but instead of water coming out, he saw
human waste, and he woke up feeling depressed. But the following night, he dreamed that he turned on another faucet, out
of which flowed fresh water, and he felt relieved and happy. He
realized that there was a connection between his dreams and
his physical state: his body needed to be purified. One night,
he dreamed he saw a curtain and heard a voice telling him: "If
you draw the curtain, you will see a world of light." In another
dream, he was standing in front of a church. He heard the words:
"Go in and follow the light." Duc began to visit churches. He
was very impressed by the fact that Christians are invited to be
open to others and to admit their failings— "Through my fault,
through my fault, through my most grievous fault". He was also
impressed by the peace greetings that they respectfully offer one
another. In due course, his spiritual pilgrimage led him to ask
for baptism.*

**"My brother was
the rock that
transformed the
life of Duc."**

---

[11] Big demonstrations calling for reforms took place in China in the spring
of 1989 on this central square in Beijing. They were put down bloodily, and
government control of the press was intensified.

What followed was what I consider to be Thuan's first miracle. A few months after my brother's death, Duc was baptized during the Easter Vigil in 2003, and he received Communion for the first time. The Resurrection of Christ had a transformative effect on him that was not solely spiritual. His body had healed completely,[12] with no scar showing. Duc prayed: "Lord, I thank You for Your light, for Your call, and for having chosen me to be Your child. My whole journey began with Bishop Thuan, who taught me and guided me toward You."

These days, Mr. Duc writes books and composes songs and poems that he offers as a gift to the Lord. He is also the author of a major piece of evidence in Thuan's beatification dossier: The Road to Faith through Francis-Xavier Nguyen Van Thuan. *Not surprisingly, the authorities refused him permission to leave Vietnam in 2013, on the occasion of the closing of Thuan's beatification process in Rome. Interviewed by Radio Free Asia, Duc reported that the reasons for their refusal to let him go were never clearly explained. Considering that he was a former Party official who had converted to Catholicism, the story of his spiritual journey was bound to upset the authorities! Moreover, in the articles he published about the problems facing our country, he showed no indulgence toward the Communist ideology.*

Other witnesses of Thuan's holiness were able to fly to Rome to give their testimony. One of the prison guards, a convert, gave Cardinal Turkson a brief summary of my brother's message:

- *Be the first to begin to love.*
- *Love each person.*
- *Love your enemies too.*
- *Love by serving and by your life.*

---

[12] The healing process began from the moment Mr. Duc started to prepare for baptism. By Easter, he had recovered his health!

The Power of the Eucharist

When Thuan gave talks after his liberation, he was often asked: "How did you manage to retain your mental stability and this capacity to love?" He invariably replied: "The Eucharist and prayer, for they are special moments of meeting with God". Right up to the last days of his life, Thuan found his inner strength in the celebration of the Eucharist.

Before his incarceration, he had not only anticipated the possibility of imprisonment but had also thought about how to keep Jesus with him. He had told his friends: "When I am in prison, if I ask you for medication for my 'stomach pain', please send me some hosts and some communion wine." When he was arrested, he was not allowed to take anything with him. Friends could receive his letters, in which he asked for soap, a toothbrush, toothpaste, and pajamas. He also complained that he had an upset stomach. His supporters immediately got the message and sent him a little bottle of communion wine. They sent it in a medicine bottle labeled: "stomach medication". Hosts were hidden in various places, including among flashlight batteries.[13]

While at Cay Vong, Thuan was physically able to celebrate Mass. At other times, especially in Phu Khanh, his second place of imprisonment, he became so weak that he was scarcely able to pray or to remember liturgical prayers, but he tried to unite his sufferings with those of Jesus. Over the long years of his captivity, he was able to write to my parents. He would always end his letter

[13] In Vietnam, I was able to meet one of the individuals who helped send the items necessary for Mass during the nine months that Archbishop Thuan spent in Phu Khanh prison. In fact, various methods were used: for example, the wine would be put into little bottles labeled "fish sauce" and the outside of the bottles doused with a very smelly sauce. Baskets containing food were sometimes sent to the prisoner, with hosts hidden between layers of rice bread.

with "Dear Mum and Dad, do not burden yourself with grief. I live each day in union with the universal Church and the Sacrifice of Christ. Pray that I have the courage and strength always to stay faithful to the Church and to the gospel and that I may live in conformity with the will of God." So it was that in his exhaustion, his life itself became a perpetual sacrifice.

Later, particularly when he was in a prison in the North, he regained enough strength to be able to celebrate Mass. He managed to put a few drops of wine and a few crumbs of bread in his hand for the consecration.

He would then pray: "This is my altar, and this is my cathedral! It is the true tonic for soul and body. I feel the very heart of Christ beating in mine. I feel that my life is His and His is mine. He lives in me and I in Him, in a kind of symbiosis and mutual immanence. He remains in me. I will never be able to express adequately such a great joy. Every day, with three drops of wine and a drop of water in the palm of my hand, I celebrate Mass."

When he was working in the field at one of the camps, Thuan found a flask buried in the soil. He began to use this little container as his chalice.

> In the reeducation camp, the prisoners were divided into groups of fifty; we slept on common beds and everyone had the right to fifty centimeters of space. We arranged it so that there were five Catholics near me. At 9:30 P.M. the lights were turned off and everyone had to sleep. I curled up on the bed to celebrate Mass, from memory, and I distributed communion by reaching under the mosquito netting covering us. We made small containers from cigarette packages in which to reserve the Blessed Sacrament. Jesus in the Eucharist was always with me in my shirt pocket. . . .
>
> At night, the prisoners took turns for adoration. . . . Many Christians regained the fervor of their faith during those days, and

Buddhists and other non-Christians converted. The strength of Jesus' love is irresistible. The darkness of prison became light.[14]

During solitary confinement, he generally celebrated the Eucharist at three in the afternoon, the hour of Jesus' death on the cross. Providentially, his guards would be having a nap right at that time, and he was free to sing the Mass however he pleased, in various languages, without fear of disturbing anyone or, worse, arousing suspicion. In all likelihood, his guards probably thought he was crazy.[15] He continued to receive his "medication for stomach upsets", and the guards did not interfere.

During the retreat he preached at the Vatican in 2000, Thuan said: "Altogether, about three hundred priests were put in prison. Their presence in the various camps was not only providential for Catholics; it was also an opportunity for protracted interfaith dialogues, which created friendship and mutual comprehension among all, not just in word but in real life."[16]

My brother had inherited his eucharistic spirituality from our forebears; it was also nurtured during his seminary training by the example of several of his teachers. I think particularly of Father Cressonnier, who gave his life for the Eucharist. From his early days in the minor seminary, Thuan had been strongly influenced by the indomitable faith of Father Cressonnier, whom he met again later when he himself became rector at Kim Long. Just after his appointment as bishop of Nha Trang, Thuan heard

---

[14] Nguyen Van Thuan, *Five Loaves*, 36–37.

[15] *When we compare the various testimonies given by my brother, it seems we can conclude that sometimes he prayed secretly, while at other times, he was free to sing the glory of God, for what mattered to the authorities was to isolate him from the outside world, not what he was actually doing in his cell. The friendships he developed with his jailers certainly enabled him to enjoy relatively more freedom.*

[16] François-Xavier Nguyen Van Thuan, *Témoins de l'espérance: Retraite au Vatican*, trans. Sylvie Garoche (Paris: Nouvelle Cité, 2000), 168–69.

that his former teacher and colleague had been murdered: in February 1968, the Communists attacked a great number of towns, including Hue and Phu Cam. The fights took the lives of many innocent victims. In our home village, a large number of Christians were rounded up and executed by firing squads. Priests were buried alive. Thinking it was safe, Father Cressonnier went to the convent chapel to retrieve the consecrated Hosts and hide them. Unfortunately, on his way back, he was stopped by Communist troops, who arrested him and killed him. His body was left in the street for two days. After things had calmed down somewhat, some of the faithful went to recover his body. A witness reported that before he died, the priest was able to consume the Hosts, in adoring respect for the Blessed Sacrament. Thuan always spoke of this priest as a saint. Later in prison, the Eucharist would, for him too, be his strength in a life defined by sacrifice.[17]

"Jesus in the Eucharist was an enormous help in His silent presence."

Cardinal Thuan said that these celebrations in prison were the most beautiful Masses of his life: on the cross, Jesus began a revolution, and we can renew humanity through the Sacrifice of the Mass. The Eucharist gave Thuan the strength always to be at the service of others. Every time he said Mass, he held out his hands to be spiritually nailed to the cross with Jesus, to drink with Him the bitter cup. Every day, reciting or hearing the words of the Consecration, he sealed with all his heart and soul

[17] Father Cressonnier went to get the Hosts with a colleague, Father Pierre Poncet, who also died there. See Antoine Fouques Duparc, *Pierre Poncet, missionnaire au Vietnam (1932–1968): Lettres à sa Famille (1956–1968)*, Églises d'Asie 19 (Paris: Archives des Missions Étrangères, 2004). The testimonies at the end of the book give an account of the fate of these two fathers in the 1968 conflicts.

a new pact, an eternal pact between Jesus and himself, by His blood mixed with his own (see 1 Cor 11:23–25). Jesus accomplished on the cross the most important action of His life: He shed His blood to save the world. On the cross, Jesus could no longer preach or heal the sick or visit people. He was in a state of total abandonment, absolute immobility, wholly united to God. And so, for Archbishop Thuan, Christ truly became the perfect example of total love for the Father. The Lord gave everything to save souls; He loved to the end, and He remains with us always.[18]

[18] Nguyen Van Thuan, *Five Loaves*, 35–41.

Tiet Do

Temperance

7

Liberation and Exile

Meeting with the Minister of the Interior, Liberation, and Residence in Hanoi

After endless, epic soul-searching, my brother had accepted his fate and resigned himself to staying in prison,[1] though he longed to see our parents again. He told us how, on the evening preceding his liberation, which was the vigil of the feast of the Presentation of the Blessed Virgin Mary in the Temple (November 21), he had prayed very intensely. Like Mary, he had to present himself before God, but he had great difficulty understanding what the Lord wanted him to do. On the one hand, he wanted to say to God: "Fiat, Your will be done: if You want me to spend the rest of my life in prison, I accept. If You want me to die in prison, give me the courage to be ready." This prayer brought him great inner peace. But at the same time, he found himself saying: "Fiat. If it be Your will, Lord, set me free. I feel I am still able to serve Your

[1] When one enjoys freedom, he does not realize just how much suffering a person endures in prison. In Germany one day, I was in a car with the cardinal. Seeing the trees that had been planted along the roadside to diminish noise from traffic, he remarked that they prevented him from seeing the horizon. Another time, in a market, we saw frogs that were trying to escape from a cage. Just looking at them nearly made him faint. These two anecdotes show the depth of the psychic wounds that prison time had inflicted on Cardinal Thuan.

Church. And if it is in Your plan, Lord, I want to go on living so that I can glorify You." The following day, while making his breakfast, he had a feeling that the guards were acting busier than usual. There was a great deal of traffic in the corridors. Eventually he heard steps coming toward his room; then there was a knock on the door, and a warden said to him: "Have you finished your breakfast?"

"No, I am boiling water for the rice."

"Hurry up, then; the minister of the interior is waiting to see you!"

"O Mary," he prayed, "today is the feast of your presentation in the Temple. Yesterday, I made two requests, A or B, to you. You know which one I prefer—to live and serve the Church—but I must learn to be ready to say, as you did, 'Fiat'."

After his breakfast, the guards said to him: "Get dressed. You cannot show up in pajamas before the minister."

They gave him a clean shirt, and half an hour later, they took him to see the minister, who offered him tea. There was also a bowl of fruit on the table. Noticing the welcome he was getting, Thuan had a hunch that he might just be set free. The minister even shook his hand and said to him: "Ah! Mr. Thuan, you have indeed caused us so many problems—at home, abroad, and all over the world! Now we'd like to get rid of you!"

"Yes, but how?"

"How long have you been in prison?"

"Thirteen years. Since I was first put in prison, many changes have taken place: different prime ministers, change of popes. If you find me such a big problem, why not just send me to some remote part of the country, out of sight, to some insignificant parish?"

"Oh no! But is there anything you'd like to ask today?"

From deep within, he seemed to hear a voice whisper: "Tell him that you want your freedom."

And suddenly Thuan felt bold enough to say: "I want to be released."

No prisoner is supposed to address a minister like that, but he had the courage to say what he wanted loud and clear: "I want my freedom!"

The minister replied: "Just like that?"

"Yes, just like that!"

Surprisingly, the minister then asked him: "When?"

And Thuan replied: "Today. Right now. Yes, I want to be freed today!"

Thuan was very surprised when the minister called his secretary: "He's leaving today. Get the papers ready. That's final!"

Turning to my brother, he added: "Drink your tea; have a banana. You are leaving prison. This way, we'll be done with you."

The minister ended the interview with a simple "Au revoir!"[2]

Thuan recalled that he almost froze; he did not even remember to thank the minister, for he just couldn't attune himself to the fact that he was free. He was taken back to his cell to pick up his things. Prior to leaving his prison, he tried to stuff his few possessions into his pajama trousers. But his guards found him a bag: it was important to give the outside world the impression that he had been well treated!

---

[2] Mai Chi Tho (1922–2007), also known as Phan Dinh Dong, was at that time the minister of the interior. In his book, Chau describes the conversation: Tho, a Communist from the South, apparently said that the Communists had changed their opinion about Diem and that they had stopped denigrating him as a puppet of the United States. According to Chau, Bishop Thuan was set free the very day of his encounter with Tho (André Nguyen Van Chau, *The Miracle of Hope: Francis Xavier Nguyen Van Thuan; Political Prisoner, Prophet of Peace* [Boston: Pauline Books and Media, 2003], 231–36). It is quite possible that, during the conversation, the minister wanted to get information about the relations between the Church and the state, relations that were in the process of undergoing modification, above all in Russia, at the time of this "transition" period.

It is possible that they took a few days to complete the formalities surrounding his release.[3] Perhaps they hoped he would, in the meanwhile, recover somewhat from his ravaged appearance, the result of so many years in incarceration. They also needed to provide him with accommodations where they could monitor his activities. They found him a room in the bishop's residence.[4] Even though he had to report to the police every day, he could now sleep in a comfortable bed; he had almost forgotten what that was like! He was fascinated with little things: a pillow, nice blankets. In his heart, he did not forget that the Virgin had answered his prayer on November 21 and given him the strength to say "I want to be set free."

Thuan was touched by the fact that the key moments in his captivity took place under the gaze of the Virgin. The day when his freedom was taken away was August 15, the feast of the Assumption of Our Lady and also Mothers' festival.[5] At the time of his liberation, he felt fully protected by the Virgin and the presence of God by his side. Even if my brother never doubted that the Lord is all powerful, stronger than evil, the evil spirit sometimes tempts us and pushes us to think that he will triumph over good. But Thuan said that this temptation helps us move forward in hope: God invites us to turn our faces even more directly toward Him.

For my brother, the Marian feasts have always had a great importance.

---

[3] A priest working at the time in the bishop's office in Hanoi confirmed this to me. He had a clear memory of the arrival of the archbishop on November 23.

[4] The diocesan house in Hanoi is very large. It occupies a large piece of land. Archbishop Thuan lived there in a building that still contains many handwritten documents that he was able to take with him when he left prison. The archbishop was also able to keep various objects, of no value to the guards, but so precious to him: his cross and the small vials that he had used to say Mass.

[5] *On that day, mothers are given flowers and do not do any cooking. It is said that the food is brought by angels.*

Around that time, I was experiencing a lot of difficulties at work, but the trust in God that Thuan had always shown greatly inspired me, and I understood that God wanted me to keep on boldly moving forward. Thanks to his testimony, I am convinced that despair has no place in a life of faith. I also experienced the power of prayer in my life: it is the soul of all Christian life. Without prayer, we have a tendency to shift responsibility for our problems, both in the world and in our daily lives, on others and to do nothing about them. But prayer sets us free, and we become useful instruments in God's hands. Otherwise, we are like dull knives that have lost their effectiveness. Prayer gives us the strength to choose. I saw that in the case of abortion, for example. It is all too easy to blame the laws that authorize it. Instead, I can vote for pro-life candidates, I can nurture in myself the desire to have children, and I can say no to abortion. Prayer makes us free to become effective instruments in the hands of God. Thuan taught us that the Lord can become everything for us, thanks to the Eucharist, the Rosary, and the strength that prayer gives us.

Thuan's Visit to His Family in Australia and to Pope John Paul II

Although officially he could not leave Hanoi, Thuan made the best possible use of his freedom: he went for walks in town or rode a bicycle. Having spent so many years separated from his compatriots, he was eager to meet people and to listen to their stories and hear about their sufferings. He was sometimes able to make secret day-long car trips to visit Christians throughout the region. Once he even made a 185-mile trip.

Shortly after his release, Thuan was able to phone our parents, who had emigrated to Australia. After a few months in Hanoi, he received permission to leave the country to visit our family and to meet Pope John Paul II in Rome. Thuan wanted to surprise our parents with his visit. He was a little afraid that the authorities in Vietnam, who had so readily agreed to his travel request, might change their minds at the last minute. But they seemed eager to get rid of him. All that mattered to them was that Thuan not be allowed to return to Saigon as archbishop, a post that the Holy See insisted he had already been appointed to a long time ago. He was allowed to fly first to Thailand. My sister Ham Tieu (Anne) and the staff of the apostolic nunciature were there to meet him at the airport in Bangkok.[6] Anne was planning to get Thuan a visa for Australia and help him financially, since he had no money.

Although all the passengers had disembarked from the plane and cleared the arrival areas, Anne and Thuan, who had been separated for so many years, could not spot each other anywhere. Anne did not see anyone who looked even remotely like our brother. She even wondered if she had the right arrival information for the flight from Hanoi. She kept looking around and then saw an elderly, thin, frail-looking man.

My brother was only sixty-one then, but the years in prison had exacted a heavy toll on his appearance. Moreover, he was wearing a hat that was much too big for him. Anne asked the strange-looking man, "Thuan, is that you?" Then they recognized each other. Anne wanted to get Thuan's luggage, but he did not have any. "I don't have anything", he said, "only my rosary in my pocket. The bishop of Hanoi lent me a shirt and a pair of trousers, and I'm wearing the shoes the family sent me. All I have is a little present for Dad and Mum." It was a little box wrapped in paper. Anne offered to carry it in her bag, but Thuan did not want to let go of it. "I want to give it to Dad and Mum myself", he added. And he later did.

---

[6] Anne had made arrangements with the nuncio's office in Bangkok. She and Thuan stayed at the nunciature, and she bought him the clothes he needed.

My parents had not been told that their son was coming. Anne had simply told them that a bishop would be visiting them. When Thuan arrived at the front door of their house in Sydney, Mum was the first to recognize him. All during his stay in Bangkok and throughout the flight to Australia, my brother had kept the little packet with him. On the evening of his arrival,  *he explained: "I am your eldest son. According to our culture, I should be taking care of you and should offer you something when I come to see you. I have no money to give, but what I do have for you is a very beautiful present that all the money in the world could not buy." He opened the box, explaining what was inside: a couple of little glass bottles and a plastic spoon, seemingly cheap trinkets, that he had used for celebrating Mass in prison. "See, you can lose everything, you can even lose your life, but you don't lose anything when you welcome the Lord in the Eucharist. Christ came down in these objects here, in this box. I lost my freedom for thirteen years, but these little vials are a reminder that we have the Lord with us. It is never right to despair." My mother kept the box until she died in 2005 at the age of 103.[7] When I visited Australia, she would gather us all together—she had a particular fondness for my children—to pray together around my brother's memorial of his prison days.*

The archbishop would have liked to travel to other countries, but he had been granted permission only for a visit to Pope John Paul II. He went to Rome and met the Holy Father on several occasions. John Paul II had been

---

[7] Today this precious memento is on display in Cologne (see appendix 2).

monitoring very closely the imprisonment of the man appointed archbishop by Paul VI. Archbishop Thuan took great pleasure in taking walks on the streets of Rome, a city so familiar to him from his days as a student. He made another short visit to his parents and then stopped in Manila on the way and met up with Cardinal Sin (1928–2005).[8] He then returned to his residence with the bishop of Hanoi, still abiding by the same police restrictions as before.[9]

The Communist world was in turmoil. In the USSR, President Mikhail Gorbachev (in power from 1988 to 1991) carried out the first reforms, known under their Russian name as *glasnost* (transparency): a first step in the country toward democracy and opening up to the West. In 1989, when Thuan had gone back to Hanoi, the Berlin Wall fell. China saw mass demonstrations in the center of Beijing, in the famous Tiananmen Square. In Asia, though they did introduce economic reforms, the Communists stifled popular appeals for more democracy.

An Operation and Various Travels

Unfortunately Thuan's calvary did not end with his release. Shortly after his release from prison, the doctors diagnosed serious prostate issues. Thuan dreaded going to a Communist hospital because he feared that an operation could provide them with an

---

[8] At the time, Cardinal Sin was one of the most important bishops in the region, and he had a great influence within the East Asian episcopal conference. Along with numerous other clerics, he criticized the regime of the Philippines president Ferdinand Marcos (1917–1981). Archbishop Thuan had known him when he was bishop of Nha Trang.

[9] Archbishop Thuan could have sought political asylum in the West, but he wanted to serve his country and chose to obey the orders of Hanoi.

*ideal opportunity to get rid of him. In view of the urgency of the
situation, however, he agreed to go to Bach Mai Hospital to have
his tumor removed.[10] Following the three-hour operation, Thuan
did not receive proper postoperative care: the surgeon had ordered
the nurses not to make any decisions on their own or dispense any
treatments without his permission.[11] A serious infection set in,
and Thuan had to be operated on again to curb it. The procedure
was poorly performed, and he thought he was going to die. Thuan
survived thanks to the intervention of a hospital staff member who
looked after him in secret. Despite the surgeon's ban, he was able
to receive clandestinely the medication he needed. Once again, he
realized that the Lord had saved him through the hands of men
and women of courage and integrity. Thuan was also aware that
many people in Vietnam and in the diaspora were praying for
him.[12] He recognized the power of prayer.[13]*

*The treatment Thuan received in Hanoi was unfortunately still
inadequate. The Sant'Egidio Community,[14] which supported
him on many occasions throughout his life, paid for a trip to*

[10] Founded in 1911 by the French, Bach Mai was the main hospital in Hanoi.
This important hospital was badly damaged in the Vietnam War.

[11] One of our uncles on the maternal side, a retired doctor who had continued to live in the North, was able to attend the operation but was not permitted
to intervene afterward and provide my brother with aftercare. Thuan and that
uncle both suffered from the situation, although in different ways.

[12] Following the victory of the Communists in South Vietnam in 1975, millions of Vietnamese fled the country. Many family members of Cardinal Thuan
were among them. They were joined by many other refugees in their prayers
for the archbishop.

[13] It is rarely mentioned that the archbishop stayed for a few months in St.
Anthony's parish near the hospital. The room he occupied has been preserved
and turned into a small memorial.

[14] This movement of Catholic laypeople, founded after the Second Vatican
Council, has put a great deal of work into the evangelization of the poor areas
in Rome. Today it can be found in a number of countries, and it has become
an important agency for peace through prayer, solidarity with those living in
poverty, work in favor of unity between Christians, and interreligious dialogue.

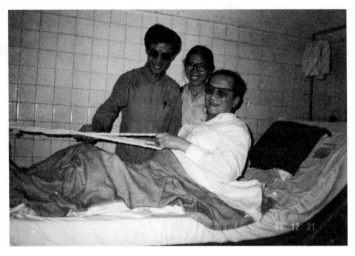

Rome for another operation. He was away from Vietnam for only a short while, and after a period of convalescence, he returned to Hanoi.[15] As soon as he arrived, Thuan was summoned to Colonel Nguyen Hong Lam's office. Lam was a high-ranking official in the Ministry of the Interior. The colonel informed Thuan that any appointment offered to him by the Holy See would need express approval by the Vietnamese government. It appeared that the Communists were even more scared of my brother at that time than in 1975. Thuan responded politely, trying to explain the Holy See's thinking in the matter of appointments: "Appointments made by the pope are of a pastoral nature", he said. "There is no intent to meddle in the politics of any country."

Lam would not listen. He advised Thuan to leave for Australia and visit his parents again. "Stay there", he suggested, "until the situation in Vietnam becomes more settled."

[15] Nguyen Van Chau, *The Miracle of Hope*, 247–48.

"I have just been there to visit my parents", my brother replied.
"Why don't you go and spend some time in Rome?" the
colonel responded.

Thuan realized that Lam meant his last proposal to be taken
seriously, and he promised to give it some thought. He telephoned
our parents, who contacted the Holy See. The Vatican response
was short and sweet: "Come to Italy." It is quite possible that
the Vietnamese government contemplated giving Thuan some sort
of role in the episcopal conference in his country, but it was completely out of the question for him to resume his appointment as
archbishop of Saigon. The Communists opted, in the end, to keep
him away from any official ministry. They even promised to allow
more freedom to other Vietnamese bishops on condition that they
distanced themselves from Thuan. The political authorities realized that, given his status as archbishop, any official role given to
him would increase his influence and create trouble for the government. As far as the Communist regime was concerned, there were
only two options: the archbishop's death or his permanent exile
from the country.[16]

In a long document dated November 9, 1991, Thuan tran-
scribed the content of various discussions and letters that shed light
on the situation. The government did not want him to have any
role in Vietnam, arguing that many citizens did not support him:
Was he not the nephew of President Diem? In reality, contrary
to what the authorities claimed, our uncle Diem was held in very
high regard by many of his fellow citizens for his spirit of nation-
alism and independence with regard to American policies. Behind
this charade, what they wanted was for Thuan to abandon the
fight against the effects of Communism on the political, moral,
and spiritual life of the people, a battle that had also defined

[16] Ibid., 243–48.

Diem's policy. The government wanted to send my brother into exile: he presented a risk because he was a potential source of inspiration for the nation.

Thuan refuted the arguments that were being put forth. After at first politely defending Vatican policy, he stated clearly that only truth can set us free. In response to the accusations made against him, Thuan wrote that he was looking only for dialogue, harmony, and peace; his sole motivation was to serve his country. He also expressed the desire that three years after his liberation his situation could finally be clarified and he could be allowed to fulfill his responsibilities toward mankind, preferably in Vietnam; he still had a lot to offer his homeland, even if it were in some very remote parish in the northern part of the country. He pointed out that he had family duties to attend to: his family's assets had been confiscated, and his brother Thanh was sick and living in poverty. Thuan was the only one still in the country and in a position to help him.

Thuan was very realistic about how people regarded him: no one—and no institution—is ever fully accepted by everyone. The only thing that mattered to him was the spirit of generosity and friendship that was characteristic of the Vietnamese. In response to criticisms of Diem's regime, he wrote: "Generally speaking, the Vietnamese[17] are intuitive enough to recognize truth, sin, and sacrifice." It was too soon to gauge the significance of such recent events; history would be the judge. And Thuan added: "The party and the government have a right to their point of view, but I doubt whether we are able today to know the whole truth."

I still have this very important document. Whenever I reread it, it renews my awareness of Thuan's perseverance and his sheer courage. He could have shown a degree of flexibility regarding

---

[17] He was speaking of the voice of the people.

government policy. He chose not to! Despite his imprisonment and the terrible abuse he suffered, he was not afraid to speak out and follow his conscience. He defended the Vietnamese spirit and his family values, and he assumed his responsibilities toward the country and the universal Church. He was deeply convinced of his priestly vocation as guardian of the flock that had been entrusted to him by the Lord. But in the end, he entrusted the decision about his future to the Holy See.

Final Exile

Thuan's third trip to Rome after his release marked the beginning of his exile. It was in late 1991. Even though 1976 was the last time he saw the South, he still considered himself the archbishop of Saigon, a fact backed by Pope John Paul II in Rome. On several occasions, Vatican representatives in charge of his dossier met a Vietnamese delegation that had specifically flown to Italy to resolve the problems they believed were caused by my brother and the Vatican. The Holy See was not ready to cave in to Vietnamese political pressure and discharge Thuan from his episcopal role. During the negotiations between the papal representatives and the Vietnamese government officials, the latter showed how much they loved Italy. They behaved very differently in Italy from the way they would back in Vietnam. They actually smiled and even drank champagne in Thuan's honor! When the issue of Thuan's return to Saigon was broached, however, they would not budge. Thuan realized very quickly that as far as the Vietnamese Communists were concerned, he was and would remain in exile.

Since his release, Thuan had had very little rest, in spite of his serious health problems. Battling cancer, like many in our family, he had to undergo several operations, but he went on working and traveling the world to proclaim the gospel. The testimony of individuals who have consecrated their lives to God is tremendously helpful to those around them. One day, when Thuan was celebrating Mass in the United States, a young Vietnamese attended the service with his brother and a young girl, but he remained outside, uninterested in religious ceremonies. There were loudspeakers around the church forecourt, delivering a live broadcast of the Mass. Although he generally paid little attention to the message of the Gospel, this young man was fascinated by my brother's homily and felt a need to hear more of it. Books written by Thuan were on sale at the back of the church. He looked at them and felt an inner impulse to study my brother's message. Little by little, he found himself attracted to the Church; he started going to Mass and eventually became a priest. Father Bao lives his priesthood as Thuan lived it; he often refers to my brother's spirituality.[18]

Activities in Rome

Archbishop Thuan's first years of exile from Vietnam were devoted mainly to visiting the Vietnamese diaspora. In 1993, he went to Sydney to attend his father's funeral. His mother showed great courage and dignity that day. She received the full support of her many children who were able to travel to Australia.[19] Archbishop Thuan evoked the memory of Am as a husband and a loving father whose quiet courage had a profound effect on his children.

In Rome, the archbishop oversaw the translation of his works into several languages. These publications were a

[18] He later obtained a doctorate in Rome. When I had the opportunity to meet him, I felt very close to him as one of many friends of the cardinal.

[19] One of her sons, Thanh (Michel), who had stayed in Vietnam, was not permitted to leave the country.

spiritual blessing not just for the Vietnamese community in exile but also for many Christians all over the world. He received several prizes for his work for world peace, honors that he regarded as an encouragement for the Vietnamese people. He was invited to many countries to give retreats and talks. During the first years after his release and the beginning of his exile, he said little in public about his spiritual journey in prison. But his mother made him understand that the exceptional graces he had received were not his to keep: he must share them outside the inner circle of family and friends. The archbishop was very aware that the physical and moral sufferings he had endured were, sadly, far from exceptional. Countless innocent victims had perished during the twentieth century, especially in Nazi and Communist camps. But the archbishop's particular experience stood out: in prison, he managed to develop friendly relationships with several of his tormentors, and some of them even converted. Alone, from the depth of darkness, he sent out a message of hope, and he experienced the power of God, thanks particularly to his clandestine celebrations of the Eucharist. A great number of people were able to meet the archbishop and listen to him. The core of his talks was about his discovery of what prison had enabled him to experience: that God alone suffices. God's presence is vital in the life of every Christian, and it matters more than all the work we can accomplish for Him.

Accompanied by his mother, Archbishop Thuan visited the headquarters of the Paris Foreign Missions Society. They spent a long time in prayer in Lourdes and then went to Rome, where they were received by Pope John Paul II. His mother was particularly moved by the pilgrimage to the Eternal City. That visit to the Vatican was a turning point in the life of Archbishop Thuan: Hiep was convinced that her son's place was now in Rome and that he needed to abandon definitively his dream of one day returning to Saigon.[20]

Following a meeting with Pope John Paul II in 1994, Thuan resigned his post as archbishop of Saigon, thus choosing to serve the universal Church in a different way. He then took part in the work of various dicasteries of the Roman Curia. The Holy Father appointed him vice president of the Pontifical Council for Justice and Peace. In 1998, he became president of that dicastery. In 2000, John Paul II invited him to preach the Lenten retreat in the Vatican, and in 2001, he was created a cardinal. The pope, who had himself experienced Communist oppression, did not simply want to honor Thuan for his courage in the face of a totalitarian regime. He saw in him an envoy who could, by his testimony, work for more justice and peace in the world.

John Paul II endorsed the foundation of the Community of Our Lady of La Vang. Its members were to see themselves as simple children of God, and, in their works, they were invited to serve the poor and encourage unity in the Church. The members of the community were also to proclaim the Word and rekindle family values.[21]

---

[20] Nguyen Van Chau, *The Miracle of Hope*, 256–60.

[21] Madame Hong has quite a bit of material about this community that Archbishop Thuan founded. It shows his great attachment to the shrine of Our Lady of La Vang and to the Virgin. He used to say that he entrusted himself to her very early in his life. We know that in 1998 he spoke in Washington about the community. He wrote various texts to explain its spirituality (April and August 2000). Although it is difficult to sum them all up, it is clear that while he talked a great deal about the spirit of the community, he said very little about its practical organization. This material is a testimony to his own spirituality too: "Mary taught me to have faith and to persevere", he wrote. "And she set me on the path of evangelization." This community is mainly alive in Australia.

While in Rome in 1995, Bishop Thuan was appointed postulator for the cause for beatification of Marcel Van, another victim of Communist oppression in Vietnam. He was also given the task of composing the *Compendium of the Social Doctrine of the Church*, a long-term project that his deteriorating health prevented him from completing; it was published after his death by Cardinal Renato Raffaele Martino, his successor at the Pontifical Council for Justice and Peace.[22]

[22] At the beginning of the work, Cardinal Martino writes: "My predecessor, the late and venerable Cardinal François-Xavier Nguyên Van Thuân, guided with wisdom, constancy and far-sightedness the complex phase of the preparation of this document; his illness prevented him from bringing it to a conclusion with its publication. This work, entrusted to me and now offered to those who will read it, carries therefore the seal of a great witness to the Cross who remained *strong in faith* in the dark and terrible years of Vietnam." Pontifical Council for Justice and Peace, *Compendium of the Social Doctrine of the Church* (April 2, 2004), presentation.

Hao hiep

Magnanimity

8

Talks and Retreats

*After his release, and while he was working at the Pontifical
Council for Justice and Peace, Thuan gave a great number of
talks and retreats on various subjects. Many of these have not yet
been published.*

The Bishop's Vocation

*In July 1999, Thuan preached a four-day retreat to African bish-
ops in Ghana. He mainly talked about chapters 14 through 17
of the Gospel of Saint John. To his fellow bishops he spoke first
about the problems they were facing: armed conflict, corruption,
galloping urbanization, and the exploitation of resources by mam-
moth multinationals.*

*In the face of such challenges, Thuan stressed the importance of
these words of Jesus: "Apart from me you can do nothing" (Jn
15:5). He encouraged the bishops to stay faithful to the gospel,
for the teaching of the Church does not bow to public opinion.
He said: "The Church offers the message of Jesus to the world as
found in the Scriptures." He also urged the bishops to reread the
Vatican II documents so as to apply them better.*

*Certain truths can be fully understood only by those who
believe. God reveals Himself to us, and we are servants called*

upon to proclaim, with evangelical enthusiasm, the greatness of His Person. The Christians of Africa must turn their continent into a new homeland for Christ. When the gospel is made incarnate in the culture, society becomes more humane. Our relationship with Jesus will enable us to establish new kinship with the poor, with families in difficulty, with the sick, and with all those who thirst to be taught.

In another talk, Thuan referred to his personal experience. With humility, he admitted that convincing a bishop of anything is a difficult task. And he should know! The life of a bishop is not his to live. To clarify his views on what a bishop should be, Thuan spoke of those who had been models for him: with their lives, they had opened his eyes to the needs of the people of

For him, to evangelize meant to transform the whole of humanity from the inside.

God and to the urgent need for evangelization. That is why he suffered so much when, in 1975, he could only watch helplessly as the Communists closed seminaries, Catholic schools, and universities and prevented him from carrying out pastoral visits. His time in prison was defining, since it was there that he felt a deep sense of abandonment, especially by some of his colleagues, just as Jesus did on the cross: "My God, my God, why have you forsaken me?" (Mk 15:34). His epiphany came with the realization that it is more important to seek God than to work for Him. He called this eye-opener a "gift of light and spiritual discernment".

Like Christ in His Passion, who did not complain about the flogging or the crown of thorns, Thuan did not rebel against his difficult situation. Thanks to the celebration of the Eucharist, he was able to rise above the sufferings of solitary confinement and the mental abuse that was inflicted on him in the indoctrination sessions. "During the Eucharist, I knew I was nailed to the cross with Jesus and His blood was mixing with mine. I contemplated Christ, immobilized by the nails but Savior of the world through His suffering. That is how Jesus, died and risen again, became everything for me." The experience of suffering leads a person to reflect on the essential.

In another lecture, Thuan mentioned an American bishop who had cancer (Thuan also suffered from cancer but did not want to talk about himself); the illness had converted him. From being a civil servant, this bishop had become a father to his diocese.

Thuan did not forget to remind the bishops of the importance of the Virgin Mary as an example of total faithfulness to the Lord.

Human Dignity

Among all the subjects that my brother tackled as a member of the Roman Curia, he held one particularly close to his heart: the respect that every person deserves due to his dignity, something that can be fully lived only in peace.

Thuan traveled all over the world to defend the fundamental rights of every person. During a congress in July 1988, he used an Asian proverb to make a point; he asked: "Who can count all the leaves in the forest?" In fact, human rights encompass a great many domains: economic and social rights, religious liberty, the right to life, the promotion of women's and children's and family *rights, immigration and the right of asylum, the rights of native peoples, international debt, and capital punishment.*

According to Thuan, Pope Saint John Paul II made himself the "voice of the voiceless" in all his travels. Defending and protecting man is an integral part of evangelization. Was Jesus not anointed to bring the good news to the poor (Lk 4:18)? Working to promote justice requires not administrators but pastors: persons serving the poor and listening to them, inculturating the gospel and dialoguing with them in humility and with hope.

The Family

Thuan and I were raised in a family steeped in Vietnamese traditions. The Vietnamese New Year, Tet, had a great place in his life: during this period, our families reunite and decorate the tombs of our ancestors. Thuan never forgot family birthdays or wedding anniversaries, as well as the feasts of family patron saints. He commemorated the deceased and took an interest in all our children. In Vietnam, the family is

"O silence of Nazareth, teach us recollection, reflection, and eagerness to heed the good inspirations and words of true teachers" (Paul VI in Nazareth, January 5, 1964).

the child's first school.[1] For Thuan, even a good school with good teachers cannot replace parents. Throughout his apostolate in his home country, he endlessly stressed to fathers and mothers the primary importance of their role.

[1] Madame Hong set out these thoughts at greater length in Élisabeth Nguyen, *La famille asiatique, dépassée ou prophétique?* Une mission extraordinaire 18 (Versailles: Éd. Amis de Van, 2014).

In exile in the West, he continued his battle for the family. For example, in a talk he gave in Paris in 1994,[2] he expounded at length on the spirituality of marriage, quoting various Church Fathers, the New Testament, Popes Paul VI and John Paul II,[3] and also his own works—especially The Road of Hope: A Gospel from Prison. *Thanks to the breath of the Holy Spirit, each family can become a missionary family by its witness. The Eucharist transforms the members of our families into a single body; through this sacrament, the family home becomes an illuminating domestic church.*

Joy

One of Thuan's last publications was devoted to the joy of living the faith.[4] This book is a synthesis of his spirituality. In it, he revisits a number of his insights. Because we have been created in the image of God, the Lord is the source of our joy and our hope.[5] Offering a smile to a neighbor is one of the ways to live the Beatitudes in our time.[6] Thuan even went so far as to advise us to welcome our enemies with a smile![7]

It is important to stay optimistic: it is easy but counterproductive to complain and criticize others.[8] I think that is the rea-

---

[2] "Familles, vous êtes l'Église!", talk given at the Chaillot-Galliera Center, Paris, January 12, 1994.

[3] Especially John Paul II's apostolic exhortation *Familiaris Consortio* (1982).

[4] François-Xavier Nguyen Van Thuan, *La Gioia di vivere la Fede*, 2nd ed. (Vatican City: Libreria Editrice Vaticana, 2014). This book contains various testimonies by the cardinal. It has been translated into Spanish: *El gozo de la esperanza*.

[5] Nguyen Van Thuan, *La Gioia*, 17, 41.

[6] Ibid., 47.

[7] Madame Hong refers to a Vietnamese book about the cardinal: Le Tien, *Đức Hồng y Cười* (private collection, California, 2017).

[8] Nguyen Van Thuan, *La Gioia*, 52–53.

son Thuan liked to slip funny little stories into his teaching. For example, once, when speaking about faith in God, he illustrated his point with the story of a person who asked the Lord to let him win the lottery. The reply from heaven was simply "I'm waiting for you to buy a ticket."[9]

On another occasion, speaking of the secret of Fátima, he told the following joke: Some cardinals wanted to find out the secret from the pope himself. He replied: "Here it is: Our Lady of Fátima wants us to close the shrine at Lourdes!"

The photos taken at the time of his final illness show him smiling a lot. Perhaps this was a virtue he had inherited from some of our family members. My uncle Thuc, who was a little younger than my aunt Giao, knew how much her tuberculosis had made her suffer. Still, he described her as "a cheerful woman who loved jokes and harmless teasing". Suffering did not dim Thuan's mood. After he was set free, while in the hospital in Hanoi, he maintained his good humor. Although he was still convalescing, some faithful who visited him wanted him to hear their confessions. "I am ready", he would say to them. But his visitors hesitated because he wasn't wearing a stole. He reassured them: "You have forgotten the Gospel! On the cross, Jesus was almost naked, and he forgave a thief. Compared with Him, I am rather well dressed." That was very much like Thuan, always eager to make things easy for others.

"A smile is the music of the soul."

The Call to Holiness

In February 2002, shortly before he died, Thuan expressed himself lucidly regarding the call to holiness. During the last retreat

[9] Ibid., 63.

that he led,[10] he spoke quite candidly on the topic of his illness: his cancer was progressing, death was inevitable, and undiminished was his desire to fulfill the will of God to the end. He hoped he would be welcomed by the Master of the vineyard, like the laborer at the eleventh hour or like the good thief, that sinner who was told: "Today you will be with me in Paradise" (Lk 23:43).[11]

Though, after being freed, he had often referred to his joy and hope, as well as his desire to stay faithful to the Church, all of which had enabled him to cope with his imprisonment, he now wanted to voice his dearest desire: that he would soon see Christ face-to-face.[12] The prospect of being welcomed by the One he so often encountered in the Masses he celebrated was already filling him with joy. The Eucharist is the road of humility that leads us to holiness.[13] It is Jesus, present in the Host, who sanctifies the priest and the faithful.[14] While Thuan admitted that he had always been afraid to speak about man's vocation to become a saint (Mt 5:48),[15] in this last retreat he encouraged his listeners to invite every individual to holiness.

---

[10] François-Xavier Nguyen Van Thuan, *Scoprite la gioia della speranza: Gli ultime esercizi spirituali predicati dal Cardinale*, 2nd ed. (Rome: Éd. Art, 2006).

[11] Ibid., 21.

[12] Ibid., 14.

[13] Ibid., 25.

[14] Ibid., 29.

[15] Ibid., 13.

Khiet Tinh

Purity

9

Death and Beatification Process

Illness and Death

On February 21, 2001, the eve of his elevation to the cardinalate, my brother found out he had advanced stomach cancer. He told his close family, who were privy to his health condition, that he wanted to continue to live in the present moment, without worrying about the future. He invited us to have dinner together, but we could not bring ourselves to eat. Shortly after the diagnosis was made public, Thuan was able to have an operation in the United States, where he spent a month. My husband and I visited him regularly, and we witnessed the kindness of the hospital staff. A Muslim doctor liked to come and chat with him. One day, he told Thuan that all the paper from all the trees in the world would not be enough for everything that could be written about Allah. In reply, my brother spoke about God's love, the greatest power in the world. He added that all the pencils made by man would not be sufficient to describe it!

Thuan resumed work as soon as he got back from the United States. Despite his decline in health in 2002, he was able to make one last trip to Australia for the celebration of our mother's hundredth birthday, which was celebrated early to allow Thuan to attend.[1] At my request, the American doctors had sent Thuan's medical report to their colleagues in Milan. Back there, he underwent another operation, during which he suffered a heart attack. The prognosis was clear: his poor state of health meant that he would not be able to withstand any more procedures. He had to be transferred to the Gemelli Hospital in Rome because of the risk that the scar from the operation would get infected. Thuan was perfectly lucid: he knew that there was nothing more the doctors could do to halt the spread of the cancer. Only palliative care could provide him with some relief. He was admitted to the Casa di Cura.[2] Among the people who visited him there were Andrea Riccardi, founder of the Sant'Egidio Community; Nicolas Buttet, founder of the Eucharistein Community;[3] the prelate of Opus Dei; political figures such as the Italian minister of justice; and, above all, many of his countrymen, including a few Vietnamese bishops. He continued to evangelize even in the throes of illness. He slept very little, and, at night, he would think about others and talk to God. During the day, he was exhausted but nonetheless spent a great deal of time welcoming his many visitors. Some priests asked him to pray for their parish; childless couples appealed to him to intercede in their behalf so they would be able to bear children.

Thuan was also sometimes asked to convey messages to Pope John Paul II. During conversations, he would keep his eyes fixed on the crucifix on the wall across from his bed. He had hardly any time for himself, and he had little opportunity to pray during

---

[1] My brother was also able to give my mother a papal medal: the title of Knight of the Order of Saint Sylvester was bestowed on her.

[2] This is a home that provides care (cura, in Italian) and emphasizes the human dimension in its treatment.

[3] A fraternity founded by Father Nicolas Buttet that focuses on Christ in the Eucharist.

the day. But he said he could be united with God by sharing his time with others. His contemplative way was to see God in the tabernacle of his brothers.

Although dying, he was the one who comforted others. He inspired them with his optimism and his joy. For example, he would tell my children where they could find good Italian ice cream. He paid special attention to the younger ones in the family. When they asked him whether he had any regrets in life, he replied that he would have loved to have spent more time with them. He was particularly happy to see Nhung, Michael's eldest daughter, and her family. Michael was the only one of my brothers who was unable to leave Vietnam.

Even at the Casa di Cura, Thuan never forgot his homeland. Ever since he was made cardinal, he had dreamed of going home to Vietnam. His illness prevented it. By inclination, he would have wanted to change his country's destiny. Now that his end was drawing near, he gave more thought to the youth in particular and wished that the history of the Vietnamese people, who had suffered so much, would not be forgotten. Once again, he chose to entrust everything to God's hands. As in his prison days, he was able to say that work in behalf of the kingdom of God is nothing in comparison with the greatness of God. The Eucharist remained the focus of his life. Initially in the Casa di Cura, he could still say Mass, provided he remained seated, but he was soon permanently bedridden and needed to concelebrate with a fellow priest. Many faithful attended, and his sick room was often too small to accommodate everybody. I was afraid he wouldn't be able to breathe properly, but he insisted on letting in as many people as possible. Right up to the end of his days, his spirit remained open.

The medical staff became very attached to Thuan. He was what they call an easy patient. He forced himself to smile when

he felt a lot of pain, such as when they dressed his wounds. He had lost a lot of weight, and seeing him waste away little by little saddened me terribly. I could not help asking him why suffering was an integral part of Christian spirituality. He listened to me very patiently, as he always did, and explained that the main issue was not the cross or the suffering but the infinite love of God. All his life, he had wanted love to be central to his faith. When I was little—and, indeed, throughout my life—I was always asking him questions. My desire to think things through for myself never bothered him—in fact, quite the contrary! According to him, God loves those who seek in the darkness. I am convinced that our conversations gave him great joy; sometimes he would laugh at my way of thinking, but he insisted on certain rules: I was not allowed to ask too many questions at once! He taught me to listen attentively to my interlocutor's reasoning. I talked to him about the doubts of our generation, especially regarding the evil endemic in creation and in humanity. He told me that he did not have an answer for every problem and that he was only a poor instrument *of God. The Lord would make things clear to me Himself. He pointed out that the love of our parents can help us understand the Creator's love: even when their child displays all kinds of shortcomings, the parents do not love him any less. When I asked him whom Jesus looked like, he replied: "Mary." "And who else?" "The Holy Spirit!" He listened very patiently when I called Saint Joseph a poor fellow who had to live with such a beautiful wife without being able to touch her. My brother simply replied that Saint Joseph was a happy man because he had the joy of living so close to the Virgin. As far as he was concerned, Saint Joseph had understood everything by the light of the Holy Spirit. Moreover, he added, Saint Joseph is particularly attentive to the forsaken, including those in our family.*

There was a "cube of love" by Thuan's bedside. It was a die that he would roll every day; then he would read the saying on the side that ended face up: "Love one another"; "Love others as yourself"; "Love your enemies"; "Be the first to love"; "Love everyone"; "Love Jesus in others." One day, when I shared with him that I had had a quarrel with someone, he gave me these last words: "Love Jesus in others"; then he invited me to look at the crucifix: "Jesus is there," he said, "but he is also in your neighbor." All these conversations I had with my brother helped me deepen my relationship with God, a process that intensified after his death.

He also confided in me over the last months of his life that he had been tempted to question his faith. He regarded that as a test from the devil. At other times, he recalled the desire he had had as a child: "I want to see His face", he would say. He was even prepared to relive all his life's sufferings if they could help him see God. And he added that he still needed to abide every day by the saying that our mother had taught us in our childhood: we must live constantly under the gaze of God.

Father Hubertus Blaumeiser, a German Focolare[4] priest who lives in Rome, summed up admirably the spirit of my brother at the end of his life:

> *I well remember what the cardinal said to me in April 2002, before the major surgery he was about to undergo in Milan. When I asked him whether he was afraid of the operation, he said to me: "No, given that there are three possibilities: I could die, and it would be the right moment because I am ready for it. On the other hand, I could stay alive, but in a state of constant pain. Or I will be able to get back to work. All three options are good." But when his physical condition deteriorated and he recognized that death was near, he had a big struggle. It was not mainly because of the physical suffering but because of the realization that he would no longer be able to spread the gospel. It was as though he regretted not having worked hard enough for God, using the talents he had received.*

On his deathbed, Thuan surrendered himself completely into God's hands, as he had done during his years in prison: "God is the guide, and I can pass on to others the responsibilities that were entrusted to me."

Various photos of him taken at the end of his life show him smiling. He would say jokingly: "It's my Gandhi smile", referring to the anorexic look of that other man of peace.

During his last days, Thuan could no longer speak, but he continued to stare at the crucifix. He was totally free of spiritual temptations. He could still write a few words, and he had a visit from Chiara Lubich, founder of the Focolare Movement, before he fell into a coma. During his last agony, Vietnamese sisters prayed the Rosary aloud in the corridor.

[4] The Focolare Movement is a Catholic association of the faithful, founded in northern Italy in 1943 by the Servant of God Chiara Lubich (1920–2008). It promotes unity among Christians and among different religions.

Pope John Paul II was already ill when my brother entered eternity on September 16, 2002, but he was able to give the homily at his funeral on September 20. John Paul II focused on Thuan's hope, "full of Christ, the life and resurrection of all who trust in him", and he summed up the character of his spirituality with a few well-chosen words.[5]

At his own request, my brother was not buried in his cardinal's cappa but was dressed in a red chasuble that recalled the blood of the martyrs of our country. "Unless a grain of wheat falls into the earth and dies, it remains alone; but if it dies, it bears much fruit" (Jn 12:24). This text was read at his funeral.

Toward Beatification

Thuan once asked me whether I had given up my studies of existentialist philosophy. To my great surprise, he added that I would have much to tell after his death. I found the idea intriguing, but, in the first few years after his death, it was mostly my sister Ham Tieu (Anne) who spread his message. Today, my sister Anh Tuyet (Agnès), who lives in Australia, and I are his only siblings still alive to do it, and—contrary to my earlier apprehensions—it has been a source of great joy to me. The beatification process has uncovered

---

[5] These words of the pope were published in François-Xavier Nguyen Van Thuan, *365 jours d'espérance*, Trésors de la spiritualité chrétienne (Paris: Sarment–Éd. du Jubilé, 2005), 17–21. The text of the homily can also be found on the Vatican website: https://www.vatican.va/content/john-paul-ii/en/homilies/2002/documents/hf_jp-ii_hom_20020920_esequie-card-van-thuan.html.

for me some aspects of my brother's life that I did not know about. I have had the privilege of making contact with many individuals who knew him, such as the prison guards who converted and came to testify in Rome. Today, we can officially present Thuan as an example for Christians, since he was declared Venerable in September 2017. He has inspired many and will continue to do so. One thing that moved me in a special way was the mention of my brother in Pope Benedict XVI's encyclical letter **Spe Salvi,** *on Christian hope (2007), and in Pope Francis' apostolic exhortation* Gaudete et Exsultate, *on the call to holiness (2018).*

Pope Francis also mentioned him in his message for the World Day of Peace (January 2019) and in his apostolic exhortation Christus Vivit *(addressed to young people, March 25, 2019).*[6]

---

[6] For more details, see appendix 3.

Binh An

Peace

Part II

The Cardinal's Family Background

10

Thuan's Ancestors

Introduction

When Thuan preached the Vatican retreat in the Jubilee Year 2000, he explained how important it is for us Asians to preserve the memory of our ancestors. Referring to the first chapter of the Gospel of Matthew, in which are listed the forefathers of Jesus Christ, Thuan said that he personally knew "the names of fifteen generations of my ancestors going back as far as 1698, when members of my family first received holy baptism. Through our genealogies, we come to realize that we are part of a history greater than we are."[1]

Paternal Ancestors[2]

In the early days of evangelization of our country, our paternal ancestors lived in the La Vang region. They soon converted to Catholicism. Forced to live their faith in secret, they endured

---

[1] Francis Xavier Nguyen Van Thuan, *Testimony of Hope: The Spiritual Exercises of Pope John Paul II* (Boston: Pauline Books and Media, 2000), 4.

[2] For more details on the family, see appendix 1.

The family home has been restored.

persecution, imprisonment, and even death. One of them figures
among the Martyrs of Vietnam, canonized in 1988 by Pope John
Paul II.[3] In the nineteenth century, the family moved to Phu
Cam, where everybody was Catholic. A cathedral was built there.
Now replaced by a more modern building, it still serves as parish
church for the residents in this part of Hue. Several members of
our family were catechists there and actively assisted Vietnamese
and French clergy. Many of our cousins entered religious orders.

In our younger days, we had access to a registry of family
members from our father's side. A great number of them suffered
for their faith. Even though several of my mother's brothers were
prominent political figures in our country's history, our parents
taught us that in our family, the gift of one's life for Christ has

---

[3] His name was Tong Viet Buong (Paul, ca. 1773–1833). Originally from Phu Cam,
this family father worked for Emperor Minh Mang, who sent him to prison when he discovered that Buong was Catholic. In October 1833, he was beheaded and his body was
burned. At the time of his execution, he proclaimed his faith in the goodness of God. The
Christians in his area deeply honor him, and there is a statue of him in Hue Cathedral.

always been considered the hallmark of excellence for the nobility. This historical context enables us to understand better my brother's personality as well as our family history. After her marriage, my mother went to live with her in-laws in a nice large house that had a big chapel inside. We always were a very close-knit family. We attended Sunday Mass together; then relatives came to lunch at our house. All of us cousins went to school together and took part in the village games. The door of our house was always open. My mother was almost always there. When the Redemptorist fathers organized parish retreats, a lot of cousins would stay in our house for the whole week. Thuan's vocation owed much to this fervent, joyful spirit characteristic of my father's family.

Maternal Ancestors

My maternal ancestors were originally from Dai Phong, a village about a hundred miles north of Hue. Our grandfather Ngo Dinh Kha (Michael, 1857–1923) first attended the local school, the minor seminary of An Ninh (at Cua Tung), and then spent several years at the major seminary, which at that time was in Malaysia. In the second half of the nineteenth century, the French occupied the South of our country and Christians were suspected of collusion with the colonizing power. Thousands of Vietnamese intellectuals opposed to foreign interference set up the Van Than militia, which targeted Christians and massacred more than eight thousand of them between 1885 and 1888. In 1885, the Christian village of Dai Phong was sacked, and the church, where the inhabitants had taken refuge, was burned down by the rioters. Our great-aunt Tien,[4] Kha's sister, was among those Christians

---

[4] Although certain works mention Lien, one of Kha's cousins, the person who escaped the Dai Phong massacre was, in fact, his sister Tien.

who had gathered in the village church. Tien often recalled how the priest addressed words of comfort to his parishioners before the flames and smoke killed them. Our great-aunt luckily survived because she remained hidden under the bodies of other burned victims that piled up on top of her. She later found sanctuary with a local Buddhist family.

At the time of the Dai Phong massacre in 1885, Kha was living in Malaysia.[5] When he heard about the tragedy, he returned home to help the members of his family who had escaped the massacre: his mother and his two brothers, absent at the time of the attack by the militia, and his sister. Kha decided to remain in Vietnam. On February 25, 1887, he married Madeleine Chiu. Their marriage was short-lived because Madeleine died in an epidemic. In 1889, Kha married Pham Thi Than (Lucia, 1871– 1964), and they raised a family of nine children.

1. **Ngo Dinh Khoi** (Paul) 1890–1945 ∞ Nguyen Thi Hoa Governor	2. **Ngo Dinh Thi Giao** (Élisabeth) 1894–1944 ∞ Truong Dinh Tung
3. **Ngo Dinh Thuc** (Pierre-Martin) 1897–1984 Archbishop	4. **Ngo Dinh Diem** (Jean-Baptiste) 1901–1963 Benedictine oblate Prime minister, then president

[5] Kha spent several years in the seminary, but he had serious doubts about whether he had a priestly vocation, doubts that his teachers shared. The Dai Phong tragedy tilted the scale for him, and he decided to go back to his family.

5. Ngo Dinh Thi Hiep
(Élisabeth)
1903–2005
∞
Nguyen Van Am

Thuan's parents

6. Ngo Dinh Thi Hoang
(Anne)
1904–1959
∞
Nguyen Van Le

Thuan's godfather

7. Ngo Dinh Nhu
(Jacques)
1907–1963
∞
Tran Le Xuan

Adviser to Diem

8. Ngo Dinh Can
(Jean-Baptiste)
1910–1964

Adviser to Diem

9. Ngo Dinh Luyen
(Michel)
1914–1990
∞
Nguyen Thi Danh (†)
∞
Nguyen Phuoc Hanh

Ambassador

My grandfather was a prominent public figure in the twentieth century. Officials of the Imperial Court were appointed and assigned various grades commensurate with their competence level. A highly cultivated man, Kha belonged to the Mandarin class, educated individuals entrusted with political responsibilities. He held various important positions in the court: tutor to the future emperor Thanh Thai; then, after the latter's accession to the throne, head of the guard responsible for the administration of the imperial household; and master of ceremonies with the job of supervising palace protocol.[6] *Kha was also the cofounder of an educational institute (Quoc Hoc—"national school") where students from all over the country were taught Eastern as well as Western cultures. An interesting detail: his son Diem and Ho Chi Minh, future political opponents, were both pupils at Quoc Hoc.*[7]

After Kha's death, our grandmother Pham Thi Than stayed very close to her daughter Hiep, whose house was only a few hundred yards away. So she saw Thuan grow up alongside her other grandchildren. Her son Thuc's episcopal ordination and the accession to the presidency of her son Diem were moments of great happiness for her. She also went through great sufferings, particularly the assassination of her eldest son, Khoi, by the Communists. When three of her other sons were murdered, she was, mercifully, already too ill to be fully aware of those new tragedies.

---

[6] Thanh Thai was the first emperor to accept Catholic Mandarins into his immediate entourage. He did not compel them to participate in festive sacrifices, which, by then, had become rare events anyway. André Nguyen Van Chau, *A Lifetime in the Eye of the Storm: Ngo Dinh Thi Hiep, a Younger Sister of Late President Ngo Dinh Diem*, 2nd ed. (Canyon Lake, Tex.: Erin Go Bragh Publishing, 2015), 9–12.

[7] Other well-known pupils of Quoc Hoc: Pham Van Dong (1906–2000), one of the most important Communist leaders after Ho Chi Minh; and Vo Nguyen Giap (1911–2013), Communist military leader from 1945 to 1973. Michael R. Nichols, "Pham Van Đông", in *The Encyclopedia of the Vietnam War: A Political, Social, and Military History*, ed. Spencer C. Tucker (Oxford: Oxford University Press, 1988), 325–26; Cecil B. Currey, "Võ Nguyễn Giáp", in *Encyclopedia of the Vietnam War*, 475–76.

Thuan's Parents

Nguyen Van Am ∞ Ngo Dinh Thi Hiep

Hiep's Early Years

The arrival of the French in the nineteenth century unleashed deep changes in Vietnamese institutions. The
colonialists started imposing more and more restrictions
on the emperor's autonomy while keeping him on the
throne. In 1907, Emperor Thanh Thai, considered too
uncooperative by the French, was forced to abdicate and
then was exiled, first to the south of the country and later
to the island of Réunion. That year, Kha was also forced to
resign his position: he was the only minister to refuse
to ratify the emperor's abdication. Thanks to his friend
Nguyen Huu Bai,[1] minister of the interior and, like him,

---

[1] Bai and Kha were very close. Bai was Thuc's godfather. Bai thought it
opportune to ratify Thanh Thai's act of resignation. He could thus retain his
position as a Mandarin in order to continue to support the nationalist cause
from the center of power. The emperor appreciated Kha's gesture but did not
encourage his minister to make it. He knew that the colonial force feared the
reaction of the Catholics present at the imperial court: they were very often
in contact with missionaries and Catholics in France. Articles by Kha and Bai
were published in Vietnamese and French newspapers. The position of Bai, the

a Catholic, along with the support of other Mandarins loyal to the emperor, Kha was spared the exile imposed on Thanh Thai. Hiep was too young to have had any clear memory of this emperor, but she did recall how he would arrive on horseback on his frequent visits to the family. Later, whenever the family chats included any reference to an emperor, it was always Thanh Thai they had in mind. Although Kha was allowed to remain in Phu Cam—little Hiep had promised to pray that her father would not be separated from the family[2]—the removal from his position and the departure of the emperor into exile constituted a harsh blow for the family. Stripped of office and without financial means, Kha, over fifty at the time, and his wife had to work very hard to be able to feed their large family. Family tradition proved to be the source of Kha's fortitude.

Family bonds were strengthened during that humiliating period, which the family endured with pride and a spirit of prayer and solidarity. My grandfather's tenacious attitude aligned perfectly with the Confucian ideal that encourages men to live according to their consciences, even at the expense of their careers. Kha told my uncles, who had to work hard during their school breaks, that manual work, integrated with their studies, is highly conducive to a solid character formation. He also wanted them to experience firsthand the plight of farmers.

The marriage of Khoi—Kha's eldest son—with Minister Bai's eldest daughter[3] in 1912 was a memorable event

---

only remaining Catholic Mandarin, seems to have been strengthened against the French after Kha's resignation. André Nguyen Van Chau, *A Lifetime in the Eye of the Storm: Ngo Dinh Thi Hiep, a Younger Sister of Late President Ngo Dinh Diem*, 2nd ed. (Canyon Lake, Tex.: Erin Go Bragh Publishing, 2015), 45–59.

[2] Ibid., 1–70.

[3] Ibid., 81–82.

in the family's history. The French government was not at
all keen on this alliance between two nationalist Catholic
families and viewed it as dangerous. Bai visited Kha quite
frequently, as did other members of the Imperial Court.
Hiep would serve tea when Kha hosted Mandarins, and
his insistence on his daughter's presence at those meetings was, in the local cultural context, unusual. A staunch
nationalist and politician concerned with the future of
the Vietnamese people, Bai was appointed regent when
Duy Tan, exiled emperor Thanh Thai's son, was still a
minor. During their conversations, Bai often spoke of
the young emperor's anti-colonialism and his plans for
rebellion against the French occupier. Duy Tan was then
very angry indeed that thousands of young Vietnamese
had been drafted into the military and sent to the city to
fight in a war that they felt had nothing to do with them.
Moreover, the Vietnamese people were being made to
support the war effort with higher taxes. The emperor
believed that the colonial power had been weakened
by Germany's military successes in France. A rebellion
planned for May 3, 1916, was foiled, however, and Duy
Tan was sent into exile, just like his father.[4]

Emperor Khai Dinh, a man with lackluster personality,
succeeded him in 1916. In a momentous turn of events
for the family, Hiep reported, Kha was rehabilitated by
Emperor Khai Dinh in 1919. He was restored to his Mandarin emeritus title, along with the emoluments his position
carried, as well as his retirement pension arrears. Now gen-
erously compensated and back with his family, Kha simply told them: "Rich or poor, let our lives be guided by

[4] Pham Cao Duong, "Duy Tân", in *The Encyclopedia of the Vietnam War: A
Political, Social, and Military History*, ed. Spencer C. Tucker (Oxford: Oxford
University Press, 1988), 111.

our consciences. In the end, God's justice will prevail."[5] As a result of his improved financial situation, Kha was able to buy some land and hire workers, and he again had the chance to enjoy his reading. Now he could also spend more time writing and passing on his extensive knowledge to his children. Until her marriage, Hiep regularly maintained her silent presence at every discussion about national and international issues. Her maturity grew with the experience.[6] Hiep also saw how deeply her mother shared the suffering of those great servants of the state so loyally serving their country, no matter the cost. Later, Hiep would often amaze her brother, now president, with the pertinence of her political analyses.

Hiep's Marriage

In those days, marriages were arranged by parents. According to common practice, Am's father, Nguyen Van Dieu, went to Kha to ask for his daughter Hiep's hand in marriage for his son. To Dieu's surprise, Kha involved his wife and his daughter in the crucial decision-making, and he nodded his approval only after making sure Hiep was in full agreement. The two families agreed on the date for the wedding, but early in 1923, Kha fell ill and was diagnosed with pneumonia. His condition worsened, and he received the anointing of the sick. All his children except Thuc, who was in Rome for his studies, gathered around their dying father. One of the children was to receive his blessing on behalf of the rest. Kha chose neither his son Khoi, the youthful

---

[5] Nguyen Van Chau, *Eye of the Storm*, 105–6.
[6] Ibid., 83–91.

governor of the province of Binh Dinh,[7] nor Diem, head of the prefecture of Hai Lang,[8] but his fifth child, his daughter Hiep. From his deathbed, Kha entrusted his daughter with the mission of speaking on his behalf every year and giving a review of her siblings' activities.[9]

He also expressed the wish that his son Luyen should continue his studies in France. Finally, he murmured in Hiep's ear: "Don't forget to pray for my soul." Exhausted, he died peacefully shortly after. Since then, every New Year, all my uncles gathered in our house and my mother spoke to them in Kha's name. Whenever she disagreed with any of them, she always expressed her difference tactfully: "Our father would have said ..." But to Diem, who frequently asked for her opinion, she would give unambiguous political advice. Thanks to my mother, our uncles remained united all their lives, in spite of their very different temperaments.

The Personality of Am, Thuan's Father

Though Vietnamese society was marked by strong class distinctions,[10] the persecution of Vietnamese Christians, which persisted

---

[7] About 250 miles south of Hue.

[8] In the Quang Tri Province, just north of Hue.

[9] In some publications, you will find it stated that Kha did not want Hiep to delay her marriage, but that, following tradition, she chose to observe the mourning period. The marriage took place on November 28, 1925. I was able to verify this date in the parish archives of Phu Cam. In one of the letters he wrote from prison, Thuan referred to the date as November 21. Perhaps he was commemorating his parents' marriage on a Marian date, the feast of the Presentation of the Blessed Virgin Mary, instead of going by the date on the marriage certificate.

[10] In traditional Vietnamese society, there are often references to the Si (the intellectuals), the Nong (the major agricultural owners and entrepreneurs), the Cong (the workers), the Thuong (the merchants), and the Binh (the military).

throughout most of their history, brought about a more solid unity among the faithful. Although my parents came from different backgrounds, we never noticed any class disparity between Dad and Mum.[11] My father's heart belonged to his wife and his children. A noble, hardworking man, with a deep concern for his workers and a dedication to fine craftmanship, he was extremely affectionate toward my mother, whom he spoiled very much. A caring husband in tune with her feelings, he could guess her thoughts even before she expressed them. My mother recalled an example of my father's great sensibility and love for her: when she was pregnant with Thuan, he knew it immediately, merely from the way she placed her hands on her belly.

My mother was greatly affected by the death of her first son. Xuan was ill for only three days before leaving his young parents. Throughout the devastating ordeal that overwhelmed both of them, my mother found much comfort with her husband. I think it was from his own father that Am had inherited his great sensitivity.

It is unfortunate that I never knew Dieu, my paternal grandfather. Having had only one child, he took great delight in doting on his grandchildren and watching them grow and blossom. Dieu always helped fellow parishioners in need. As a catechist, he also visited the sick, which resulted in his contracting tuberculosis. When his illness prevented him from running his business, my father took over and specialized in the restoration of large buildings, such as cathedrals, monasteries, and hospitals. Am and Thuan drew up the plans and oversaw the construction of Hoan Thien Minor Seminary. World War II and then the Indochina War caused business to slow down, sometimes even stopping it

---

[11] Through some of his ancestors, Am was related to the imperial family. The difference between the two families lay mainly in their respective political affiliations.

The new cathedral. Am was responsible for the foundations, but his forced departure to Saigon and his subsequent exile prevented him from seeing it through to completion.

altogether, but activity resumed after the Geneva Accords (1954). Then business boomed; Am reaped such huge profits that he was able to buy himself a beautiful villa by the sea.[12]

My father was very caring toward his family and the household workers. Often on Saturdays, weather permitting, we would all go to some picturesque location for a picnic and spend an enjoyable

[12] The building still stands, though it is now uninhabitable, due to its decrepit state.

The Phu Cam presbytery is one of the few buildings
constructed by Am that has survived.

*day there. Even if it was only a few miles from home, it provided
us with a delightful opportunity to relax and unwind from our
daily routine. I always eagerly looked forward to those carefree
moments when my father would forget about work, if only for a
few hours.*

12

Thuan's Brothers and Sisters

Thuan's brothers and sisters were all born in Hue. All his life and throughout his incarcerations, Thuan always managed to stay in touch with them by writing.

Whether as a seminarian, a priest, a bishop, or a member of the Roman Curia, Thuan readily became a brother, a father, and a friend to many. But his close bond with members of his family was never jeopardized by the spirit of universal fraternity that he chose to live with those entrusted to his care during his priestly ministry.

His brothers and sisters were as follows:

- *Xuan* (Jean-Baptiste), Am and Hiep's first son, died before Thuan was born.
- *Niem* (Bernadette) was close in age to the future cardinal and married an Englishman living in Saigon.
- *Tuyen* (Joseph), the fourth child, set out on a military career in Vietnam but later emigrated to the United States, where he lived among many of his exiled compatriots until his death.
- *Truyen* (Paul) was stillborn.
- *Thanh* (Michel), close to his uncle Can, was the only one who never left Vietnam. Like his brother the bishop, he spent time in jail.

- *Ham Tieu* (Anne-Cécile) went to work in Australia and was thus able to prepare for the arrival of her parents and her siblings when they went into exile there.
- *Anh Tuyet* (Agnès) still lives in Australia and has provided precious information to the historical commission that is working on the beatification of the cardinal.
- *Thuy-Tien* (Anne-Thérèse) studied with Élisabeth in France. In 1975, she and her family were granted asylum in Australia.
- *Nguyen Thi Thu Hong* (Élisabeth, born on October 17, 1949), whose testimony makes up the bulk of this book, is the youngest of the family. Educated in France from the ages of eight to sixteen, she completed her university studies in Australia, where she studied philosophy. At present, she lives in Canada with her husband and has five grandchildren.

Given our age difference, Thuan was not only a brother; he was also a little father to me. When he was a seminarian, spending his holidays at home, he sometimes babysat me.

At the end of my high school years, he helped me decide on a university. During my studies in philosophy and literature, I was fascinated by existentialism, a philosophical mode of thinking fashionable at that time, and my favorite author was the poet Paul Valéry. While I was writing my thesis, Thuan never attempted to influence me; he left me free to write what I thought. But toward the end, having read my manuscript, he asked me: "Have you found the road to happiness?"

This brought me to tears, because I had not found it—not at all! "What do I do now? I have almost finished my thesis", I said to him. He replied: "You can tell the truth that you were passionate about your research but now that you are finishing

Élisabeth Thi Thu Hong, coauthor of this book,
in the arms of her brother Thuan

*your thesis, you have serious questions. The teachers must accept
freedom of thought." It was very moving: a priest, a brother who
advocated independence of mind but was always there to enlighten
consciences. This had a great impact on my thinking, on my life,
and on my faith.*

*When I was nineteen, my brother suggested that I volunteer
with Mother Teresa's sisters in Calcutta. The experience proved
to be both a shock and a revelation. I was deeply moved by the
great suffering in which numerous inhabitants of that city lived,
a suffering that has left a profound mark on my soul. But I was
impressed, above all, by the sisters: they truly saw Christ in
the faces of the poorest of the poor. I also saw how much their
silent prayers in front of the tabernacle nourished their love for
one another.*

*Before, it was mainly other members of my family who took an
interest in my brother while he was alive. But since his death, and
the deaths of my mother and other family members, many things*

have changed in my life. I have read and reread Thuan's writings. Little by little, his testimony has touched me. I have immersed myself in his spirituality, and, through him, the Lord has revealed to me more and more of His great love. Sharing Thuan's thinking is a task that is close to my heart. I have the impression that he is pressing me to launch a "crusade" to spread this precious message, and I hope with all my heart that the beatification process—very strongly supported by my compatriots all over the world—will reach a happy conclusion in years to come and be a blessing for the Church in Vietnam and the universal Church.

It is for this that I live and pray.

13

Family Life and the Ngos' Commitments

The Ngo Uncles and Aunts

I still hold fond memories of the times I spent with my uncles, particularly with Can, my mother's younger brother. My sister Thuy Tien (Anne-Thérèse) and I went to school in France between 1950 and 1960, but every year we returned home to Vietnam for our Christmas and summer breaks.

Can and I were very close. I visited him each day during our breaks, and we went fishing near his cottage or crabbing along the beach. He was a very practical man, engaging us young children in solid conversations about our country, food, trees, the imperial tombs, rivers, and forests. He would teach us geography in a very playful manner. These are very beautiful memories of my childhood, and Can's tragic death came as a devastating spiritual cross for me.

My uncle Diem was a very stubborn and independent child. Family members and friends were surprised that Kha paid particular attention to Diem's education, for he was not the eldest son.[1]

---

[1] Throughout Diem's youth, Kha encouraged him to progress quickly. He sent him to Quoc Hoc at the age of fifteen. In his studies, Diem was struck by the numerous similarities between Christian and Confucian values. Confucianism does not encourage individualism because each person is invited to place

It is equally surprising that Khoi was in perfect agreement with his father's decision. Kha firmly believed that Diem should work harder to control his temper. He sent him away for six months to a novitiate of brothers who ran the Pellerin School,[2] not as a novice but as a boarder, with the hope that he would be inspired by the brothers' self-discipline. Diem was very close to his brothers Nhu and Can. Nhu later became a political confidant, and Can, who showed little interest in studying, would prove a valuable asset to him on account of his vast practical sense.[3] My uncle Luyen was a real mischief-maker but otherwise was very gifted in everything he undertook, at school or outside. My grandmother was forever calling on Diem to punish Luyen for his numerous escapades, but the eldest brother would often arrive too late: Luyen ran for cover with us, and my parents would hide him. This is why he stayed very close to Mum and spent his last year in Australia with my parents before returning to France, where he died of a heart attack.

Despite their great differences in temperament, the brothers and sisters shared the same ideals and remained solidly united once a decision had been made, no matter how difficult it was. My grandfather had told them repeatedly that the greatest dangers are ignorance and lack of unity. Nhu, for example, did not desert Diem as he faced death, even though they had different ways of tackling politics.

---

his talents at the service of the common good. Confucius dreamed of a society in which individuals would sacrifice their personal interests and would first and foremost serve the good of all: that of the family, of the local community, and of the country. Diem harmonized this ideal with his faith.

[2] This school, run by the Brothers of the Christian Schools, was also a place of formation for the novices of the congregation.

[3] *My uncle Thuc provided more information about Can's activities: he had a great practical intelligence and managed to acquire considerable wealth through the cinnamon trade. He knew Central Vietnam like the back of his hand. The money he had earned would serve later to reestablish a degree of stability in this region.*

Diem

In 1921, Diem brilliantly completed his studies in law and administration at the Hau Bo Institute in Hue. He finished at the top of his class. Thanks to the excellent relations between Kha and Nguyen Huu Bai, but due mostly to his personal competence, Diem was soon promoted to the position of head of the district of Huong Thuy in the Thua Thien-Hue Province. In 1925, he was made head of Hai Lang, in the Quang Tri Province. It was perhaps not solely due to their devotion to the Virgin Mary that Am and Hiep went to pray at La Vang after their wedding. The shrine was in the district of Hai Lang, which comprised almost two hundred villages, all under Diem's supervision at the time. Hiep and her husband had long conversations with Diem. It was the start of the mission that Kha had entrusted to his daughter.

Hiep would constantly urge her brother to bear in mind Kha's teaching on the need to act according to one's conscience. Knowing better than anyone the depth of her brother's commitment, Hiep was not at all surprised to learn that he visited every village on horseback in order to get to know his district better. Diem was very mindful of the conditions of vulnerable individuals. He was afraid that colonialism and the hierarchical structure of Vietnamese society might marginalize them. He showed impartiality toward Buddhists and Confucianists, battled corruption, and focused so much on his work that he hardly took time to eat properly. Hiep wondered why he never seemed in a hurry to get married. But Diem appeared to have chosen to serve his country, whatever that would take. All his life, he lived an ascetic lifestyle—his only indulgence being smoking. He considered his austere way of life too demanding for a wife and family.

In the 1930s, Bai appointed Khoi governor of the Quang Nam Province and, a little later, appointed Diem governor of Binh Thuan,[4] two prominent positions for men so young. In April 1933, Bai handed in his resignation as minister of the interior and was replaced by Diem. The young emperor Bao Dai had just returned from France to assume power.[5] Diem worked to further radical reforms that were not appreciated by either Bao Dai or the French. Faced with this opposition, Diem resigned after having served only three months. After that, he lived in Phu Cam and decided to travel the country and establish contact with other nationalists.[6] In addition, he spent a lot of time

---

[4] From 1927 to 1930, Diem had been governor of Ninh Thuan, a province in the South.

[5] Bai considered that the imperial system had had its day—and his bold personal opinion conflicted sharply with the position expected of a politician of his standing. He admired "revolutionaries" such as the Confucianist poet Phan Boi Chau (1867–1940), founder of a nationalist party and close to the exiled prince Cuong De (Pham Cao Duong, "Cuong Đê", in *The Encyclopedia of the Vietnam War: A Political, Social, and Military History*, ed. Spencer C. Tucker [Oxford: Oxford University Press, 1988], 88; Rodney J. Ross, "Phan Bôi Châu", in *Encyclopedia of the Vietnam War*, 326). Bai also respected Phan Chu Trinh (1872–1926), an anti-monarchist who, toward the end of his life, attracted a considerable number of followers (Ross, "Phan Bôi Châu", 326). See also André Nguyen Van Chau, *A Lifetime in the Eye of the Storm: Ngo Dinh Thi Hiep, a Younger Sister of Late President Ngo Dinh Diem*, 2nd ed. (Canyon Lake, Tex.: Erin Go Bragh Publishing, 2015), 127.

[6] It is difficult to retrace Diem's movements over these years. The political and religious world was increasingly restless. The Communist Party was established in 1930. On the Buddhist side, Huynh Phu So (1920–1947) founded the Hoa Hao sect, which immediately attracted millions of followers in rural areas. Later, its members took up arms, and the sect presented itself as an anti-Communist and anti-colonialist force (Rodney J. Ross, "Hòa Hao", in *Encyclopedia of the Vietnam War*, 177–78; Pham Cao Duong, "Huỳnh Phú Sổ", in *Encyclopedia of the Vietnam War*, 185). It seems that initially it was with Phan Boi Chau that Diem was in contact.

going on long walks, reading, and meditating. While visiting his sister Hiep, he took the time to chat with his young nephew Thuan. Diem also developed a friendship with Father Thich, who was to become Thuan's spiritual adviser and longtime family friend.

The Second World War

Various events affected the family from 1938 onward. In January of that year, Thuc was appointed bishop of Vinh Long, a diocese south of Saigon. Around that same time, Nhu came home after completing his studies at the École Nationale des Chartes in Paris.[7] He planned to marry Tran Le Xuan, a member of the imperial family.[8]

At the beginning of World War II, the Japanese invaded the country. The early bombings left Phu Cam devastated, and its inhabitants, including my parents, fled. After the ceasefire, Japanese troops occupied the country but left the French administration in place. My parents were able to return to the village. Thuan remembered the family's return home: the Japanese had built a small station in the middle of our large garden. There was no way for my father to resume his business again. He was forced to sell some properties and work the land with my mother in order to feed our family and the numerous needy people who came to ask for help.

But good comes out of bad. Because the Christian communities had been dispersed, they bore witness to their faith in the heart of the non-Christian world. During these difficult times, some

[7] A prestigious institution that trains archivists and library and national-heritage conservationists.

[8] Xuan was the granddaughter of Emperor Dong Khanh.

Buddhists would join Christians in prayer—prayers of trust in God in spite of the horrors of war. Uncle Khoi, a provincial governor, was the only person authorized by the French to carry on with his political duties, but only on the condition that he distance himself from his brothers, especially Diem. Both men, however, continued to make contact with nationalists, especially with the Cao Dai Buddhists.

At the time of the Japanese occupation, Diem continued his clandestine political activities. He remained faithful to the practice of his Christian life, lived under the gaze of Divine Providence, and was, above all else, a man united with God. Personal prayer, meditation, and reception of the sacraments were at the heart of his activities. He resigned himself to live a difficult life that constantly put him at risk. In the summer of 1944, the French, who were aware of his secret nationalist activities, decided to arrest him and put him in prison in Laos. Old friends from the imperial palace alerted him about the plan, and he eluded the surveillance team posted at the family home, escaping at night through the garden. Thanks to his contacts, he was able to escape to Saigon, where he drew closer to the Caodaists[9] and the Hoa Hao Buddhists. He also had the opportunity to visit my uncle, the bishop of Vinh Long. Luyen, who lived in the South, passed on news of Diem to the family.

---

[9] Caodaism is one of the main religions in Vietnam. It was founded in 1926 in Tay Ninh in the south of the country. It contains key elements of Confucianism (ancestor worship), Taoism (self-cultivation), and Buddhism (rebirth). The members believe that the Spirit of God can be found everywhere in the universe. Ngo Van Chieu (1878–1932) is considered the first disciple of Cao Dai (supreme being), beginning in 1921, and Le Van Trung (1876–1934) gave Caodaism a structure similar to that of the Catholic Church in 1926. Although Caodaism was very critical of French colonization and the regime of Ngo Dihn Diem, it became strongly anti-Communist. The new religion was banned from 1975 to 1997. Victor Hugo (1802–1885), Sun Yat Sen (1866–1925), and Nguyen Bihn Khiem (1491–1585), a Vietnamese Confucianist poet, are depicted as the three main saints in the colorful Caodaist temples.

The end of the war in Europe, the fall of the Vichy regime, and its replacement by the provisional government of the French Republic placed the Imperial Japanese Army in direct conflict with the French. Western priests were put in prison. Rice was requisitioned to feed the Japanese troops, and this resulted in terrible famine among the civilian population. Two million Vietnamese died, the majority of them northerners, for the North was more affected by the shortage of rice, which was mainly cultivated in the South.[10] It was chaos! Emperor Bao Dai proclaimed the independence of the country, but, in reality, Vietnam was under Japanese control. Bao Dai sent out tentative invitations to Diem to form a new government, but Diem refused: he was not prepared to accept any new form of colonialism.[11]

The dropping of atomic bombs on Hiroshima and Nagasaki (August 6 and 9, 1945) put an end to Japanese domination in Indochina. Bao Dai was removed from office by the Communists, who proclaimed the independence of the country. Khoi and his son were killed by the Viet-Minh,[12] who also arrested Diem. Sick and imprisoned in the North, Diem was abandoned by his jailers in an isolated village near the Chinese frontier, where he was looked after by the Mèo tribe locals.[13] The Viet-Minh left him

[10] For further information, see Chizuru Namba, *Français et Japonais en Indochine (1940–1945): Colonisation, propagande et rivalité culturelle* (Paris: Éd. Karthala, 2012), 118.

[11] For further information, see Nguyen Van Chau, *Eye of the Storm*, 212–28. Nhu's father-in-law was one of the politicians who chose to enter the government.

[12] Ibid., 255. Can was very disturbed by the fate of his elder brother. From that time on, he began to involve himself in the political battle being waged by his brothers. He also supported his mother, devastated by the death of her son and her grandson.

[13] There were more than a million members of minority tribes living in the North. The Mèos' land is more than three thousand feet above sea level. Their way of life—in habitat, agriculture, and beliefs—differs from that of their compatriots. Hanoi has attempted to integrate these tribes into the Communist system. The Mèos retained a profound attachment to Diem.

there until Ho Chi Minh was informed that the French intended to recover their former colony, a project that led to the Indochina War. He brought Diem to his headquarters in Hanoi, hoping to find in him an experienced collaborator who would help him fight the French. Following his refusal to cooperate with Ho Chi Minh, Diem was greatly surprised to be set free,[14] and he took refuge for a few days with some sisters in Hanoi, where he met Nhu. Despite being ostensibly a free man, he had to remain in hiding for a lengthy period, and, to that extent, he shared in the plight of his countrymen in times of war.

[14] Ibid., 262–68. Unlike Bao Dai and Bishop Le Huu Tuu, who accepted the role of councillor in the new régime, Diem dared to resist Communist power. Tuu, bishop of the Diocese of Phat Diem, about sixty miles south of Hanoi, had a private army. He was a nationalist and was close to the emperor. In 1954, he distanced himself fairly quickly from Ho Chi Minh, however, and left for the South when the North became Communist.

14

Troubles at the End of the War

Diem in Hiding

After a brief stay at a convent in Hanoi, my uncle took refuge in Thai Ha Ap, in a monastery of the Redemptorist fathers outside the town.[1] Disguised as a priest, he continued his political work in secret. This seems to have been an almost classic formula in Diem's life: leading the battle for the political well-being of our country while living a life of prayer in places that were strongholds of faith, often convents or monasteries. As a fugitive whose life was constantly at risk, he found strength and wisdom in private prayer while the country was readying itself for a new onslaught. Between the Japanese departure and the Indochina War, Communists and nationalist movements were at loggerheads. While the rivals locked horns, Diem sought to build relationships with ordinary, honest people, especially those who did not put their personal interests first. Over these difficult years of clandestine activity, he learned a lot about the depth of the Vietnamese soul. It taught Diem that there was a great potential for sacrifice among many of his compatriots. He met with Vietnamese of all religious

---

[1] Founded in 1928, the monastery proved a great draw, but it was suppressed by the Communists in 1954.

confessions who were ready to work for the emancipation of the people by peaceful means. Historians generally tend to skim over these details about this side of Diem. However, the policies that he pursued as president and his spirituality cannot fully be understood if we ignore this episode in his life.

In the Redemptorist monastery, Diem met a person who had a big impact on his life: Marcel Van,[2] who was at his side for several months.[3] This brother had had a very difficult childhood, but in spite of that, his life was suffused with prayer—and even with a mystical contact with Christ as lived by Saint Thérèse of Lisieux. This encounter transformed Diem's period in hiding into a spiritual experience. By his words and by his spirit of service, Van breathed the power of God into him. Even though Diem was a very learned man who had occupied elevated political positions, he was transformed by this simple brother who radiated the freedom and peace of the children of God. Van had suffered greatly from the presence of the French in Vietnam. Living far from the centers of political power, he had been able—thanks to his intense life of prayer—to let his hatred morph into forgiveness.[4] As for Diem, his friendships with numerous missionaries had led him to desire to work peacefully for the departure of the colonizers. That's how the politician and the praying brother found, each in

---

[2] For further information on Van, see chapter 15. Like Thuan, Nguyen Tan Van (Marcel, 1928–1959) has been proclaimed a Servant of God. In his writings, he speaks often, like Saint Thérèse of Lisieux, of the love of God. He died of tuberculosis and exhaustion in a concentration camp in North Vietnam. See Élisabeth Nguyen Thi Thu Hong and Olivier de Roulhac, eds., *Two Lives, One Mission: Parallel Views* (Versailles: Amis de Van Éditions, 2018), 112–14. See also Antonio Boucher, *Petite Histoire de Van* (Paris: Saint-Paul Éd. Religieuses/Les Amis de Van, 2006).

[3] Father de Roulhac places this long collaboration in the period when Diem stayed in the monastery near Hanoi. Nguyen Thi Thu Hong and de Roulhac, *Two Lives*, 75–76.

[4] Ibid., 77.

his own way, a response to the sufferings inflicted on our country by colonization.

At the same time in Phu Cam, the family was going through difficult times. Giao and her husband succumbed to tuberculosis. Am and Can, the least politicized members of the family, were obliged to sleep in a different place each night, for fear of being captured by the Communists. Other nationalists dug defensive trenches in Hiep's garden, hoping that this would enable them to fight off the French, whose eventual return was daily presenting a growing threat.

By the end of 1946, negotiations between the Communists and the French were leading nowhere. Each side wanted to control the whole territory. In December, the Viet Minh launched its first significant attack on French positions. The Indochina War was about to devastate a country already reeling from famine. For a few months, Phu Cam was under control of the Communists, who destroyed more than a thousand books that had been carefully preserved in the library belonging to Kha, my grandfather. My parents, my grandmother My, and my brothers and sisters escaped to Vy Da, a small village on the outskirts of the town, where my paternal grandparents owned a country house surrounded by rice paddies. My uncle Can, my grandmother Pham Thi Than, my aunt Hoang and her daughter, and Nhu's wife and daughter found refuge with the Redemptorists in Hue.[5] Beginning in February 1947, my father dispensed with the traditional Vietnamese New Year festivities and instead spent a lot of time with his family in fervent prayer. The very precariousness of the situation brought them closer to the Lord. It seems this period enabled them to acquire a deeper understanding of the suffering that our ancestors, those persecuted Christians, went through. When they

---

[5] Nhu was also forced to seek refuge elsewhere.

returned a month later to Phu Cam, my parents found the area devastated, the imperial palace burned down, and the French back in control.

Diem's Departure

In 1947, my uncle was free to move around again and was able to rejoin the family in Phu Cam in the spring. My mother noticed a great change in this brother she had not seen for so many years. He had aged, of course, but he seemed less tense, more mature, though still standing by his political convictions. In Hue, he rejected the proposal of the French, who were then fighting the Viet Minh, that he form a government. He went off to Saigon and paid two visits to Bao Dai, who was in Hong Kong at the time. In 1949, the former emperor returned to the country, and the French named him head of state. During that time, Diem often remained in the area, staying with his mother. Thuc was convinced that Diem should expand his political experience by traveling abroad. This would enable him to meet nationalists in the diaspora and to observe how Europe, Japan, and the United States were emerging from the aftermath of war, while Vietnam was bogged down in endless conflicts. As for Diem, when he learned that 1950 had been proclaimed a Jubilee Year by Pope Pius XII, he relished the idea of visiting Rome, the heart of the Catholic Church.

That explains my uncle's absence from his home country for four years. Accompanied by Thuc, he first visited Japan, where he met Cuong De, an exiled imperial prince. Thanks to his bishop brother, he managed to secure an audience with Pius XII in Rome. He then spent a year or two in the United States, living mainly in a New York monastery. The time he spent there helped him acquire a feel for American culture and establish numerous contacts

TROUBLES AT THE END OF THE WAR   207

with political personages—among others, the future president John F. Kennedy. The contacts he made then were to prove meaningful in the future. Like his father, Kha, Diem was particularly interested in the encounter between Eastern and Western cultures. He cofounded the Center for Asian Studies at Seton Hall University in New Jersey.[6] In May 1957, the university conferred an honorary doctorate on him. During the ceremony, he gave a speech in which he stressed the place of spiritual values in the political world of Vietnam. In such talks, Diem strongly defended the dignity of every human being.[7]

Following this notable period spent in the United States, he left for Europe, where he became an oblate at the Belgian Benedictine monastery of Saint Andrew, near Brugge.[8] Circumstances had led Diem to stay in different religious establishments, but it was this monastic community that he opted to join. On February 10, 1954, on the feast of Saint Scholastica, the sister of Saint Benedict, my uncle took his first vows. He chose the name of a saint of the Benedictine Order, Odilo, who had worked for the establishment of the commemoration of the faithful departed on November 2.[9] My family in Vietnam did not understand why Diem had

---

[6] The establishment of the Institute for Far Eastern Studies (now Asian Studies) at Seton Hall University involved other eminent members, such as the president of South Korea. Asia Center, *When Heaven Meets Earth: Confucian and Christian Explorations of the Social Order*, symposium, Seton Hall University, April 2002.

[7] In his speech of 1957, he spoke of "the transcendent values of the human person whose free, harmonious and complete development on the individual as well as on the communal plane must be the object of all state activity". Ibid.

[8] An oblate in the Benedictine Order is a person who lives the spirituality of Saint Benedict in ordinary life. Diem took his vow in the monastery community itself, but when he left it in 1954 to return to his homeland, he continued to live his commitment faithfully until his death.

[9] Saint Odilo (961–1048) was the fifth abbot of Cluny (994–1048), which had been founded in 909. Medieval monks were exhorted not to dwell on their sufferings and spiritual trials but to direct their gaze at the victorious Cross. The monks had the custom of sending around "rolls of the dead". When a monk died, a letter was drafted and carried from monastery to monastery. Saint

chosen as patron of his life as a religious this saint so little known among us. Later, my mother was impressed by the fact that my uncle Diem was assassinated on November 2, All Souls' Day, as established by Saint Odilo.

Diem's Return

Shortly after Diem had taken his vows as an oblate, Bao Dai asked him to come back to his homeland to take up the post of prime minister. Diem had no desire whatsoever to leave the Brugge monastery. After much hesitation and prayer and discussion with the monks of the abbey, Diem agreed to return home. The country had become one of the epicenters of the Cold War. On July 21, 1954, the day the Geneva Accords were signed, the Indochina War ended. Sadly, this was not to be the end of the conflicts, which would tear the country apart for many years, engulfing Diem and our family in a maelstrom of violence. A man of prayer, Diem, now president, wanted the Vietnamese people to become masters of their destiny. Whether from a distance or from close quarters, his people always supported his commitment to a free Vietnam.[10]

Odilo established the practice of commemorating all the faithful departed on November 2. The attention he paid to the deceased did not prevent him from showing great charity toward the living; for example, he fed the victims of numerous famines. On Saint Odilo, see, for example, Jacques Hourlier, "Odilon (de Cluny)", in *Dictionnaire de spiritualité* (Paris, Éd. Beauchesne, 1982), vol. 11, 608–613. On his writings, see *Les saints abbés de Cluny*, ed. and trans. Raymond Oursel, *Les Écrits des Saints* (Namur: Éd. du Soleil Levant, 1960), 89–161.

[10] The political situation during this period will be analyzed more closely in part 3.

15

Exile of the Family

Saigon

Diem and Nhu were assassinated on November 2, 1963. The putschists who had plotted their deaths decided also to rid themselves of Can, who was executed on May 8, 1964. I was in the country at the time, and the death of this uncle who was so close to us affected me deeply. Thuan had been able to visit Can in prison but could not pray with him on May 8. A priest was present at the execution, and he told us that Can had faced his death with courage and dignity. Wishing to extend a gesture of fraternity to the Buddhists, he had expressed a desire to be buried in a Buddhist cemetery.

Supported by Thuan and Tuyen, my mother went to retrieve his body from the prison.[1] Bishop Hoa Nguyen Van Hien helped us organize the funerals of our uncles. A few years later, the remains of Diem and Nhu were transferred to a public cemetery in Saigon, where family and friends could go and pray at their graves for peace in the country. Our maternal grandmother, Pham Thi Than, who had been sick for a long time, also left us on January 2, 1964.

---

[1] Later, Can's remains were exhumed and transferred to a Saigon public cemetery, near the graves of his murdered brothers.

All those deaths happening so close together took a toll on my mother's health. In 1965, she was hospitalized for six months in Saint Paul Hospital.[2] *My father visited her every day. The sufferings that my parents had to endure strengthened their love for each other. From the beginning of their marriage, my father had chosen to stay away from political debates, although he was familiar with the positions of the persons involved. Diem's assassination resulted in the downfall of his family; it spelled the end to the aspirations of the Ngo family to play an important role in the construction of a free Vietnam. Throughout all our trials, my father proved to be the rock in the storm on which the whole family could rely. He drew his strength from his own father, who had faithfully gathered his family around him each evening for the family prayers.*

Suspected of collusion with the Diem regime, Catholics were the object of discrimination by the military authorities.[3] *The fate of our sister Ham Tieu (Anne) was a good example: she was fired from her position at the Vietnam Embassy in Australia.*[4] *Living in Phu Cam became impossible for my parents, and they decided to live in Saigon with my brother Tuyen.*[5] *They stayed there for twelve years. When my mother's health was restored, their house*

---

[2] *She had problems mainly with her heart and kidneys.*

[3] On June 7, 1964, in a demonstration in Saigon, forty thousand Catholics protested the discrimination they were subjected to on religious grounds (André Nguyen Van Chau, *A Lifetime in the Eye of the Storm: Ngo Dinh Thi Hiep, a Younger Sister of Late President Ngo Dinh Diem*, 2nd ed. [Canyon Lake, Tex.: Erin Go Bragh Publishing, 2015], 540). During the Vietnam War, politicized Buddhists were, in turn, kept out of public life by the Americans. Ibid., 544.

[4] *Ambassador Tran Van Lam (Charles, 1913–2001), afraid of losing his position, obeyed the putschists' orders.*

[5] *Tuyen was able to continue with his military career, but he was sent to dangerous areas, such as Plei Ku, a mountainous part of the country where there were frequent attacks. He was wounded there. Later, he was sent to Korea, and when the Communists took power in South Vietnam (1975), he emigrated to the United States.*

became a place of meeting for numerous persons who had fled the bombardments. Although the family was kept under surveillance, they were allowed visits by friends, former members of the Diem party, and military personnel. Their home was in the center of town, and it had a large veranda, which my mother adorned with plants. My parents liked to rest there, especially in the evenings.

This was a period of deaths but also of new life. Shortly after the putsch, my sister Niem (Bernadette) gave birth to a daughter, Kim Lan (Anne-Marie). My father doted on his granddaughter and played happily with her. He was especially fond of his son-in-law Brian Smith, Bernadette's husband.

My father led a quiet life: he played long games of chess with his children and welcomed visits from his friends. As my mother did not go out often, my father went shopping by himself at the market and enjoyed the walks and chats. When I was in Saigon, he was always very attentive to me. Thanks to the telephone, my parents—especially my mother—were able to keep in touch with Thuc and Luyen.[6] Dad also maintained close contact with his cousins. Three of my brothers and sisters got married. My parents did not have time to get bored!

A particularly happy year was 1967, when Thuan was made bishop. All the family gathered in our home village to prepare the house, which Thuan had looked after, and to organize hospitality for the numerous guests. This home, with its large garden, was one of the few assets the family had been able to hold on to.[7] During her visit to the former capital, Hiep took the

[6] Thuc spent some time in Rome and then moved to the United States. Luyen worked as an engineer in France, where some of his children still live. He remained in contact with his brothers and sisters until he died. Luyen went to America when Thuc was very ill and was able to give the family an account of Thuc's peaceful death.

[7] This house has been restored, and it is an important memorial to the cardinal.

opportunity to pray at her father's grave and those of other family members.[8] That would be the last time she was able to do so. For Am, the joy of hugging his son, now bishop, was tinged with sadness: the cathedral that Thuc had told him to build was unfinished. The year 1963 had tolled the end of his dreams. His visit in 1967 confirmed it.

The Tet Offensive early in 1968 was particularly bloody. Am's last hopes were dashed: the prospect of going back to live in Central Vietnam had vanished forever.[9] In Saigon, less within reach of attacking Communist forces, everyone anxiously watched the war unfolding.

All those years, Hiep went to daily Mass. Studying the Bible, reading religious books, and praying the Rosary structured her days. As before, the evenings were devoted to prayer and the remembrance of ancestors. My mother kept a private diary, which I treasure. She noted in it not political events or family news but her reception of the sacraments. The diary shows, for example, how important confession was for her and my father. Thanks to their faith, my parents were able to overcome despair and even to pray for their enemies.[10]

The direct intervention of the United States set the country on fire. When possible, my father took my mother to the seaside or

---

[8] I have been able to visit these graves, and I have seen for myself that it would be very difficult to restore them. They are in a deplorable state, which is very surprising in a country with such reverence for ancestors.

[9] A hundred or so towns, as well as some parts of Saigon, were attacked on the Vietnamese New Year in 1968 (the Tet Offensive). Hue was almost completely destroyed in the bloodiest battle of the war.

[10] *Hiep was very sad when President Kennedy was assassinated. Unlike some of her compatriots, who described the death of the president as a punishment sent from heaven and even said that the blood of Diem shed in Saigon was coloring the White House red, Hiep did not see any connection between Kennedy's death and her brother's. According to her, this kind of talk encouraged a false image of a vindictive God. She had thoroughly internalized the idea of the value of suffering.*

*up the mountains in the Da Lat area. On those excursions, Hiep
came across young American soldiers thrown into a war that was
not theirs, and she pitied them.[11] Thuan often talked to those
foreign soldiers, who knew nothing about the politics of their own
country and felt very lonely, lost in a faraway land where their
lives were constantly in danger.[12] He even preached a few retreats
for the American soldiers stationed in the area.[13] This may seem
surprising, given that his uncle Diem had been assassinated with
the complicity of the American authorities. But Thuan reported
to us the substance of a conversation that made his attitude com-
prehensible. One of the American military chaplains asked him
one day: "Did your uncle hate America?" It was not easy for
my brother to explain Diem's feelings about the United States
in a few words, so Thuan replied with some of Diem's words:
"America is a great country, capable of surviving the thousands of
mistakes that her leaders may make. South Vietnam is a small
country that will fast disappear from the map if we make even a
few mistakes. That is why we cannot permit or even tolerate the
Americans making mistakes for us." After making this point,
Thuan went on to speak freely with the American chaplains,
troops, and officers. He did not see in them men representing a
country or a policy but rather men who were often demoralized
and suffering from being away from their homeland.*

*The peace negotiations that took place in Paris at the start of
1973 concluded with a ceasefire and the progressive withdrawal*

---

[11] In the end, Hiep chose to remain in Saigon since it had become clear that one could not travel in Vietnam at this time without witnessing the horror of war. Nguyen Van Chau, *Eye of the Storm*, 559–60.

[12] More than 2.5 million American soldiers fought in Vietnam. About 150,000 were wounded and more than 58,000 died there.

[13] André Nguyen Van Chau, *The Miracle of Hope: Francis Xavier Nguyen Van Thuan; Political Prisoner, Prophet of Peace* (Boston: Pauline Books and Media, 2003), 176–77.

of American troops. Everyone was well aware of the significance of the peace agreement: the Americans had sold us to the Communists. My father long hesitated to sell his Saigon property.[14] He lost it for good in 1975, when the Communists took over the whole country. In the face of the Communist victory, a given consequence of the withdrawal of the Western military, the only way out for my family was emigration to Australia.

Australia

On Friday, April 25, 1975, when Thuan had just been appointed archbishop, my parents were able to board one of the last planes to take Vietnamese out of the country. The Communists were already at the gates of Saigon. Anh Tuyet (Agnès) and her son, Duc, and Thuy Tien (Anne-Thérèse) and her daughter, Pascale, left Vietnam with my parents to immigrate to Sydney, Australia, as refugees. My sisters' husbands, fighting in the army, were able to flee Saigon later by boat. Remaining in the country, Thuan and Thanh would soon see the inside of prison. Having now acquired Australian citizenship, my sister Ham Tieu (Anne) was able to help the refugees settle in that country. As for myself, I was already living in Canada. It was the first time my father had left his homeland, and he knew that he would never be able to go back. Although my family had the good fortune to be able to emigrate safely rather than risk their lives with the Boat People, they permanently left behind them a country that had fallen into Communist hands after the capitulation of the commanding generals.

Initially my parents had great difficulty adapting to life in Sydney.[15] Everything was different: language, food, environment.

---

[14] The properties in Hue had been entrusted to the parish of Phu Cam.

[15] They lived in a house near the beach (25 Curtin Crescent, Marouba, New South Wales).

Little by little, Australia, like other Western countries, became aware of the frightful conditions in which the Boat People were fleeing the dictatorship,[16] and they expressed solidarity with them when they welcomed them in. When my mother arrived in Australia, it was almost as if something had broken within her, and only prayer seemed to help her cope. Little by little, however, visits to refugee camps reawakened in her the energy

Nguyen Van Am

that she had shown all her life. She found the inner strength to begin a new life. She took up religious books again and began to share with us memories from her rich past. Every day she called on the Virgin Mary for the grace of the liberation of my brothers who were in prison. My mother used every opportunity to inform the Australians about the conditions in which the Vietnamese people had to live under the iron rule of Communism. Working for the refugees provided her with greater insight into the efforts that Diem and Thuan had made in behalf of migrants. The presence of a Vietnamese diaspora gradually helped her cope with exile. Many refugees, both Buddhists and Catholics, developed fervent communities. These Vietnamese offered the Western world the example of a people who were patient, hardworking, and disciplined and who stressed the importance of education.

As in Saigon, my parents began receiving visits from people who were fighting for the rights of man and from bishops concerned about the situation of my brothers in prison. Despite his advanced

---

[16] The measures taken by the Communists are described in chapter 18.

age and his halting English, my father offered help to neighbors, starting with those who were working on the construction of their house. Examining the plans for their future home, my father offered them advice. His prayer life was different from my mother's. I remember that he was very devoted to the Angelus, and he stopped to pray it wherever he found himself, even if he had visitors.

Hiep was especially pleased at the election of Pope John Paul II. She immediately had an intuition that he could change the face of Communism, which he knew from experience. Had he not begun his pontificate with the words "Be not afraid"? My sister Ham Tieu (Anne), who traveled a lot and had visited Rome, had told her about the enthusiasm that this election had aroused in many Vietnamese. John Paul II's decision to canonize the Martyrs of Vietnam in 1988 was seen by the whole Vietnamese Catholic community as a sign of hope.

For my parents, Thuan's liberation was a gift from heaven. They had never stopped praying for him. It was only after he recovered his freedom that my brother realized how many people—including Pope John Paul II—had worked and prayed for it. Thuan was always infinitely grateful for all the anonymous individuals who supported him. While he saw himself as alone, forgotten in his cell, he was surrounded by the mysterious communion of the living and the dead! From our remote ancestors down to Dad and Mum, the invisible world was present in his prison. For several years, Am still had the joy of Thuan's presence and of sharing the story of his long imprisonment. With my mother, he lived the last years of his life in a nursing home, where they could attend Mass every morning. My father's health declined. One morning, he had difficulty breathing, and later that day, he had a heart attack. He went to his eternal reward in 1993, twelve years or so before Mum.

Hiep in her garden in Sydney, Australia

In those days, parents and children were not in the habit of openly sharing their feelings for one another, but after our father's death, Thuan gave a talk in which he expressed very tenderly his great love for Am. My mother herself found the courage to do a reading at the funeral Mass for this man whom she had known since her childhood and who had always been at her side, in moments of joy and in moments of pain. They had always been united in the face of adversity. Even death could not separate them.

My sister Ham Tieu (Anne) took our mother in to live with her after my father's death. My mother had a very strong constitution. Once Thuan had been set free, she was still able to accompany him on a few trips. They stayed in regular contact until Thuan died. My mother was very ill at the time of his death, so she was perhaps not fully aware of it. But God alone knows the depths of a mother's heart! Hiep's whole being was steeped in Vietnamese culture.

In his memoirs, my uncle Thuc wrote that she was the sweetest person in the family, the most devoted, and, indeed, the most patient. She played a fundamental part in the character formation of my brothers and sisters, and she provided the foundation for our religious and social life. Later, she became a model for the nation, especially after 1963 and the assassination of her brothers. Despite the sufferings that she had endured, she did not want any talk of vengeance.[17] Many Vietnamese acknowledge today the great injustice done to her brothers and see my mother as representing all those who dream of a free and democratic Vietnam.

My mother longed for the restoration of the dignity of the people. Many Vietnamese faithful in the diaspora, some from abroad, came to pay their respects to this remarkable woman who had lived times of suffering and of glory and peace, always with the same faith in God, with the same human dignity, and believing in the power of forgiveness and reconciliation.

Thuan dedicated to our mother the published version of the retreat that he preached in the Vatican in 2000. Our mother had a great devotion to Saint Thérèse of Lisieux, whom she considered a model of virtue.

---

[17] In Vietnam, I met people who had known Hiep and who had not realized at the time how exceptional a person she was. Like many Vietnamese, she was discreet and prayerful. Her greatness consisted, above all, in her capacity to overcome bitterness in the face of extremely painful situations.

In his book, Thuan also spoke of Hiep as a "strong woman" who was able to forgive when four of her brothers were murdered. She was his support during his imprisonment. She would say to everyone: "Pray for my son to be faithful to the Church and pray that he stays where God wants him to be."

The Communion of the Saints

I would like to mention two events in my mother's life after Dad's death, events that I myself witnessed. I consider them miracles.

The first concerns Van,[18] the Vietnamese Redemptorist whose life and sufferings paralleled those of my brother. The Marcel Van Association, which works for his beatification and promotes his writings, was looking for a postulator. They approached Thuan, who was working in Rome, but he was hesitant about accepting the task.

As for me, I was absorbed in reading works on Marcel Van. In 1993, my mother and my sister visited me in Canada after my father's death. My sister and I shared a bedroom with Mum so that we could help her more easily. Mum had a different rhythm of life from ours. At five in the morning, my sister and I had to recite the Rosary with her. That is how she always began her day. Then Anne and I would go back to sleep while Mum had her breakfast. One day, she did not want us to stay in bed. She said: "We have to have that boy join us." But there was no boy in the house, and the children were still asleep. Anne and I thought she was merely showing signs of Alzheimer's. But she insisted: "I mean the boy who said the Rosary with us."

---

[18] Van has already been mentioned in connection with Diem's time with the Redemptorists.

"Oh dear", said Anne quietly, "she is losing it."

But Mum kept saying: "I don't want to have breakfast with you without that boy. We have to get him to join us." We were thinking perhaps she caught sight of a boy outside, in the street or in the garden. But as my mother passed my bed, she saw a book about Marcel Van, with his photo on the cover. She exclaimed: "That's him! He talks about the love of God", and she recited a whole page of the book, written in French, although she had never read it. Moreover, my mother read only books in Vietnamese. We went to the kitchen for breakfast, and Anne later telephoned my brother to tell him what had happened.

Thuan was very surprised, especially by the fact that Mum had recited a page from a French book that she had never read or even opened. My brother saw in this a sign that he must agree to be postulator.[19] Mum did not understand why Marcel Van needed a beatification process. For her, the matter was settled. "He is a saint", she would say. When she was asked how she could be so certain of that, she would simply reply: "Because he came with the angels!" What happened that day had a powerful effect on us, and my brother and I began to collaborate with the Marcel Van Association.

My mother experienced another supernatural event. In 2001, I went to visit her in Australia. She was by this time very elderly, and she needed a great deal of care. She slept in a bed with a rail to prevent her from falling out. By the side of her bed was a statue

---

[19] In my visit to Vietnam, I had the impression that Van was not well-known there. In the context of all the suffering endured by the Vietnamese people over the course of the last century, the suffering of this Servant of God does not look at all exceptional. Moreover, some people are surprised that the Marcel Van Association connects his life with Thuan's. But in agreeing to be his postulator, the cardinal seemed to have seen in this Redemptorist more than just one of the many courageous victims of the totalitarianism of the period. Thuan discerned the depth of Van's message—which I admit regretfully that I do not know well myself—as very close to that of Saint Thérèse of Lisieux: a call to us to give ourselves to God, the Father of all mercies.

of the Virgin and Child, as well as the little box that my brother had brought as a present when he first visited Australia.

Every morning, we would dress my mother and seat her in a chair. One day, Anne, who usually looked after her, had gone to Mass. My cousin Marie Claire Le, who was also visiting, stayed home but didn't help my mother out of bed as early as usual. But after going to her, Marie Claire called to me, stunned. When she went to get Mum up, she found her already dressed and sitting in her chair. Her nightgown was folded and placed at the side of her seat. How had she managed to do that? When Anne got back, we confirmed that neither my sister nor anyone else had helped my mother out of bed.

When they asked her how she had managed to get up, dress, and sit in her chair, she replied simply: "I looked at the Virgin and said to her: 'My daughters are keeping me waiting, I must get out of my bed to pray. You carry your Child, who has the universe in His hands; you can carry me too!'"

I think it was because my parents always made their house a true house of prayer that such events could take place in my mother's life. We who were aware of marvels that happened in her life have been inspired by her example and by her prayer, just as my father was. Their shared faith enabled them to bear the crosses they had to carry in the course of their lives.

Part III

Historical Background

NOTE

The testimonies that Élisabeth has devoted to her brother and to her family make up the core of this book. The reader will not, however, be able to grasp the book's message in all its depth without some familiarity with the history of Vietnam. That is the reason this third part is devoted to various contemporary events, specifically ones that affected the life of the cardinal and his family.

There has frequently been mention of the emperors of Vietnam. The home of the cardinal's ancestors was in the center of the country, near the imperial palace. Several members of the family exercised important political functions. Because their lives were often interwoven with the life of the court, a brief presentation of the emperors seems relevant.

A sketch of the history of the evangelization of this country will enable us to understand the reasons Thuan loved the Church in Vietnam so much. The archbishop's life in prison can be viewed as an extension of the story of the Vietnamese martyrs.

I want to focus especially on the key elements in twentieth-century political life. Several well-documented books have been published recently, providing new perspectives on this period.[1] This historical part contains

---

[1] In the United States, the archives for this period have been opened to historians.

enough information to give the reader a basic idea of the many sufferings the Vietnamese people have endured. From the time that he entered the seminary, Thuan was living in a country torn apart by conflicts. War followed war without respite. Profoundly moved by the sufferings of his compatriots, Thuan chose to respond to violence with peace, justice, and hope, a counterbalance to so many acutely painful events. His peaceableness certainly exemplified truly heroic virtue.

16

Imperial Culture in Vietnam:
The Nguyen Dynasty

Over its long history, Vietnam, as it is now known, has been called by various names: Annam, Tonkin, Cochinchina, Indochina. These names referred to different areas of the country in which Thuan lived. Like China, Vietnam bore the hallmark of the Confucian culture. The father's role and family values were central. The quest for the common good and moral integrity were more important than the accumulation of wealth. An educated man was more respected than a soldier.

The king, or the emperor, whose power was absolute, was regarded as the father of the people; he ruled at the summit of the royal world, that "intermediate" place between heaven and earth. By the imposition of his own calendar, the emperor took over custody of the cosmic order, an order equally reflected in the architectural organization of the palace. An elite group, the Mandarins—senior lettered civil servants—acted as the emperor's advisers.

While deeply infused with the values preached by Confucius, political morality also displayed the influence of Buddhism, Taoism, and ancestor veneration.[1]

When I talked to the cardinal, I discovered how eager he was to see future Vietnamese priests familiarize themselves with this ancestral culture and morality in their philosophical and theological formation. Despite the collapse of the imperial regime and the introduction of Marxism—a Western atheistic philosophy—the old traditions continue to suffuse the daily life of many Vietnamese.

Founded in the nineteenth century by Emperor Gia Long, the Nguyen dynasty was the last to reign over the country.

- *Gia Long* (1759–1820). Ruled from 1802 to 1820.[2] With the support of the French military, he undertook the unification of the country and gave it the name Vietnam.
- *Minh Mang* (1791–1840). Ruled from 1820 to 1840. He reaffirmed the sanctity of his position as emperor and worked toward the centralization of national policies. Regional administration was closely supervised from the imperial palace in Hue. Unlike his father, Minh Mang pursued anti-European and anti-Christian policies.
- *Thieu Tri* (1807–1847). Ruled from 1841 to 1847. It was at this time that the Opium War began, during

[1] Pierre Huard and Maurice Durand, *Connaissance du Việt Nam* (Paris: Éd. Imprimerie Nationale, 1954), 71–72, 218–20.

[2] The dates of the reigns of the emperors differ slightly in various sources. The ones given here were taken from Huard and Durand, *Connaissance du Việt Nam*, 34–35, and from Philippe Devillers, "Vietnam: Histoire", in *Encyclopædia Universalis*, vol. 23 (Paris: Encyclopædia Universalis, 1996), 571–72.

which the British forced China to open her ports to international trade.[3] Thieu Tri refrained from executing missionaries out of fear of reprisals first by the British and then later by the French, who were on his doorstep.

- *Tu Duc* (1829–1883). Ruled from 1847 to 1883. He resumed the persecution of Christians suspected of affinity toward the European presence in Asia. These persecutions provided the French with an excuse to intervene militarily from the 1850s onward. Initially they invaded only the South of the country (Cochinchina), which became a French colony. Tu Duc was forced to sign treaties with the colonial powers.

- The short reigns of *Duc Duc* (1883), *Hiep Hoa* (1883), and *Kien Phuc* (1884). During Kien Phuc's reign, France conquered the North (Tonkin), which became a French protectorate.

- *Ham Nghi* (1870–1947). Ruled from 1884 to 1885. He plotted against the colonial forces and was banished to Algeria.

- *Dong Khanh* (1862–1889). Ruled from 1885 to 1889. The French imposed very severe restrictions on his powers.

- *Thanh Thai* (1879–1954). Ruled from 1889 to 1907. As emperor, he remained in tune with his people's wishes and opposed the French colonial forces peaceably. He was banished in 1907 but returned to Vietnam in 1946 and died on March 15, 1954, in Saigon.

[3] There were, in fact, two Opium Wars. The first (1839–1842) was waged by the United Kingdom. In the second (1856–1860), France, the United States, and Russia supported the British. These wars inflicted heavy blows on China's prestige. In the longer term, the Western powers put an end to the last imperial dynasty in China in 1911. See Louis Wei Tsing-sing, *La politique missionnaire de la France en Chine (1842–1856): L'ouverture des cinq ports chinois au commerce étranger et la liberté religieuse* (Paris: Nouvelles Éditions Latines, 1960).

- *Duy Tan* (1899–1945). Ruled from 1907 to 1916. He was brought to power by the French colonial authorities but was later deposed by them because of his active resistance. He was exiled to the island of Réunion, where he met up again with his father, Emperor Thanh Thai.

- *Khai Dinh* (1885–1925). Ruled from 1916 to 1925. The French appointed him emperor and left him on the throne until he died.

- *Bao Dai* (1913–1997). The only son of Emperor Khai Dinh. Officially, his reign began in 1926, when he was only thirteen years old. Bao Dai was educated in France, in the same school as Luyen, Diem's younger brother. He stayed close to the French all his life. He exercised power only from 1932 to 1940, and it was a power constrained by the colonial authorities. He broke with a great number of rules of etiquette in the Imperial Court and abolished polygamy. He was the first emperor to marry a Catholic, Nguyen Huu Thi Lan (Marie-Thérèse, 1914–1963), who became Empress Nam Phuong. During World War II, he collaborated with the Japanese occupiers, but he abdicated on August 25, 1945, by which time the Communists controlled the majority of the country. He was brought back to power by the French in 1949 as head of state in Vietnam. When the French withdrew in 1955, President Ngo Dinh Diem, Thuan's maternal uncle, opted for a republic. Bao Dai spent the rest of his life in exile and was the last emperor of Vietnam. In 1988, a few years before he died, he was baptized and received into the Catholic Church.

17

Evangelization of Vietnam

The Early Days of Evangelization in Vietnam

The first missionary who left a visible mark on the country was the French Jesuit Alexandre de Rhodes (1591–1660), who evangelized the country from 1623 to 1645.[1] With the help of the Holy See and French compatriots, he recruited missionaries for this region to proclaim the gospel there outside the Padroado, the "guardianship" that the Portuguese exercised over missions in almost all of Asia.[2]

Mission to Vietnam and Spiritual Life in France

De Rhodes got in touch with well-known spiritual figures who, following the Council of Trent (1542–1563),

---

[1] Most of this information is the fruit of my research on the history of the Church in East Asia. See my book *Siméon-François Berneux (1814–1866): Missionsbischof und Märtyrer in Korea* (Cologne: Böhlau, 2000). Siméon-François Berneux was initially a missionary in Vietnam.

[2] In the fifteenth century, the Portuguese extended their commercial dominance to the entire Indian Ocean. Evangelists who went to Asia could do so only with authorization from the king of Portugal. Jean Comby, *Deux mille ans d'évangélisation: Histoire de l'expansion chrétienne*, Bibliothèque d'histoire du christianisme 29 (Paris: Éd. Desclée 1992), 63–114.

were working at that time for the spiritual renewal of the Church in France. The initial evangelization of Vietnam can be better understood if we familiarize ourselves with this religious awakening in France; devotion to the Blessed Sacrament was closely linked with charitable institutions: the establishment of women's orders by Saint Vincent de Paul and Saint Francis de Sales made up of uncloistered nuns whose mission was to bring comfort to the afflicted.

Established in 1658, the Paris Foreign Missions Society (MEP) specialized in the creation and organization of local churches in Asia, relying on the training and support of indigenous clergy assisted by a great number of catechists.[3] For directives in their apostolate, the MEP missionaries consulted their *Instructions aux Missionnaires* manual, which reminded them not to become involved in local politics,

> Inculturation is an encounter between the gospel and the values embodied in the culture of each country.

[3] Madame Barbara Acarie (the Carmelite Blessed Marie de l'Incarnation, 1566–1618), Saint Francis de Sales (1567–1622), Cardinal Pierre de Bérulle (1575–1629), Saint Vincent de Paul (1581–1660), Saint John Eudes (1601–1680), and Jean-Jacques Olier (1608–1657) were part of a renewal movement called the French Spirituality Movement, or the School of de Bérulle. The Company of the Blessed Sacrament was part of this renewal and actively supported missionaries in Asia—particularly Alexandre de Rhodes. See, among others, Raymond Deville, *L'école française de spiritualité*, Bibliothèque d'histoire du christianisme 11 (Paris: Éd. Desclée, 1987); Alain Tallon, *La Compagnie du Saint-Sacrement (1629–1667): Spiritualité et société* (Paris: Éd. du Cerf, 1990); and Françoise Fauconnet-Buzelin, *Le père inconnu de la mission moderne: Pierre Lambert de la Motte, premier vicaire apostolique de Cochinchine (1624–1679)* (Paris: Archives des Missions Étrangères, 2006). For the connection with Alexandre de Rhodes, see Comby, *Deux mille ans d'évangélisation*, 65–69.

to keep their distance from European powers, and to learn the culture and language of the country.[4]

In Vietnam, Bishop Pierre Lambert de la Motte, MEP (1624–1679),[5] established a new local congregation, the Amantes de la Croix (Lovers of the Cross), comprising uncloistered sisters aligned with the latest French women's orders. It was within this Church rooted in Vietnamese society that Thuan grew up. His primary school teachers were Amantes de la Croix members.[6] They accompanied him in prayer all his life and were at his bedside at the moment of his death.

Thuan knew many MEP priests. His family included several evangelical catechists, administrative members not just of the MEP but of the indigenous clergy as well.

Persecutions

Christians still remain a minority in the country. Right from the beginning of the evangelization, they often had to practice their faith clandestinely: royal decrees prohibited anyone from being Catholic or from organizing liturgical celebrations. From 1820 on, Emperor Minh Mang

---

[4] François Pallu and Pierre Lambert de la Motte, *Monita ad Missionarios: Instructions aux Missionnaires de la S. Congrégation de la Propagande, rédigées à Ayuthaya, Siam, en 1665* (Paris: Archives des Missions Étrangères, 2000).

[5] He practiced his ministry in much of Vietnam, where dioceses had yet to be set up. The Diocese of Nha Trang considers the missionary its first bishop; hence, Thuan is his distant successor.

[6] The Amantes de la Croix sisters still play a crucial role in the life of the Vietnamese Church. In each diocese, these sisters, living in conformity with the spirituality of their founder, are at the service of the local bishop, so that the form of their ministry varies according to the needs of the region they are in. A superior general is therefore not needed in the congregational hierarchy.

had numerous Christians executed.[7] As a religion imported from Europeans, Christianity was viewed as an internal threat to the established order. Indeed, while continuing to accept Confucianist values, Christians abandoned ancestor worship and refused to partake in its formal celebrations, regarded at the time as superstitious by the missionaries.[8] Since the introduction of Christianity into Vietnam in 1644, however, Christians have rarely contested the authority of kings or emperors.[9]

The Vietnamese Clergy

From the time of their arrival and despite risking persecution, the missionaries invested a great deal in the formation of sisters and of indigenous clergy and catechists. It was much easier for native individuals to elude government surveillance. For several centuries, nonetheless, it was French priests and bishops who were responsible for managing the missions.[10] In the twentieth century,

---

[7] Of the 117 martyrs canonized by Pope John Paul II on June 19, 1988, 58 were executed during Minh Mang's reign.

[8] The Roman Catholic Church later accepted this "ancestor worship" as compatible with the Christian faith, seeing no hints of superstition in expressing gratitude to one's ancestors, paying homage to their memory, and commemorating them in prayer.

[9] Generally speaking, the missionaries were faithful to the *Instructions*, which they received from their founders, and stayed away from local politics. Through the assistance he gave to Emperor Gia Long, the MEP bishop Pierre Pigneau de Béhaine (1741–1799) was the first exception to this long tradition. In this, he was followed in 1850 by members of the MEP who pleaded with the French government to sign treaties that guaranteed the liberty of the Vietnamese Church.

[10] I repeatedly asked many elderly native Vietnamese priests about their relationship with the French missionaries. Those who had been involved in local

Pope Benedict XV (reigned 1914–1922) and his successors encouraged missionaries to entrust management of the young churches to native members of the local clergy.[11]

Minister Nguyen Huu Bai had, in fact, gone to Rome to promote the emancipation of the Vietnamese clergy. In 1945, a native Vietnamese rector assumed the management of the minor seminary for the first time. In 1960, Jean-Baptiste Urrutia, MEP (1901–1979), archbishop of Hue, decided to retire. Thuan's uncle Ngo Dinh Thuc was his successor and thus became the first Vietnamese archbishop of Hue.

Cardinal Thuan eminently embodied the missionary policies inspired by Pope Benedict XV. The Communists would expel the foreign missionaries whenever they took power in countries such as China and Vietnam, but they were unable to eradicate the religion itself because the local Christians had long prepared themselves to take over the local churches completely.

---

parish work spoke French fluently. In the major seminaries, French remained the working language. For a long time, the missionaries held important positions in the local churches. Although they were in positions of authority over the Vietnamese priests, the latter deemed this state of affairs perfectly natural. They respected the French priests and considered them their elders, but they never felt humiliated by them. They unanimously expressed their admiration for the commitment of those missionaries, even though—as everywhere else in the Church—their apostolic spirit was not always expressed by all in the same way.

[11] Paragraphs 7 and 8 of Pope Benedict XV's apostolic letter *Maximum Illud* (November 30, 1919) are particularly clear: the formation of a native clergy carries particular requirements that must be met before those members of the clergy can be ordained bishops. Pope Pius XI took up the same themes in his encyclical letter *Rerum Ecclesiae* (February 28, 1926), especially in paragraphs 35–38. The lecture given by Françoise Buzelin on World Missions Day (October 2019) is also very helpful: Françoise Buzelin, *Des Instructions aux vicaires apostoliques (1659) à l'encyclique Maximum Illud (1919): Permanence et inflexions de la stratégie missionnaire du Saint-Siège* (Paris: Missions Étrangères, 2019).

18

Military Conflicts in the Nineteenth and Twentieth Centuries

Introduction

Even though history cannot be neatly compartmentalized into distinct periods, undeniable facts help us follow the sequence of events, such as the French colonization, the Indochina War, and the Vietnam War, all of which had an impact on the cardinal's destiny. It is difficult to put our finger on the motivation of the French in colonizing Vietnam, although the economic arguments all too often come to the fore. The justification given has varied with the times. At first, the argument for the defense of persecuted Christians was put forward to legitimate French intervention in Vietnam. Later, the anticlerical French regime stated that it wanted to liberate "inferior races" from obscurantism. After the Second World War, the fight against Communism became the principal motivation for foreign interference in the country. While the identity of those responsible for the violence meted out to the Vietnamese has changed in recent history, the people's suffering has continued unabated.

Colonization

The French decided to conquer Vietnam in the 1850s.[1] Fearing the persecutions by several emperors, some of the missionaries decided to break off with the *Instructions* and appealed to the French government for support in their evangelization project. Although this move was not, in and of itself, an appeal for the colonization of Vietnam, it went against the injunctions that the missionaries had received in the seventeenth century. That is why the appeal to France to impose freedom of religion was not supported by certain members of the Paris Foreign Missions Society. Bishop Siméon-François Berneux, for example, himself formerly a missionary in Vietnam and vicar apostolic in Korea, wrote various letters criticizing this request. He personally refused, in the case of Korea, to call for the support of Western forces to ensure religious liberty for his mission. He was convinced that a French military presence in Vietnam would not be in the best interest of the local Church.[2]

---

[1] The struggle of Thuan's family against colonization was mentioned in the second part of this book. It is set out in detail in André Nguyen Van Chau, *A Lifetime in the Eye of the Storm: Ngo Dinh Thi Hiep, a Younger Sister of Late President Ngo Dinh Diem*, 2nd ed. (Canyon Lake, Tex.: Erin Go Bragh Publishing, 2015), 1–335. The reader can also consult Philippe Devillers, "Vietnam: Histoire", in *Encyclopædia Universalis*, vol. 23 (Paris: Encyclopædia Universalis, 1996), 572–75, and Mark Moyar, *Triumph Forsaken: The Vietnam War, 1954–1965* (New York: Cambridge University Press, 2010), 8–9. On the ecclesial situation during this period, see Charles Keith, *Catholic Vietnam: A Church from Empire to Nation* (Berkeley: University of California Press, 2012), 41–241, and Jacob Ramsay, *Mandarins and Martyrs: The Church and the Nguyen Dynasty in Early Nineteenth-Century Vietnam* (Stanford, Cal.: Stanford University Press, 2008), 139–72.

[2] See Stefaan Lecleir, *Siméon-François Berneux (1814–1866): Missionsbischof und Märtyrer in Korea* (Cologne: Böhlau, 2000), 347.

During that time, European nations were colonizing a great many places all over the world, with economic gains in mind. In 1858, the French attacked the Port of Tourane (Da Nang), and, in 1859, they occupied the South, which became one of their colonies (French Cochinchina). From around 1870, large parts of Cambodia, Laos, and Vietnam came under French control. From 1887 to 1954, the entire area thus occupied was officially known as French Indochina. Some parts of the country were simply French colonies, while others, such as Central Vietnam, where Thuan's family lived, were given protectorate status.

The French governors exercised de facto power there, but they left the emperor in place as a figurehead in that part of the country. Conquering Indochina took about thirty years. Once they arrived, the French encountered hostility not only from Vietnamese Catholics but also from a great number of missionaries who lived among their Catholic faithful and were afraid that the intruders would spread the secularist ideas endemic in the mother country.[3]

In the Hue area, for example, the missionaries had established good relations with the local population. Indigenous Catholics and missionaries such as Father Eugène-Marie-Joseph Allys[4] worked very closely together there in proclaiming the gospel. As soon as he arrived in Vietnam, the priest was based in Hue (Kim Long) and later in Duong Son (Bac Kan Province), and he witnessed firsthand the

[3] Keith, *Catholic Vietnam*, 18–54.

[4] That is, Père Ly (1852–1936). In 1908, Father Eugène-Marie-Joseph Allys was ordained bishop and remained in close contact with Thuan's family. Gérard Moussay and Brigitte Appavou, *Répertoire des membres de la Société des Missions Étrangères (1659–2004): Ordre alphabétique suivi de l'ordre chronologique* (Paris: Archives des Missions Étrangères, 2004), no. 1272.

disturbances—and, indeed, numerous massacres—in the wake of the French colonization. Afterward, he returned to Hue and was appointed parish priest of Phu Cam, where Thuan's paternal ancestors helped him catechize thousands of converts.[5]

Despite their patriotism, Catholics were, in the minds of many of their fellow citizens, identified with the colonizing powers and bore the brunt of popular hatred during the long years of territorial conquest.[6] Among Vietnamese nationalists, those non-Christians who knew very little about Western culture and made no distinction between colonization and evangelization put to death a great number of their Catholic compatriots.[7] The suffering of Thuan's paternal and maternal ancestors during that period was just one horrible case in point. Yet Thuan's family gave a powerful example of how being a Christian was perfectly compatible with love of country and respect, not just for the local culture and moral values but also for other religions.

The anti-colonial struggle was initially led by various emperors, followed by intellectuals and Buddhist and Catholic movements, although the Communists became the best organized and most violent power. In 1930, Ho Chi Minh (1890–1969) created the Indochinese Communist Party (ICP, Dang Cong San Dong Duong) and, in 1941, the League for the Independence of Vietnam (Viet Minh), which, as its name indicated, focused mainly on

---

[5] Among these converts was a Buddhist monk, Prince Huong Thuyen, a grandson of Emperor Minh Mang and a forebear of Vinh Thua. This Buddhist convert to Catholicism was a great friend of Kha and the godfather of Diem and Can.

[6] Keith, *Catholic Vietnam*, 48–51; Ramsay, *Mandarins and Martyrs*, 156–72.

[7] Ramsay, *Mandarins and Martyrs*, 151–66.

the struggle to end colonial occupation. The Viet Minh rapidly set up an armed branch, the People's Army of Vietnam (PAVN, from the North) and later the National Liberation Front (NLF, or Viet Cong, from the South). After 1954, when the Republic of the South was established, the Viet Cong became especially active in villages in the South: the goal was the reunification of the country under a Communist regime.

The Second World War

The Japanese invaded Indochina in 1940.[8] While the Vichy regime in Europe was collaborating with Nazi Germany, the French colonial administration, under the command of Governor-General Jean Decoux (1884–1963), did the same in Vietnam with Japan.[9] Propaganda in favor of the Pétain regime was rife, and the local press was muzzled.[10] Gaullist resistance against the authorities was practically nonexistent, since the life of the French in Indochina was not much impacted by the war raging in the mother country.[11] The Japanese military presence was concentrated mainly in strategic locations such as airports. At the end of the war, the country was completely disorganized and briefly slipped under Japanese domination, but following Japan's defeat, it was mainly the Communists who filled the power vacuum.

[8] Chizuru Namba, *Français et Japonais en Indochine (1940–1945): Colonisation, propagande et rivalité culturelle* (Paris: Éd. Karthala, 2012).
[9] Ibid., 23, 53–57.
[10] Ibid., 122–44.
[11] Ibid., 50–51, 66–67. Namba describes the French milieu in Indochina as an oasis in a world tormented by war (249).

The Indochina War (1946–1954) and the Beginning of a Country Divided

Driven out of Indochina by the Japanese at the end of the Second World War, the French Expeditionary Corps in the Far East undertook the reconquest of the territory but ran up against Vietnamese Communist opposition. An eight-year war followed, during which the French troops failed to halt the progress of the Viet Minh. By then, the Cold War, which in Asia set Mao's China against the allies of the United States,[12] was already underway. At the battle of Dien Bien Phu in 1954, the French suffered their worst military defeat of the war, which led them to sign the Geneva Accords with the Communists in July of that year. The country was divided in two at the seventeenth parallel. In the North, Ho Chi Minh imposed a Communist regime, and in the South, Bao Dai was officially kept in power, with Diem as prime minister.[13]

The Situation in South Vietnam (1954–1963)

My uncle Diem had grown up in an environment in which human dignity and depth of faith went hand in hand with a peaceful struggle for the liberation of our country.[14] In 1954, Diem was a

[12] Devillers, "Vietnam: Histoire", 576–78.

[13] See Moyar, *Triumph Forsaken*, 33, and Geoffrey D. T. Shaw, *The Lost Mandate of Heaven: The American Betrayal of Ngo Dinh Diem, President of Vietnam* (San Francisco: Ignatius Press, 2015), 41. For an analysis by a U.S. diplomat at the time, see Frederick Nolting, *From Trust to Tragedy: The Political Memoirs of Frederick Nolting, Kennedy's Ambassador to Diem's Vietnam* (New York: Praeger Publishers, 1988), 9.

[14] For various reasons, this book adopts a nonpartisan position on Diem's policies. At his liberation, Archbishop Thuan declared that it was difficult to evaluate recent history. Although nowadays there are more sources available

Benedictine oblate in the monastery of Saint Andrew in Brugge. Bao Dai, who was living in France when the Geneva negotiations were underway,[15] suggested that Diem become prime minister. When Diem visited him, Bao Dai led him into a room with a crucifix and gave him time for silent prayer. Bao Dai apparently said: "Before this cross, you cannot refuse the sacrifice that God is asking of you for the country." Diem was moved and eventually agreed to return to Vietnam, where he became prime minister and then president in 1955. The situation facing Diem was particularly chaotic.[16] He miraculously survived numerous assassination attempts. Surrounded by a competent staff, he managed to set up

---

on the period, there is a wide difference of opinion among their authors as to the policies of the republic (1954). The reader will find a variety of books in the richly annotated bibliography. In order not to overload my text, I will limit myself to presenting the reader with Élisabeth's testimony. Certain points of historical clarification have been included in the notes.

The speeches that Diem gave during his presidency have not been referred to very often here. Nonetheless, he explicitly declared in them that the freedom and democracy he desired for his country in no way disavowed the people's gratitude for the benefits brought by the Western powers. There is no trace of xenophobia in his policies. Ngo-Dinh-Diem, *Quelques discours politiques importants du président* (Saigon: Présidence de la République du Vietnam, Service de Presse, 1956).

[15] The former emperor, who had gone to France for his studies, often resided there and eventually died there.

[16] A few examples must suffice: (1) In October 1954, Edward Lansdale (1908–1987), an American colonel, foiled an attempted coup by Nguyen Van Hinh (1915–2004) aimed at overthrowing Diem; (2) The Cao Dai Buddhist movement, which held power in the area northeast of the Mekong, had twenty thousand soldiers, while Hoa Hao Buddhism controlled the area southeast of Saigon with the help of thousands of soldiers; (3) About thirty tribes held the mountains in the center of the territory. In Saigon itself, there was a powerful criminal organization, the Binh Xuyen Force, whose main revenue derived from drug trafficking and prostitution; (4) In 1960, eighteen prominent politicians and intellectuals signed the Caravelle Manifesto (named after the Caravelle Hotel in Saigon), which contained strong criticism of the president. This group of non-Communist opponents became known as the Caravellists. Seth Jacobs, *Cold War Mandarin: Ngo Dinh Diem and the Origins of America's War in Vietnam, 1950–1963* (Lanham, Md.: Rowman and Littlefield, 2006), 61–62; Moyar, *Triumph Forsaken*, 32–59, 105–7; and Shaw, *Lost Mandate*, 49.

policies to fight corruption. Thanks to foreign aid, the country was able to absorb nearly a million refugees fleeing the Communist regime in the North. Diem shared in the suffering of all these people and placed his trust in the help and the light of the Lord.

Eager to fulfill the mission entrusted to her by Kha, Hiep maintained close contact with her president brother, often by telephone, and offered encouragement. As for Thuan, he knew that Diem lived an ascetic life and that he was a man of profound integrity, eager to serve his country. When people spoke negatively of our uncle in front of my brother and ranted about his intransigence over international demands, he would remain silent, but he felt they were talking about someone other than the man he knew so well.

Although Diem's relations with envoys from the United States were often strained, he harbored no animosity whatsoever toward the American people; his only fight was for the Vietnamese people to become masters of their own destiny. All his life, Diem had been a man of prayer; he went to Mass and prayed the Rosary every day. Throughout his political career as well as in his private life, he remained an oblate, and he was sometimes compared to a monk.[17] Diem faced huge problems[18] and was frequently

[17] Although he worked with great diligence and displayed true statesmanship when receiving diplomats, meeting with his staff, and addressing the people, Diem lived a very austere life in the presidential palace. He had one simple bedroom, and his bed was surrounded by books. He had maintained a quasi-monastic lifestyle. On December 17, 1957, he wrote to his fellow brothers in the Brugge monastery: "Pray for my country and for myself, dear Father; we have such a need for the good God."

[18] One of the tactics employed by the Viet Cong was the installation of secret bases in each village in the South. They began by eliminating thousands of local leaders, teachers, and health workers. Geoffrey Shaw estimates twelve thousand victims between 1960 and 1961. The Republic of the South thus lost the support of a substantial part of the rural population, from which the Viet Cong afterward recruited many of their fighters. The latter intensified their operations in 1960, backed by soldiers from the North, who sneaked along

slandered[19] by those who wished to remove him from power.[20] In 1963, he encountered strong opposition from the Buddhists. Claiming that they were the victims of unfair policies imposed by a Catholic president, some of the Buddhists engaged in violent clashes with the police. In July 1963, Buddhist monk Thich Quang Duc (1897–1963), a high-profile preacher, doused himself with gasoline and burned himself to death in the middle of the street. Photos of that suicide were flashed all over the world and heavily impacted international public opinion. It is easy to understand the indignation of the Western world when the press reported systematic killings of Buddhists or the burning of their

---

the notorious Ho Chi Minh Trail through Laos. An American commentator summed up the situation laconically: "We built; the Viet Cong destroyed." From the start of his presidency (1961–1963), John F. Kennedy decided to boost the American military presence in South Vietnam, for the democratic republic was considered to be a strategic part of the battle against Communism in Asia. American ambassador Frederick Nolting (1911–1989), stationed in Vietnam from 1961 to 1963, struggled to understand his president's strategy at that difficult time. According to Diem, the thing to do was to prevent armed contact between the Communists in the North and those in the South. Unfortunately, neither the republic itself nor the Americans proved capable of stemming the flow of weapons and soldiers from the North into the South. See Devillers, "Vietnam: Histoire", 579; Howard Jones, *Death of a Generation: How the Assassination of Diem and JFK Prolonged the Vietnam War* (Oxford: Oxford University Press, 2003), 1–12, 377; Moyar, *Triumph Forsaken*, 87–105; John M. Newman, *JFK and Vietnam: Deception, Intrigue, and the Struggle for Power*, 2nd ed. (New York: Warner Books, 2016), 4, 9–29; Nolting, *From Trust to Tragedy*, 9; Shaw, *Lost Mandate*, 41–45, 84, 178.

[19] Recent publications confirm that Diem was indeed the victim of what Élisabeth calls "calumnies". See also Nguyen Thi Viet, *Việt Nam: Histoire d'une nation* (Paris: Éd. du Jubilé/Hachette, 2017), 478. In her work, Madame Viet puts it in her unique way: "A French proverb says: *Qui veut tuer son chien l'accuse de la rage.* ["Give a dog a bad name and hang him."] Ngo Dinh Diem was a victim of such an injustice. The Communists and their sympathizers pulled out all the stops to denigrate his entire government agenda in order to destroy it and take over South Vietnam."

[20] More details can be found in Edward Miller, *Misalliance: Ngo Dinh Diem, the United States, and the Fate of South Vietnam* (Cambridge, Mass.: Harvard University Press, 2013), 271–72.

pagodas. But the newspaper reports accusing Diem of being the instigator of such violent acts against Buddhists were completely unfounded.[21] During his eight years in government, the number of pagodas actually increased. The pagodas we had visited in our childhood were old and decrepit, but Diem helped with their renovations. Throughout his presidency, Buddhists and Confucianists made up more than half of the ministerial or administrative staff.

American ambassador Nolting was away on vacation at the time of these events and was thus unable to provide his government with objective information. The American administration, therefore, somewhat hastily concluded that Diem was responsible for serious religious discrimination. Eager to clarify the situation for the international community, Diem happily welcomed a visit to Vietnam by a United Nations commission of inquiry in 1963. The conclusions reached by the inquiry were conclusive: there was no discrimination against Buddhists in South Vietnam. It is perplexing that the report was not presented to the American Senate until several months after Diem's assassination.[22] That year, Kennedy replaced Nolting with Republican Henry Cabot Lodge,

---

[21] Paul Rignac confirmed this. He mentioned that under Diem's presidency, more than four thousand pagodas were built between 1954 and 1962, which represented an increase of 200 percent. More importantly still, he added that "the various Buddhist sects enjoyed total freedom of worship." Rignac also provided precise figures on the political responsibilities fulfilled by Buddhists, whose representation in the government exceeded that of the Catholics. He spoke of the "myth", disseminated all over the world, that Diem marginalized the Buddhists. Paul Rignac, *Ngo Dihn Diem: Une tragédie vietnamienne* (La chaussée d'Yvry: Éd. Atelier Fol'fer, 2018), 226–29.

[22] Few commentators paid any attention to this report drawn up by the commission sent in 1963 to South Vietnam by the United Nations. Invited by Diem, it concluded its inquiry by stating that it had found no evidence whatsoever of a violation of the rights of Buddhists: "There was no religious discrimination or persecution, no encroachment of freedom of religion.... It is a political question, not a religious question." United Nations, "The Violation of Human Rights in South Vietnam", document A/5630, in Shaw, *Lost Mandate*, 231–32. Shaw's conclusion is confirmed in Rignac, *Ngo Dinh Diem*, 236.

Diem receiving a Buddhist leader in Saigon

Jr. (1902–1985), a media celebrity.[23] *Shortly after his arrival in Vietnam, Lodge became convinced that a coup against the president must be mounted for the sake of stability in the country and for American interests.*[24] *Western pragmatism could hardly imagine that Diem would stand his ground and face the danger or that his heroic behavior would lead to his demise.*[25]

On November 1, 1963, the rebel forces swung into action. On November 2, very early in the morning, Diem and Nhu took refuge in a church in Saigon's Chinatown. Nhu would have

[23] Anne E. Blair, *Lodge in Vietnam: A Patriot Abroad* (New Haven, Conn.: Yale University Press, 1995), 14–15.

[24] Ibid., 37–47.

[25] Shaw, *Lost Mandate*, 257–58; Moyar, *Triumph Forsaken*, 276; Blair, *Lodge in Vietnam*, 69; Jones, *Death of a Generation*, 9. These commentators suggest that the Americans offered the Vietnamese president the possibility of escaping. What mattered most to them was to be rid of a man who was a nuisance to their administration. It seems that a great number of Vietnamese generals who also wanted to be rid of Diem had nevertheless not expected him to be killed. Jones thinks that the Americans, like the Vietnamese implicated in the putsch, should have foreseen that their strategy could lead to the death of the two brothers. Jones, *Death of a Generation*, 416, 455.

preferred to leave the country—which was indeed an option offered by the Americans—but Diem was convinced that he could resolve the crisis by staying home and engaging in dialogue. Nhu showed an exceptional solidarity: he clearly saw that their lives were in danger, but he supported his brother until the end. Both men went to confession and attended Mass. Then Diem telephoned the generals to set up a meeting. The putschists sent a vehicle to pick them up.[26] *We will never know for sure whether the two brothers were killed in the vehicle or upon their arrival at the military headquarters, as has been suggested.*[27] *In any case, Diem had far too many supporters among some segments of the population for the insurgents to let him live.*[28]

As Madame Nhu was out of the country with her eldest daughter, the military contacted my cousin Nguyen Thi Hoang Anh and told her to retrieve the two bodies. Anh telephoned my sister Niem (also living in Saigon), to ask her to accompany her. In a hot country (and at a particularly hot time of the year), bodies decompose very rapidly, and given their advanced stage of

---

[26] A small detail: On November 1, the conspirators had encircled the presidential palace, but the two brothers had been able to escape and take refuge in another government building. From there, they made their way to a church in Chinatown. On the site of the palace, since then completely destroyed, a prestigious building has been erected, which is now a museum and a conference center.

[27] Fathers Guimet and Lajeune (MEP), priests attached to the church in which the brothers had taken refuge, drew up a report on the last hours of the president and his brother. This typewritten text was given to me by a Vietnamese priest who wishes to remain anonymous. The two priests formally confirm having seen Diem and Nhu alive as they left in a car: they were therefore not killed on the spot.

[28] Future prime minister Tran Van Huong would later say: "The top generals who decided to murder President Diem ... knew very well that having no talent, nor moral virtues, and no popular support whatsoever, they could not prevent a spectacular comeback of the President and Mr. Nhu if they were alive." Moyar, *Triumph Forsaken*, 273.

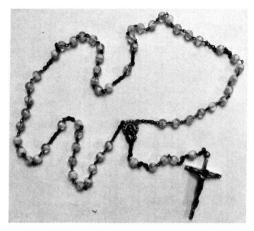

Diem's rosary found in the pocket of his blazer

degradation, Niem (Bernadette) and Anh were not able to identify them.

Bernadette even wondered whether the bodies they were asked to identify were really those of Diem and Nhu. "Perhaps they were able to escape", she hoped. Bernadette called my mother to seek her advice. Mum suggested, "Look in their pockets. If you find a translucent white rosary, it is surely Diem's, since he always carried that rosary with him. And if you find a copy of the Prayer to the Holy Cross [Prière a la Sainte Croix], it will be Nhu's. He always recited it in preparation for death. No one else carries that French prayer around, anywhere."

My sister found both the rosary and the prayer, which we have kept, and proceeded to organize our uncles' funerals.

Those deaths came as a terrible shock to the family. Thuan rarely aired his views concerning Diem's policies, but he was always capable of making a point in a very succinct way. Twelve years later, when he was himself arrested by the Communists—on August 15, 1975—they told him that Diem had been a lackey

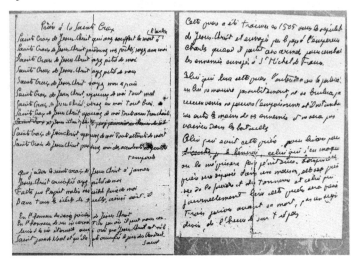

Nhu's Prayer to the Holy Cross found in the pocket of his shirt

of the United States. At that moment, Thuan summed up my uncle's life in a single sentence: "Diem was a patriot who died because he refused to be anyone's lackey." By then, my brother had suffered a lot, not just because of his uncles' assassinations but also because of the deep sadness he felt in watching the chaotic situation in which our dear country was mired. Although Thuan never officially adopted any political stance, he always wanted to awaken the faithful to the repercussions that our country's struggles could have on their personal lives and on the fate of our Church. With so much violence being unleashed around, Thuan could have turned bitter, but he did not. He had learned to love his enemies long before his incarceration, and he amply displayed a capacity for bridge building when he came face-to-face with Diem's old enemies. In 1966, a few years after the Buddhist crisis and Diem's death, a South Vietnamese general, Ton That Dinh (1926–2013), was sent to the central part of Vietnam.

In the Hue region, various groups—among them, politicized
Buddhists—were opposing the army, the nationalist parties, and
Catholics. While South Vietnam was already at war with the
Communists in the North, the danger of a civil war breaking
out in the country loomed large. Several churches were attacked,
including Tam Toa. A true opportunist, General Dinh had initially supported Diem's government, but then he succumbed to the
blandishments of the conspirators, even taking an active part in
the 1963 coup and the assassination of Thuan's uncles.[29] It was
surprising to see him renew contact with Thuan three years later:
the Catholics were beginning to regroup to defend their churches,
and there was a risk of a violent confrontation between Buddhists
and Catholics in Hue. Unable to restore order in that area of the
country, Dinh asked Thuan for help. Thanks to an agreement
between Thuan and the monk Thich Tri Quang Gia,[30] another
former Diem opponent, hostilities came to an end. Thuan even
gave General Dinh refuge in the minor seminary to save him from
attacks by the Communists.

One lesson that Thuan remembered for the rest of his life was
that human helplessness and weakness should not stop anyone
from facing up to the more powerful. Integrity is an inner force
that disconcerts bullies. Diem showed that one can be an apostle in
politics. As Christians, we can work for equity among our fellow

---

[29] This general was initially close to Thuan's family (Michael R. Nichols,
"Tôn Thất Đính", in The Encyclopedia of the Vietnam War: A Political, Social,
and Military History, ed. Spencer C. Tucker [Oxford: Oxford University Press,
1988], 404). Dinh, who took part in politics in the South until 1975, left that
year for exile to the United States, apparently after expressing remorse over the
part he had played in Diem's fall.

[30] Thich Tri Quang Gia, who was born in 1922 and was a key figure in the
Vietnamese Buddhist movement, had opposed Diem. In contrast with Dinh,
the Americans exercised less leniency toward this politicized monk and had
him locked up in a Saigon hospital. Charlotte A. Power, "Thích Trí Quang",
in Tucker, Encyclopedia of the Vietnam War, 401.

citizens. In this world, however, we must be ready for sacrifices and persecution. Our lives will then become lives "in the footsteps of Jesus". We need to carry His cross. There is always a price to pay if one wants to be an apostle in politics.

Vietnam between 1963 and 1965

The putsch, led by General Duong Van Minh (1916–2001), aimed at eliminating all opposition; hence the assassination of Diem and Nhu.[31] The political agenda drawn by the general did not include much in the way of social commitment. It provided the Viet Cong with the opportunity to take advantage of the peasants' helplessness in order to consolidate its power in the villages. The corruption that Diem had always fought was back with a vengeance.[32] As for the Buddhist monks, they continued to display their resentment.[33]

At the end of January 1964, there was yet another putsch: General Nguyen Khanh (1927–2013) overthrew the Minh government. Khanh was more amenable to political freedom, but unfortunately, he did not surround himself with competent men.[34] Any time there were protests against his regime, Catholics ended up being the main victims of the riots: houses, schools, churches, businesses, and press offices were attacked, pillaged, and burned down. Patients were even massacred in a hospital.[35]

---

[31] This chapter mentions only a few key elements that help explain how, after Diem's fall, the country was dragged into the most terrible war in its history.

[32] "The general's regime was more corrupt but more liberal. Everyone exploited his position as the Americans poured more money into Vietnam." Blair, *Lodge in Vietnam*, 129. See also Moyar, *Triumph Forsaken*, 273.

[33] Moyar, *Triumph Forsaken*, 276–87.

[34] Ibid., 295; Blair, *Lodge in Vietnam*, 133.

[35] Moyar, *Triumph Forsaken*, 316.

Under pressure from international public opinion, Ambassador Lodge intervened to try to save the life of Ngo Dinh Can, who had been imprisoned and sentenced to death.[36] His efforts were in vain. Can was coldly executed in May 1964. With American backing, Khanh managed to stay in power for a while.[37] South Vietnam was on the way to becoming a satellite country of the United States.[38] A great number of American senators and advisers called for strong military action.

Following his assassination on November 22, 1963, Kennedy was temporarily replaced by Vice President Lyndon B. Johnson (1908–1973). The latter was in full agreement with the military strategy promoted by his entourage and wished to maintain a strong military presence in Vietnam. But Johnson preferred to wait for the result of the presidential elections scheduled for November 1964 and the confirmation that he would continue in power before considering any military intervention.[39] Meanwhile, still in 1964, the Soviet Union elected a new leader, Leonid Brezhnev,[40] who increased strategic aid to the Communists in the North.

After his accession to the presidency, Johnson realized that the Hanoi regime was intensifying its military penetration in the South via Laos.[41] At the beginning of 1965,

[36] Blair, *Lodge in Vietnam*, 136–37. Pope Paul VI had made contacts all over the world with various influential figures in hopes of saving Can's life.

[37] Ibid., 318, 326–27.

[38] Anne Blair writes that the United States readily accepted Lodge's recommendations and acted accordingly. The Americans considered the republic to be "the keystone for all Southeast Asia", that is to say, Thailand, Cambodia, Laos, Burma, and Indonesia. If they won, the Communists would be on the doorstep of Australia and the Philippines. Ibid., 134–35.

[39] Moyar, *Triumph Forsaken*, 305, 309, 319–25.

[40] President of the USSR from 1964 to 1982.

[41] Moyar, *Triumph Forsaken*, 332–33.

Johnson decided to punish the Communists in the North by launching air raids after each act of aggression by the Viet Cong.[42] Military logic prevailed, and weapons and troops were deployed in Vietnam. War became the preferred option. There was no chance the Americans would be negotiating with the Chinese or Russian Communists,[43] nor would they even seek help from the United Nations. Later in the conflict, the Americans ignored pleas for a ceasefire from the French, who had experienced firsthand the Communists' determination and ruthlessness. The Americans wanted to maintain their stranglehold on Asia, albeit at the cost of millions of civilian and military lives. Already, under Diem's presidency, the United States had refused to support his efforts toward a peaceable solution to the conflict.[44] Diem's death ushered in a period of political instability in the Southern republic, and it was the prelude to a war that would prove extremely costly in terms of human and material losses.[45]

The Vietnam War (1965–1973)

In June 1965, General Nguyen Van Thieu (1923–2001) took control of the armed forces and acceded to the presidency of the Republic of the South.[46] The Vietnamese

[42] Ibid., 352–53.

[43] According to Lodge, that would have involved recognition of the Chinese government. Blair, *Lodge in Vietnam*, 146.

[44] In the 1960s, Diem had intensified diplomatic contacts with other countries in order to extract the politics of his country from the grip of the United States, which was monopolizing Western influence in Asia. He had even set up contacts with the Viet Cong. Shaw, *Lost Mandate*, 238–40.

[45] Moyar, *Triumph Forsaken*, 275–391.

[46] He remained there until 1975. For a description of the series of different governments, see Blair, *Lodge in Vietnam*, 133–34.

people were about to live their worst nightmare. It is reckoned that the American bombardments in the summer of 1965 marked the beginning of what is generally known as the Vietnam War.[47] The conflict escalated rapidly. The Communists received aid from China and the Soviet Union, while the Americans were supported by South Korea and Australia and were soon joined by Spain, New Zealand, Taiwan, and Thailand. Both sides committed war crimes. The Americans were guilty of massacres of civilians and rapes, and the Communists (Viet Cong), not to be outdone, executed about three thousand of their compatriots in Hue, including a great number of intellectuals in 1968. The notorious photo of a naked little girl, burned by a napalm bomb explosion, symbolized the horror of the murderous conflict.[48] American human losses and the exorbitant cost of that distant war drew stronger and stronger criticism in the United States and elsewhere in the Western world. The issue frequently made editorial headlines in American and international presses. Supporters of the war tried in vain to defend U.S. intervention in the media; despite this, the war grew increasingly unpopular in American public opinion. A great number of veterans were returning home permanently traumatized, scarred by the cruelty of the war. Intense battles—which devastated large parts of Vietnam and Cambodia—continued until the Paris Peace Accords, signed in January 1973. American troops left the country for good in 1975, which allowed the Communists to occupy several towns in the South. The fall of Saigon (Ho

[47] Devillers, "Vietnam: Histoire", 579–81.

[48] She survived to tell her story in Kim Phuc Phan Thi, *Fire Road: The Napalm Girl's Journey through the Horrors of War to Faith, Forgiveness, and Peace* (Carol Stream, Ill.: Tyndale, 2017).

Chi Minh City since 1976) marked the decisive victory of
the Viet Minh and the end of the Vietnam War.

The Communist Regime from 1975

The totalitarianism of the Communist regime established
after 1975 in the whole country very quickly revealed itself
through the violent elimination of any form of resistance:
censorship, the complete takeover of education, concentration camps,[49] forced labor, deportations, executions,
absolute rejection of any form of opposition to the regime,
restriction of liberties, and oppression of all religions.[50]
Marxist principles were rigorously applied: abolition of private business, nationalization of industry, collectivization of
agriculture, and confiscation of private assets. Opponents
who had not fled or who had escaped execution must, in
Communist parlance, be "reeducated". Thuan was only
one of the numerous victims of those policies.

The South, a prosperous area that had enjoyed much
greater political liberty, was now at the mercy of the dic-
tatorial Hanoi regime. American bombardments had seriously damaged the infrastructure in the North. The national
economy was in ruins, and food had to be imported on a
massive scale from the USSR and China.[51] The massive
exodus of the Boat People was indicative of the predicament

---

[49] For details on the camps, see Nguyen Van Cahn and Earle Cooper, *Vietnam under Communism (1975–1982)* (Stanford, Cal.: Hoover Institution Press,
1985), 188–225. Cahn and Cooper drew up a list of more than one hundred
known new prisons and reeducation camps, dispersed throughout all the provinces (202–3).

[50] Ibid., 164–87. The main victims were Buddhists and Christians.

[51] Ibid., 124.

that non-Communist Vietnamese found themselves trapped in. It was mainly after 1978 that between one and two million of them tried to leave the country.[52] The exodus constituted one of the greatest human tragedies in modern history.[53]

In the mid-1980s, just like other Communist countries, Vietnam undertook economic reforms (the Doi Moi, or "renovation"). The straitjacket that pinioned the country was gradually loosened to enable the renewal of diplomatic contacts with democratic countries. Today, relations between Communists and Catholics seem to be more relaxed than they were in Cardinal Thuan's days, even though it is much easier to present the magnificent figure of the cardinal abroad than in his own country.

[52] The chaos that engulfed the country at this time makes it almost impossible to estimate the number of refugees. In addition, a large number of the Boat People perished on the journey, drowned or victims of pirates. Ibid., 128–36.

[53] Nghia M. Vo called this exodus "the biggest sea escape in the twentieth century". He compared it to the influx of refugees from the North in 1954. Nghia M. Vo, *The Vietnamese Boat People, 1954 and 1975–1992* (Jefferson, N.C.: McFarland, 2006), 2, 193.

EPILOGUE

I had the great joy of meeting Cardinal Thuan and talking with him on several occasions. Reading his writings and meeting many times with his sister Élisabeth have enabled me to get to know him better. Before my recent visit to Vietnam, I had begun to write this book in collaboration with Élisabeth. Getting to know the cardinal's native country and the places where he lived, as well as meeting with individuals who were in contact with him, have encouraged me to publish the present work.

In the West, whenever I talk about the cardinal, I am asked a lot about the Church and Vietnamese society. Throughout my trip to Vietnam, I focused mainly on the influence the cardinal had on the local Church. I discovered that it is still difficult, in a Communist country, to speak openly about one's social commitment. Those who knew the cardinal remember him with great respect. Nuns have followed in his footsteps, and, along with Hope Community (Hy-Vong), which he founded, they give renewed hope to the poor and devote themselves happily to pastoral tasks. Cardinal Thuan always had a particular fondness for this secular movement, which seemed to have been uppermost in his thoughts when he was drafting his main projects. Quite simply, its members put themselves at the service of all, especially those who suffer. What inspires these men and women is an apostolic missionary zeal combined with a life of prayer. Like leaven in the dough, they blend in with society, eschewing all political involvement and merely working hard to improve living conditions for their fellow citizens.

Religious freedom is narrowly defined in Vietnam. The appointment of a bishop is often made in conjunction with civil authorities. Catholics are not allowed to open any schools or hospitals. And yet the Catholic youth there are more attuned to Christian life than in the West; solid charitable involvements with the sick and the poor are more noticeable there than in our secularized societies here.

Although this book deals with the cardinal's imprisonment, it places less emphasis on his suffering than on his capacity to forgive his enemies and on the message borne out of his unique writings, scribbled in prison and smuggled out. His long stints of solitary confinement led him to abandon himself unreservedly to the Lord. Charity was quintessential to his life. According to 1 Corinthians 13, the giving of one's life finds real meaning only in love.

The testimonies collected in this book include references to the political involvement of the cardinal's family. Rather than pulling the curtain over the family history, I wanted to highlight the human aspect hidden behind certain events that have been the subjects of controversy. The cardinal always maintained warm relations with his nearest and dearest and never distanced himself from any family member involved in politics. The battle he fought for greater justice, his social commitment in behalf of refugees, and his work for the emancipation of illiterate minorities, however, had nothing to do with any kind of ideological crusade. His opposition to Marxist thought never prevented him from seeing other sons of God in his Communist fellow citizens and extending his hand to them.

Élisabeth often told me that her brother was a true shepherd all his life, never abandoning his flock and never forgetting his country. His magnanimity and his message were readily shared with the universal Church, but they were first and foremost addressed to *his* Church in Vietnam, a living, fervent, joyful Church, born from the blood of martyrs. His motto, "Joy and Hope", remains a source of inspiration. His sense of humor, his wisdom, his patience, and his openness of mind combined to bring out a most engaging personality. The decision in Rome to acknowledge the cardinal's heroic virtue relates to the whole of his life.

My thanks to Élisabeth Thu Hong and to so many Vietnamese who have helped me love the cardinal so much.

—Father Stefaan Lecleir

My brother would say: I have worked and written to give hope to my people, especially to the young, that they may meet Jesus. The beauty of the Lord and His face are infinitely above our comprehension. Great spiritual people always reveal an aspect of God. One speaks of His majesty, another of His tenderness. Thuan's life shows us that God is the ultimate hope of our existence. Our greatest happiness is to be able to forgive our neighbor and to love him. Thuan invites us to share the joy of recognizing our poverty and finding our strength in our weakness.

It is my desire that each reader, in his own way, may discover Jesus, whom Thuan knew interiorly and loved deeply.

—Élisabeth Nguyen Thi Thu Hong

APPENDIX 1

Family Members: Additional Information

Thuan's Paternal Ancestors

Nguyen Van Vong ∞ Tong Thi Lai
Thuan's great-grandparents

Nguyen Van Dieu ∞ Nguyen Thi My
Thuan's grandparents

Nguyen Van Am ∞ Ngo Dinh Thi Hiep
Thuan's parents

My paternal ancestors, fervent and committed Catholics since the seventeenth century, came from a small village called Co Vuu (now Nha Tho Tri Buu), north of Hue, a village with about 140 Catholics.

This village is not far from La Vang, a site of Marian apparitions. From the beginning of the evangelization, being a Christian required a great deal of courage, and the proclamation of Christ and liturgical celebrations had to take place clandestinely. Hence, Christians tended to move together into small villages.[1] Christians

---

[1] Today, Christians are to be found scattered over many places. However, villages that are entirely Catholic still exist in the countryside. In the cities, some areas are inhabited almost exclusively by Christians.

were heavily persecuted in the period prior to French colonization (1858). In the nineteenth century, under Emperor Minh Mang, in search of greater security, the family moved to Phu Cam, near Hue, but unfortunately this did not save them from persecution.

Emperor Tu Duc took up a posture of defiance in the face of the French forces that sought to invade the country, but he considered—wrongly—that the Catholics represented a big risk for Vietnam. After all, did not the religion they had in common with Western invaders make them inclined to collaborate with those invaders? In 1860, the emperor decreed the "law of separation" (phan sap, "to separate and integrate"): Catholic families must be split up, and each of the faithful was forced to live with at least five non-Christians. Their lands were confiscated, and "Ta Dao" ("wrong way", "bad religion") was branded on their cheeks to prevent them from escaping.

- *Nguyen Van Danh. This ancestor of ours was a victim of this repressive policy: he was thrown into prison and the members of his family were split up.*
- *Nguyen Van Vong. This son of Danh was fifteen years old in 1860, when he was placed on a farm, where he was quite well treated. The farmer, a pious Buddhist, allowed him to take food to his father in prison.*

Vong showed a great deal of courage: he would get up at three in the morning, ready for the daily twelve-mile walk to make sure his father had enough to eat.

In 1862, the French colonizers negotiated treaties with the emperor that were sympathetic to Christians. Danh was freed, and the members of the Nguyen family were able to come back to live in Phu Cam. Vong and his children grew very close to Father Allys. Vong spent fifteen years evangelizing non-Christians south of the capital. On his return to Phu Cam, he became president of the parish council. My brother was fortunate enough to know this courageous great-grandfather who told him the history of our family. Vong's wife, Tong Thi Lai, was part of the family of Saint Tong Viet Buong (Paul).

- *Nguyen Van Dieu. Our paternal grandfather and the son of Nguyen Van Vong. Our father, Am, is the only child of Dieu. Lac, one of Dieu's sisters, had married Ung De, a member of the emperor's family.*[2]
- *Nguyen Van Am (Tadéo, 1901–1993). Our father. Am married Ngo Dinh Thi Hiep (Élisabeth).*

It would not be practical to list all the members of the family on our father's side who were close to Thuan, especially the descendants of our great-uncles, brothers of our grandfather Dieu.

Thuan's Maternal Uncles and Aunts

As Thuan's father was an only child, the Ngos were his only uncles and aunts:

- *Ngo Dinh Khoi (Paul, 1890–1945).* In 1912, he married Nguyen Thi Hoa, the eldest daughter of Nguyen Huu Bai, minister of the interior and a friend of Kha. Khoi held the post of governor of Quang Nam Province, in the coastal region. When the Communists assumed power at the end of World War II, he was

[2] Through his father, Prince Huong Thuyen, De was a descendant of Emperor Minh Mang. Seven sons of Ung De were catechists, and two of his daughters became religious.

executed along with his son Ngo Dinh Huan on August 31, 1945.[3]

- *Ngo Dinh Thi Giao* (Élisabeth, 1894–1944). A very pious woman with a profoundly charitable heart, she was the mother of four nuns.[4] Struck down with tuberculosis, like her husband, Truong Dinh Tung, she was often visited by Thuan when he accompanied the priest who came to bring her Communion.

- *Ngo Dinh Thuc* (Pierre-Martin, 1897–1984). Ordained to the priesthood in 1925, he pursued studies in Rome, where he was a fellow student of the future Pope Paul VI, and later in Paris (the Sorbonne), where he acquired a degree in French literature. On his return to Vietnam, he became a teacher at the major seminary in Hue. In 1938, he was appointed bishop of Vinh Long, south of Saigon, and on April 12, 1961, he became archbishop of Hue. During that time, he promoted the shrine of Our Lady of La Vang. He put his brother Diem in touch with Cardinal Francis Spellman (1889–1967), who was close to the Kennedy family. Thuc took part in the Second Vatican Council and then spent the rest of his life in exile.

After the Council, the archbishop got involved in the schism of the Sedevacantists, stating that there was no legitimate pope, and he ordained a few bishops without prior approval from the Holy See.[5] The support that he consistently received from his family in

[3] Ngo Ngoc Trung, "Ngô Đình Khôi", in *The Encyclopedia of the Vietnam War: A Political, Social, and Military History*, ed. Spencer C. Tucker (Oxford: Oxford University Press, 1988), 291.

[4] *Mémoires de Ngo Dinh Thuc*, a manuscript given to me by Élisabeth, 18.

[5] Ngo Ngoc Trung, "Ngô Đình Thục", in *Encyclopedia of the Vietnam War*, 293; Joseph Ratzinger, Sacred Congregation for the Doctrine of the Faith, *L'Osservatore Romano*, English edition (April 18, 1983), 12, https://www

Australia helped him, toward the end of his life, to seek reconciliation with Pope John Paul II, for whom he had a profound admiration.

- *Ngo Dinh Diem* (*Jean-Baptiste*, 1901–1963).[6] In 1933, he succeeded Nguyen Huu Bai as minister of the interior under Emperor Bao Dai. He was soon expelled from the political arena because of his independent stand against the French, and he settled in Phu Cam, close to his family. He left the country in 1950 and visited Japan, Italy, the United States, France, and Belgium. In 1954, he became prime minister and then president of the Republic of the South. He was assassinated in 1963. His name is well-known in Vietnam, France, America, and throughout Asia on account of his close involvement in the recent political history of Vietnam.[7]

- *Ngo Dinh Thi Hiep* (*Élisabeth*,[8] 1903–2005). Thuan's mother.

- *Ngo Dinh Thi Hoang* (*Anne*, 1904–1959), wife of Nguyen Van Le (François-Xavier), Thuan's godfather. Hoang was very close to her sister Hiep and her brother Diem, whom she supported financially at the time of his clandestine political activities between 1933 and 1950.

- *Ngo Dinh Nhu* (*Jacques*, 1907–1963). He studied in France and was a political adviser to Diem.

.vatican.va/roman_curia/congregations/cfaith/documents/rc_con_cfaith_doc_19830312_poenae-canonicae_en.html.

[6] Between Thuc and Diem, a boy was born who died in infancy.

[7] William Head, "Ngô Đình Diệm" and Cecil B. Currey, "Ngô Đình Diệm, Overthrow of", in *Encyclopedia of the Vietnam War*, 289–91.

[8] It was not surprising for several children to have the same baptismal name: in everyday life, it was only the Vietnamese first name that was used. In the family, they called Élisabeth Hiep, for example.

He married Tran Le Xuan (1924–2011), known as Madame Nhu.[9] He was assassinated at the same time as Diem.[10]

- *Ngo Dinh Can* (*Jean-Baptiste*, 1910–1964). He was a man close to the people, especially the Buddhists. During Diem's presidency, he was one of his close advisers, working mainly in his home district.[11] He was executed by the putschists on May 8, 1964.

- *Ngo Dinh Luyen* (*Michel*, 1914–1990). Sent to France as an adolescent, he was the most Westernized of Kha's children. On his return to his homeland, he married Nguyen Thi Danh (Lucie), who came from the South, and they had five children. He was widowed and then married Nguyen Phuoc Hanh (Marie), with whom he had eight children. He was based in Saigon and was then appointed ambassador in various places, including London.[12] He went into exile after his brothers' assassinations.

Thuan's Siblings

- *Nguyen Van Xuan* (*Jean-Baptiste, 1926–1927*). *He fell victim to cholera at age two, a few months before Thuan was born.*

[9] Arthur T. Frame, "Ngô Đình Nhu, Madame (Trần Lệ Xuân)", in *Encyclopedia of the Vietnam War*, 293.

[10] Ibid., 292.

[11] Cecil B. Currey, "Ngô Đình Cẩn", in *Encyclopedia of the Vietnam War*, 288–89.

[12] Ngo Ngoc Trung, "Ngô Đình Luyện", in *Encyclopedia of the Vietnam War*, 292.

- *Nguyen Thi Niem (Bernadette, 1930–1997). Our eldest sister spent a few years in the Hue Carmel,[13] when Thuan was studying not far from there in the major seminary. She had to leave the convent for health reasons. After studying, she became secretary at the British Consulate in Saigon, and in 1962 she married Englishman Brian Smith, who also worked there. The couple had two children. She was very close to my brother, and he went to England to preside at her funeral Mass.*

- *Nguyen Linh Tuyen (Joseph, 1932–2002). He was also very close to Thuan. Wanting to serve his country, he went to a military school in France. He was later appointed colonel in the military of the Republic of Vietnam and held the post of military attaché at the Vietnam embassy in Seoul, Korea. In 1975, he fled to the United States with his wife and their three children. He represented the family there when Diem's assassination was commemorated. He published various articles advocating a free Vietnam. Except for Thuan, who was by then gravely ill, the whole family gathered for his funeral in February 2002.*

- *Nguyen Van Truyen (Paul). Stillborn.*

- *Nguyen Van Thanh (Michel, 1935–2009). He was gifted in literature and poetry and worked as a detective. He had a child from his first marriage and two others from his second. He was imprisoned in 1975 in a Communist reeducation camp and was freed shortly before Thuan. Accompanied by*

---

[13] She took the name Bernadette in Carmel and was thenceforth known by that name. Her baptismal name was Anna (Archives of the parish of Phu Cam). The archives in Phu Cam provide information that is slightly different from this list. They give the Christian names, as they were used in the families in their Western form. But Joseph appears as Giuse, Michel as Micae, and Élisabeth as Isave.

his family, he visited Thuan in Bach Mai Hospital. He fell away from the Church for a long period. Struck down with liver cancer in his last years, he was cared for by a nun whom Thuan knew well. Amid those painful circumstances, he returned to his childhood faith and was surrounded on his deathbed by Vietnamese Catholics. We were unfortunately not able to get back to our homeland to attend his funeral.

- Nguyen Thi Ham Tieu (Anne-Cécile, 1938–2005). She played a providential role in the life of our family, both for my parents and for some of my sisters. While she was working at the Vietnamese embassy in Australia, the 1963 coup took place, immediately followed by the change of government in the country. Anne was fired from her post, but she was able to obtain Australian citizenship. The loss of her job turned out, in the long run, to be a blessing in disguise. In that same year, she told us, my brother wrote to her: "My dear sister, stay there: one day, you will be called to help the whole family." Indeed, for many years she campaigned relentlessly for Thuan's release from prison, seeking help from Amnesty International, Australian bishops and ministers, and friends and members of our family. Anne said: "I remember that Thuan always wanted to become a priest. He used to set up little altars when he was very young. He was, above all, a model of charity for his brothers and sisters. He was kind, and I was ready to do anything to rescue him. I visited a great number of countries and thousands of letters were written all over the world, addressed to the Communist government calling for his liberation. I was even received by Pope John Paul II, and I asked him to pray for my brother and to intervene for his release."

Anne published the English translation of the first book Thuan wrote in captivity and stayed by his side in Rome *throughout his illness—and, indeed, right up to his death in 2002. She also cared for our father and our mother until they died. When she herself fell ill in 2004, I joined her in Australia and stayed with her and with our elderly mother. Anne died in January 2005, followed by Mum seven days later.*

- *Nguyen Thi Anh Tuyet (Agnès, b. 1941). In 1962, she tried her vocation in Carmel for a year. She has always had a great devotion to the Virgin Mary and Saint Thérèse of Lisieux. She and her family have had a great number of trials and have offered their many sufferings in behalf of us all.*

- *Nguyen Thi Thuy Tien (Anne-Thérèse, 1945–2015). A multitalented woman, she possessed among other things a great knowledge of Vietnamese culinary arts. In 1975, she and her husband (a math teacher) and their daughter moved to Australia, where she studied to be an interpreter. She did a great deal of social work in behalf of Vietnamese refugees. Like so many of my brothers and sisters, she died of cancer.*

- *Nguyen Thi Thu Hong* (Élisabeth, b. 1949), coauthor of this book.

APPENDIX 2

The Cardinal Commemorated in Cologne

The various places that marked the life of Cardinal Thuan, some in Vietnam and some in Rome, have become memorials to him. Of particular note is the place where the cardinal is buried: the Church of Santa Maria della Scala in the heart of the working-class district of Trastevere, near the offices where he used to work and that have now become a major center for the spreading of his message.

But the cardinal is also commemorated in Germany, specifically in Cologne. Why?

In 1957 and 1958, Father Thuan spent the holidays in the Cologne Diocese with the Cellitinnen sisters, where he filled in for their chaplain at their provisional motherhouse in Hürth-Fischenich and learned German. After he returned home, he wrote regularly to the sisters. When he became a bishop, he visited them in 1973 and again in 1974 during a trip to Rome and Belgium. While he was in prison, the sisters received messages from him asking them to pray for him. They managed to send him medicines. Immediately following his liberation in 1988, he contacted them by telephone. The superior general, Mother Julitta, visited him in Rome in April 1989. Before and after his definitive exile in 1991, he stayed regularly in the sisters' motherhouse in Cologne-Longerich (in 1990 and between 1992 and 2001)—sometimes several times a year. In Cologne, Cardinal Thuan was easily able to get in touch with the dispersed Vietnamese. It was difficult for the Vietnamese Communist regime to track him down in Germany, and he was at liberty to phone all over the world. On various occasions, I was able to catch up with him during his holidays in Cologne. I also joined him during my research into the history of the Church in East Asia between 1997 and 1999. I remember that he paid great attention to everything that had to do with persecuted Christians.

He made his last phone call to Mother Julitta on August 10, 2002. He was dying and found it very difficult to talk, but he was determined to express his gratitude for the sisters' help: they had given generous financial support for his charitable works. It was in Cologne, too, that German translations of his writings were published. The Cellitinnen sisters have undertaken the great mission of keeping alive Cardinal Thuan's memory and disseminating his writings: a small seed that, in time, will take on universal dimensions, for so many Christians all over the world feel they have been bequeathed his message. Among other things, in the sisters' archives are all the correspondence they maintained with him over the years, a detailed history of their mutual contacts, and a testimony that Mother Julitta gave for his beatification.[1] Élisabeth visits Cologne regularly and has entrusted to the congregation a great number of her brother's relics, including chasubles

---

[1] A manuscript in German titled *Erinnerungen an Se. Eminenz Kardinal Fr. X. Nguyen Van Thuan (1957–2002)*. Mother Julitta and the current superior, Mother Bernharda, have strongly encouraged Élisabeth and me to compose this book of testimonies.

and—the most precious gift of all—the pectoral cross that he fashioned when he was a prisoner, along with the little flasks that served as his chalice. Cardinal Meissner inaugurated a fine little museum at the entrance to their convent on October 26, 2013.[2]

This deep friendship with the Cellitinnen sisters has also led to the creation of a foundation whose center holds precious documents for those interested in learning about Cardinal Thuan, the "Apostle of Hope". This memorial enterprise was encouraged by Cardinal Turkson during his visit in October 2017. The first forum devoted to Cardinal Thuan took place in Cologne from September 13 to 15, 2019, under the auspices of the foundation of the Cellitinnen sisters.[3]

[2] There is an internet site devoted to him: https://www.kardinal-van-thuan.de/index.php/.

[3] The two speakers were Father Dinh Anh Nhue Nguyen, O.F.M.Conv., and Father Hubertus Blaumeiser, introduced by Élisabeth and by Mr. Wolfgang Allhorn.

APPENDIX 3

Papal Testimonies

There is no question that contemporary popes are highly appreciative of the witness of Cardinal Thuan, now Venerable. John Paul II invited him to preach the retreat for the Roman Curia in 2000.[1] Pope Benedict XVI, as a cardinal, often had dealings with Cardinal Thuan in the context of their respective roles in the service of the Holy See. In his encyclical letter on Christian hope, *Spe Salvi* (2007),[2] he presented Thuan as a witness to hope for the whole world.

Spe Salvi: Encyclical Letter on Christian Hope (November 30, 2007)

When no one listens to me any more, God still listens to me. When I can no longer talk to anyone or call upon anyone, I can always talk to God. [...] When I have been plunged into complete solitude ...; if I pray I am never totally alone. The late Cardinal Nguyen Van Thuan, a prisoner for thirteen years, nine of them spent in solitary confinement, has left us a precious little book: *Prayers of Hope*.

---

[1] François-Xavier Nguyen Van Thuan, *Témoins de l'espérance: Retraite au Vatican*, trans. Sylvie Garoche (Paris: Nouvelle Cité, 2000).

[2] All the pontifical texts mentioned can be found on the website www .vatican.va.

During thirteen years in jail, in a situation of seemingly utter hopelessness, the fact that he could listen and speak to God became for him an increasing power of hope, which enabled him, after his release, to become for people all over the world a witness to hope—to that great hope which does not wane even in the nights of solitude....

Cardinal Nguyen Van Thuan, in his book of spiritual exercises, tells us that during his life there were long periods when he was unable to pray and that he would hold fast to the texts of the Church's prayer: the Our Father, the Hail Mary and the prayers of the liturgy. Praying must always involve this intermingling of public and personal prayer. This is how we can speak to God and how God speaks to us. In this way we undergo those purifications by which we become open to God and are prepared for the service of our fellow human beings. We become capable of the great hope, and thus we become ministers of hope for others. Hope in a Christian sense is always hope for others as well. It is an active hope, in which we struggle to prevent things moving towards the "perverse end". It is an active hope also in the sense that we keep the world open to God. Only in this way does it continue to be a truly human hope. (nos. 32, 34)

Under the pontificate of Pope Francis, Thuan's heroic virtue has been recognized and may be presented to the people of God as an example to be followed. Three papal documents explicitly mention the cardinal.

Gaudete et Exsultate: Apostolic Exhortation on the Call to Holiness in Today's World (March 19, 2018)

At times, life presents great challenges. Through them, the Lord calls us anew to a conversion that can make his grace more evident in our lives, "in order that we may share his holiness" (Heb 12:10). At other times, we need only find a more perfect way of doing what we are already doing: "There are inspirations that tend solely to perfect in an extraordinary way the ordinary things we do in life." When Cardinal François-Xavier Nguyên van Thuân was imprisoned, he refused to waste time waiting for the day he would be set free. Instead, he chose "to live the present moment, filling it to the brim with love". He decided: "I will seize the occasions that present themselves every day; I will accomplish ordinary actions in an extraordinary way. (no. 17)

Good Politics Is at the Service of Peace: Message for the Fifty-Second World Day of Peace (January 1, 2019)

In this message, the pope talked about a political life that should be at the service of human rights and peace. Significantly, before citing the "beatitudes for political life", enunciated by Thuan in Padua in 2002, Pope Francis stressed that commitment to the common good is required of "all politicians, whatever their culture or religion". He continued with these words: "In this regard, it may be helpful to recall the 'Beatitudes of the Politician', proposed by Vietnamese Cardinal François-Xavier Nguyễn Văn Thuận, a faithful witness to the Gospel who died in 2002":

Blessed be the politician with a lofty sense and deep understanding of his role.

Blessed be the politician who personally exemplifies credibility.

Blessed be the politician who works for the common good and not his or her own interest.

Blessed be the politician who remains consistent.
Blessed be the politician who works for unity.
Blessed be the politician who works to accomplish
    radical change.
Blessed be the politician who is capable of listening.
Blessed be the politician who is without fear. (no. 3)

Christus Vivit: Post-Synodal Apostolic Exhortation Addressed to Young People and to the Entire People of God (March 25, 2019)

In the third part of his exhortation *Christus Vivit,* Pope Francis spoke about the importance of living the present in depth. "Today's trouble is enough for today" (no. 147; see Mt 6:34), he wrote with the Gospel writer: each small joy can be lived as a gift of the love of God. The pope illustrated his theme with reference to the way in which the cardinal lived this word of the Lord during his incarceration:

Cardinal Francis Xavier Nguyên Van Thuân, when imprisoned in a concentration camp, refused to do nothing but await the day when he would be set free. He chose "to live the present moment, filling it to the brim with love". He decided: "I will seize the occasions that present themselves every day; I will accomplish ordinary actions in an extraordinary way". As you work to achieve your dreams, make the most of each day and do your best to let each moment brim with love. This youthful day may well be your last, and so it is worth the effort to live it as enthusiastically and fully as possible. (no. 148)

APPENDIX 4

Yesterday and Today

In 1642, Alexandre of Rhodes visited Dai Phong and baptized three hundred people, some of whom may have been maternal ancestors of the cardinal. His paternal ancestors were present at apparitions of the Virgin Mary that took place in La Vang in 1798. Various persecutions drove these families to take refuge in Phu Cam. Their profound faith nurtured the cardinal's spirituality, and it continued to spread through followers dedicated to Cardinal Thuan's social work.

While in Vietnam in January 2019, I was able to visit various charitable organizations, thanks to Dr. Vinh Thua (Tom). After completing medical studies in Belgium, this cousin of the cardinal emigrated to the United States, where he worked as a pediatrician in his own clinic. Never forgetting his native country, he devoted a large part of his free time to helping to alleviate the suffering there. A distant relative of the emperor Minh Mang, who persecuted Christians, Tom was the son of Buu Te, Thuan's adviser in aiding refugees. Like the cardinal, Tom's father was once imprisoned by the Communist regime. A great admirer of Cardinal Thuan, Tom provided considerable help toward the renovation of the family home. He also offered valuable advice in the editing of this book. He died in September

Dr. Vinh Thua

2020 while caring for COVID patients, and he leaves a great emptiness in the lives of his family and friends.

During my trip, I was able to visit a poor parish in which the priest, a friend of Tom's, and a hundred or so volunteers helped widows and the handicapped enjoy a more dignified quality of life. The parish set up a food bank. Thanks to donations, it was possible to purchase the materials needed for the construction of small houses to provide a decent living environment; everyone helped with the construction. Burial expenses for the poor are assumed in their entirety by the parish so that in the event of a death, the family is able to pay homage to the deceased in accordance with Vietnamese tradition.

Cardinal Thuan was convinced that Scouting provides a fine education for life and the formation of the young. I have had the joy of taking part in the activities of Scouting programs set up by the cardinal that are still thriving.

When he was bishop of Nha Trang, Thuan went to help the Raglai people in the Khanh Hoa Province. Tom told me about a fine project set up at Suoi Dau by the Franciscan sisters and brothers for this ethnic group. Poverty, drunkenness, an almost complete lack of health infrastructures, and a lack of professional training are the daily lot of inhabitants of remote villages. Since 2008, the Franciscan family has been cooperating with the local school, assisting with tuition and opening two residences to accommodate

Present dwelling of a widow

Construction of a small house

Some members of the Scouting group in Hue,
founded by Cardinal Thuan

girls and boys while they attend school. Thus, despite their
background of family illiteracy, these young people are able
to complete their studies, and some of them, wishing to
pursue higher education to become doctors or teachers,
receive financial support. The sisters are particularly mindful
of improving the status of women. I was deeply impressed
by the way the girls blossomed in an atmosphere of friendship and respect for their dignity. It is so different from what
they have often been subjected to that they simply cannot
believe it at first. But the discovery of a fervent church life
in which music and dancing also play a big part leads them
to witness the Christian message to those who have not had
the benefit of a fortunate upbringing. These young people
share the joy and the hope they have received.

The sisters showed me how much happiness comes
from the little things of life. Each child is respected in his

A girl playing a handmade musical instrument at the
boarding school of the Franciscan sisters in Suoi Dau

development. The young people form a united team, and
many of them attend daily Mass, go to confession regularly, and take part in parish activities. The youth tried to
enlist me in their choir, but they soon gave that up! On the
other hand, I believe I was a diligent student of their cooking classes. A sister who is a physician took me along on
her rounds. She toured the country on her motorcycle and
stopped by the villages to check on children and help families. Her presence, her warmth, and all her attentive gestures
produced smiles among those otherwise forsaken people.

I had gone to Vietnam as a historian eager to verify my
sources and find out more about certain chapters in the life
of the cardinal. I developed a deep appreciation of who
Cardinal Thuan truly was not by studying the archives but
by visiting these places where charity is lived in daily life.

A Franciscan sister physician helping the
Raglai people in Suoi Dai

"Joy and hope": that was his motto. The gospel, introduced centuries earlier and lived courageously by Cardinal
Thuan, was for him a source of joy even in the darkness of
his imprisonment. Now he brings joy to those who suffer
and, above all, to those who help them.[1]

"It is more blessed to give than to receive" (Acts 20:35):
such is the reality lived by Tom and those Vietnamese so
deeply imbued with the spirituality of Cardinal Thuan.
Wanting to live that spirituality in daily life, these men and
women present to the world the face of hope. Watching
the way they live has enabled me to understand why Dr.
Vinh Thua has supported them so devotedly. I spent the
most beautiful days in my visit to Vietnam among them.

[1] In Cologne, the Cellitinnen sisters have created a repository for Cardinal
Thuan's writings in an exhibition devoted to him, and they also provide finan-
cial support, along with many Vietnamese refugees in North America where
Dr. Vinh Thua lived, for the impoverished people of these villages.

APPENDIX 5

Important Dates in the Life of the Cardinal

Childhood and Education[1]

- April 17, 1928: Birth in Phu Cam
- April 19, 1928: Baptism
- December 8, 1935: First Communion
- December 21, 1937: Confirmation
- 1941: Attends the minor seminary
- September 2, 1945: Ho Chi Minh declares the independence of Vietnam
- Indochina War (1946–1954)
- 1947: Attends the major seminary

Priestly Life

- June 11, 1953: Priestly ordination in Hue
- 1953: Vicar in the parish of Tam Toa, in the town of Dong Hoi; December: diagnosed with tuberculosis
- April 1954: Hospitalized in Saigon; recovery and convalescence

---

[1] Different publications seem to be uncertain about dates. The ones listed here are those that are most likely to be correct.

- 1954–1955: Pastoral activities in Hue
- 1954: A country divided; Diem becomes president of the South
- October 1956–June 1959: Studies in Rome, receives doctorate in canon law, and visits Ireland, France (Lourdes), Portugal (Fátima), Canada, Germany, Belgium, and the United States
- 1959–1967: Professor and rector of the minor seminary in Hue
- 1963: Diem's assassination
- 1964–1967: Vicar-general in Hue
- 1965–1975: Vietnam War; his family is forced to live in Saigon

Episcopate

- 1967–1975: Bishop of Nha Trang; ordained on June 24, 1967
- April 1975: Coadjutor archbishop of Saigon
- April 30, 1975: Communist takeover of Saigon

Prisoner: August 15, 1975– November 21 (23), 1988

- Under house arrest in Cay Vong (Nha Trang); writes *The Road of Hope*
- March 19, 1976:[2] Prisoner in Phu Khanh (Nha Trang); solitary confinement

---

[2] Some sources specify March 18, the vigil of the feast of Saint Joseph.

- November 29, 1976: Transfer to Thu Duc prison (north of Saigon) and journey with fifteen hundred other prisoners by boat to the North (December 1)
- December 1976: Prisoner in the Vinh Quang Reeducation Center (124 miles north of Hanoi)
- February 5, 1977: Prisoner in Thanh Liet (Hanoi)
- May 13, 1978: Prisoner in the parish of Giang Xa, south of Hanoi; writes more books
- November 5, 1982: Start of a long period of solitary confinement under surveillance by security police in Hanoi; compiles various dictionaries during this time
- 1988: Canonization of the Martyrs of Vietnam; Thuan spends nine out of these thirteen years in solitary confinement

Liberation

- November 21 (23), 1988: Liberation;[3] residence with the archbishop of Hanoi
- 1989: Permission to visit his family and Pope John Paul II
- December 1989: Surgery in Hanoi
- October 1990: Second surgery in Rome; audience with Pope John Paul II
- March 1991: Return to Hanoi
- December 1991: More travel, including to Rome; beginning of his exile

[3] It seems that he did not leave the prison until a few days after the announcement of his liberation on November 21.

Exile

- 1991–1994: Accommodation in a convent of Amantes de la Croix sisters, the Foyer Phat Diem guesthouse in Rome; preaches retreats and works in behalf of Vietnamese refugees
- 1992: Member of the International Catholic Migration Commission (ICMC)
- 1993: Consultant for the pontifical Congregation for the Evangelization of Peoples

Member of the Roman Curia

- November 15, 1994: Vice president of the Pontifical Council for Justice and Peace
- Until his death: Participates in various congresses and preaches retreats
- August 1995, 1996, and 2000: Participates in the Vietnamese Marian Congress in Missouri
- May 1996: Honorary doctorate, Notre Dame Seminary— School of Theology, New Orleans
- 1997: Writes *Five Loaves and Two Fish*, a book addressed to young people
- June 24, 1998: President of the Pontifical Council for Justice and Peace
- August 22, 1998: Establishment of the Community of Our Lady of La Vang
- March 12–18, 2000: Preaches the Lenten Retreat for the Roman Curia in the Vatican
- February 21, 2001: Created a cardinal

- March 2002: Journey to Sydney for his mother's hundredth birthday
- May 8 and July 22, 2002: Surgeries in Rome

Death and Beatification Process

- September 16, 2002: Death in Rome
- September 20, 2002: Funeral Mass celebrated by Pope John Paul II
- 2007: Introduction of the beatification process
- 2010: Public opening of the process
- June 2012: Transfer of his body to Santa Maria della Scala Church (Trastevere, Rome), which was his titular church, near the Pontifical Council for Justice and Peace
- July 2013: Closure of the process
- May 4, 2017: Pope Francis recognizes the cardinal's heroic virtue; he is given the title Venerable

APPENDIX 6

Maps

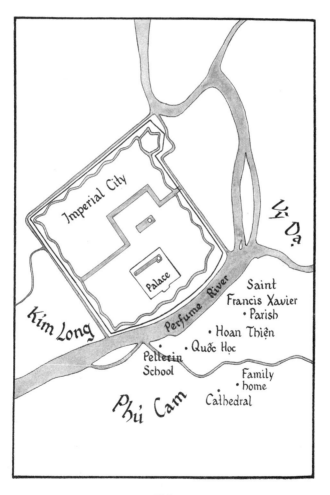

Province
Thira
Thiên-Huế

Huế

Huế

District
Hương
Thủy

Monastery
Thiên An

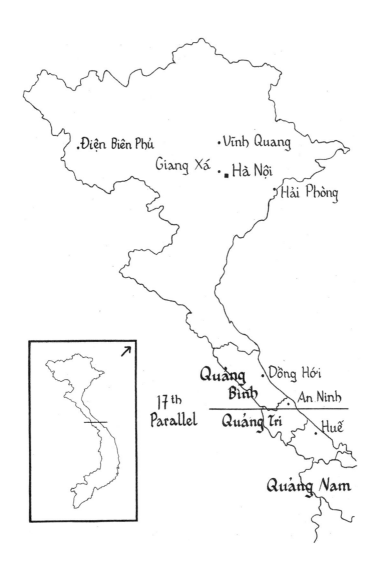

Điện Biên Phủ

Vĩnh Quang

Giang Xá   Hà Nội

Hải Phòng

Quảng Bình   Đồng Hới

An Ninh

17th Parallel   Quảng Trị

Huế

Quảng Nam

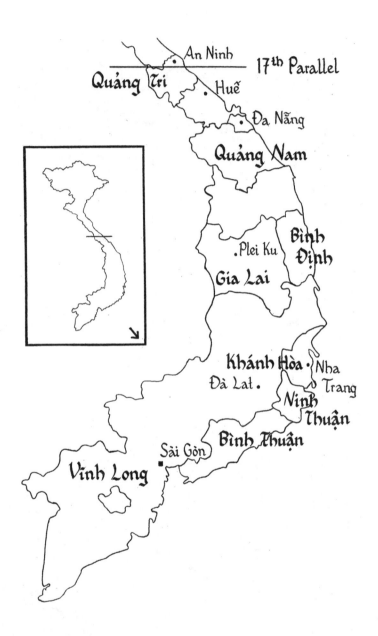

BIBLIOGRAPHY

Writings of Cardinal Thuan

In order to understand the cardinal's spirituality, it is useful to have a brief explanation of the context and content of his works.

Writings Translated into English

- *Five Loaves and Two Fish*. Boston: Pauline Books and Media, 2003.

  In this work, originally published in Italian under the title *Cinque pani e due pesci*, Thuan explains to young people that he was imprisoned for Christ and that the Lord taught him to live each day in intimate union with Him.
- Pontifical Council for Justice and Peace. *Compendium of the Social Doctrine of the Church*. London: Bloomsbury Publishing, 2006.

  The cardinal guided the preparatory phase of this document. It speaks of the value of the human person in his family and in economic and political relationships. It defines the family as the most vital cell of society.
- *Prayers of Hope, Words of Courage*. Boston: Pauline Books and Media, 2002.

  This collection of ninety prayers was written in prison, originally in Vietnamese. By wrapping it in old newspapers, he was able to smuggle the manuscript out of prison.

- *The Road of Hope: A Gospel from Prison*. Translated by John Peter Pham. North Palm Beach, Fla.: Wellspring, 2018.

    This is the best-known work from the cardinal's captivity, written in Cay Vong (1975–1976). Many of the cardinal's books have the word "hope" in their titles.

- *Testimony of Hope: The Spiritual Exercises of Pope John Paul II*. Boston: Pauline Books and Media, 2000.

    This is the text of the retreat the cardinal preached at the Vatican in 2000—one of the most important resources to get to know his life and spirituality.

Writings Not Translated into English

- *365 jours d'espérance*. Trésors de la spiritualité chrétienne. Paris: Sarment–Éd. du Jubilé, 2005.

    This book brings together four writings by the cardinal: *The Road of Hope*, *Pilgrims on the Road of Hope*, *The Road of Hope in the Light of the Word of God and the Council*, and *Prayers of Hope*. The texts of the four books are not presented chronologically but are grouped thematically. Also included is the text of the homily that Pope John Paul II delivered at the funeral of Cardinal Thuan, some biographical notes, and a meditation for each day of the year.

- *Dieci A da ricordare nella vita*. Rome: Ed. Citta Nuova, 2013.

    In about thirty pages, this book takes up the main ideas developed in the spiritual exercises that the cardinal preached.

- *La Gioia di vivere la Fede*. 2nd ed. Vatican City: Libreria Editrice Vaticana, 2014.

  This book is a collection of testimonies given on different occasions, along with spiritual and pastoral reflections.

- *Le Chemin de l'espérance: A la lumière de la Parole de Dieu et du Concile*. Des chrétiens/Vérité. Paris: Éd. Le Sarment–Fayard, 1994.

  Written in 1980 while the cardinal was still a prisoner, this book takes up the same themes as those of his 1975 and 1979 works, *The Road of Hope* and *Les pèlerins du chemin de l'espérance*. Texts from the Second Vatican Council have been added. This book forms a trilogy with the two previous publications.

- *Les pèlerins du chemin de l'espérance*. Des chrétiens/Vérité. Paris: Éd. Le Sarment–Fayard, 1993.

  Written in 1979, this book is a continuation of *The Road of Hope*, the cardinal's first book written in captivity (1975). The chapters and themes are placed in the same order as those of the 1975 writing.

- *Lettere Pastorali sulle orme del Concilio Vaticano II*. Vatican City: Libreria Editrice Vaticana, 2013.

  This book contains the letters the cardinal wrote as bishop of Nha Trang, detailed information on his life and works, and contributions from various authors about his person, his spirituality, and his social doctrine.

- Preface to *Autobiographie*, by Marcel Van. In *Œuvres completes*. Vol. 1. Versailles: Éd. Amis de Van, 2000.

- Preface to *Petite Histoire de Van*, by Antonio Boucher. Paris: Saint-Paul Éd. Religieuses/Les Amis de Van, 2006.

- *Scoprite la gioia della speranza: Gli ultime esercizi spirituali predicati dal Cardinale.* 2nd ed. Rome: Éd. Art, 2006.
- *Témoins de l'espérance: Retraite au Vatican.* Translated by Sylvie Garoche. Paris: Nouvelle Cité, 2000.

Unpublished Writings

The commission preparing for the beatification of the cardinal is in possession of unpublished writings, such as some small works written during the time he taught at the minor seminary. His doctoral thesis is titled "Studium comparativum de organisatione capellanorum militum in mundo" (1959). Many works that the cardinal wrote in captivity, such as grammars and dictionaries, reflections on youth ministry, an exposé on liberation theology, practical advice for preaching retreats, and so forth, are preserved in the diocesan archives of Hanoi.

Letters are also listed. Madame Hong offered me copies of other works that the cardinal wrote during his captivity, including a translation of his *Message from Father Maximilian Kolbe*, as well as postcards. There are many writings before and after his liberation: homilies, conferences, and retreats, to which this book refers in particular. Here are a few in particular:

- *The Church and Social Justice in the Next Millennium: New Directions and the Pope's Call*
- *Jesus Christ the Savior and the Mission of Love and Service of the Church in Asia: A Reflection in View of the Synod of Bishop for Asia*
- *Political Problems of Asia and Their Solutions*

① Aimez Jésus

a) l'amour de Dieu :
- Dieu le 1er aime l'homme, il a fait le 1er pas.
- La plus gde preuve de son amour révélé ... le fait qu'il se révèle ... le Xt, et qu'il offre à l'homme, par le Xt et sa mort, la Rédemption
- l'amour de Jésus p' nous est un amour personnel.

b) la réponse de l'homme.
- ... l'amour et de l'accueil de la révélation et de l'amour de Dieu, manifestés ... la foi qui lui est manifestée amour donné par le Créateur —

c) actualité.
- Jésus est une personne vivante, spécialement de l'Eucharistie.
- les temps d'aujourd'hui réclament une foi personnelle ... fortement et personnellement convaincu que le Salut c'est Jésus.
- Une foi chrétienne superficielle ou de type sociologique ne suffit plus
- cet amour doit se concrétiser ... la disponibilité envers le prochain.

d) Jésus présent : de l'Eucharistie
    - l'Église par ses prêtres
    - la famille par les parents
    - ceux qui souffrent

Bibliographical Works Related to the Cardinal and His Family

Bernet, Anne. *Monseigneur Thuan: Un évêque face au communisme.* Paris: Éd. Tallandier, 2018.

Gutiérrez de Cabiedes, Teresa. *Van Thuan: Libre derrière les barreaux.* Récit. Bruyères-le-Châtel: Éd. Nouvelle Cité, 2018. Translated from Spanish.

Le Thien Si, Anre. *Đấng Đáng Kính Đức Hồng Y Phanxicô Xaviê Nguyễn Văn Thuận (1928–2002).* Garden Grove, Calif.: Number One Graphic & Printing, 2012.

Melo, Louisa, and Waldery Hilgeman. *François-Xavier Nguyên Van Thuân: Uomo di speranza carità e gioia.* Messageri d'Amore (Blu). Turin: Éd. Velar, 2015.

Nguyen Van Chau, André. *A Lifetime in the Eye of the Storm: Ngo Dinh Thi Hiep, a Younger Sister of Late President Ngo Dinh Diem.* 2nd ed. Canyon Lake, Tex.: Erin Go Bragh Publishing, 2015.

———. *The Miracle of Hope: Francis Xavier Nguyen Van Thuan; Political Prisoner, Prophet of Peace.* Boston: Pauline Books and Media, 2003.

Nguyen Thi-Thu-Hong, Élisabeth, and Olivier de Roulhac, eds. *Two Lives, One Mission: Parallel Views.* Versailles: Amis de Van Éditions, 2018.

Phan Van Hien, Paul. *My Father, the Cardinal Francis Xavier Van Thuan as He Was in My Life.* Published by the author, 2006. Original in Vietnamese.

Scott, Helena, and Ethel Tolanksky. *Cardinal Nguyen Van Thuan.* CTS Biographies. London: Catholic Truth Society Publishing, 2017. Kindle.

Tien, Le. *Đức Hồng y Cười.* Private collection. California, 2017.

Velasco, Miguel Ángel. *La luz brilla en las Tinieblas: Cardenal Van Thuan: Historia de una esperanza.* Arcaduz. Madrid: Ed. Palabra, 2015.

Interviews with Nguyen Thi Thu Hong (Élisabeth)

This book contains interviews for Radio Maria (NL) from 2014 onward, as well as most of the interviews I had with Élisabeth during my two-week stay in Canada. Thanks to her, I was able to go through many unpublished documents. I also took notes on our exchanges during Élisabeth's annual visits to Europe, and she gave a long talk at the Onze Lieve Vrouw van het Fiat Monastery, of the Sisters of Bethlehem, the Assumption of the Virgin, and Saint Bruno (Opgrimbie, Belgium, 2015).

Élisabeth also gave me the text of two of her lectures:

- Conference, June 17, 2008, at the Forty-Ninth International Eucharistic Congress, Quebec, June 15–22, 2008
- National Eucharistic Congress, Cologne, June 5–9, 2013

The History and Culture of Vietnam

Blair, Anne E. *Lodge in Vietnam: A Patriot Abroad.* New Haven, Conn.: Yale University Press, 1995.

Boot, Max. *The Road Not Taken: Edward Lansdale and the American Tragedy in Vietnam.* New York: Liveright, 2018.

Cahn, Nguyen Van, and Earle Cooper. *Vietnam under Communism (1975–1982)*. Stanford, Cal.: Hoover Institution Press, 1985.

Currey, Cecil B. "Ngô Đình Cẩn". In Tucker, *Encyclopedia of the Vietnam War*.

———. "Ngô Đình Diệm, Overthrow of". In Tucker, *Encyclopedia of the Vietnam War*.

———. "Vô Nguyễn Giáp". In Tucker, *Encyclopedia of the Vietnam War*.

Devillers, Philippe. "Vietnam: Histoire". In *Encyclopædia Universalis*. Vol. 23. Paris: Encyclopædia Universalis, 1996.

Duong, Pham Cao. "Cuong Đề". In Tucker, *Encyclopedia of the Vietnam War*.

———. "Duy Tân". In Tucker, *Encyclopedia of the Vietnam War*.

———. "Huỳnh Phú Sổ". In Tucker, *Encyclopedia of the Vietnam War*.

Frame, Arthur T. "Ngô Đình Nhu". In Tucker, *Encyclopedia of the Vietnam War*.

———. "Ngô Đình Nhu, Madame (Trần Lệ Xuân)". In Tucker, *Encyclopedia of the Vietnam War*.

Head, William. "Ngô Đình Diệm". In Tucker, *Encyclopedia of the Vietnam War*.

Huard, Pierre, and Maurice Durand. *Connaissance du Việt Nam*. Paris: Éd. Imprimerie Nationale, 1954.

Jacobs, Seth. *Cold War Mandarin: Ngo Dinh Diem and the Origins of America's War in Vietnam, 1950-1963*. Lanham, Md.: Rowman and Littlefield, 2006.

Jones, Howard. *Death of a Generation: How the Assassination of Diem and JFK Prolonged the Vietnam War*. Oxford: Oxford University Press, 2003.

Miller, Edward. *Misalliance: Ngo Dinh Diem, the United States, and the Fate of South Vietnam.* Cambridge, Mass.: Harvard University Press, 2013.

Moyar, Mark. *Triumph Forsaken: The Vietnam War, 1954–1965.* New York: Cambridge University Press, 2010.

Namba, Chizuru. *Français et Japonais en Indochine (1940–1945): Colonisation, propagande et rivalité culturelle.* Paris: Éd. Karthala, 2012.

Newman, John. M. *JFK and Vietnam: Deception, Intrigue, and the Struggle for Power.* 2nd ed. New York: Warner Books, 2016.

Ngo-Dinh-Diem. *Quelques discours politiques importants du président.* Saigon: Présidence de la République du Vietnam, Service de Presse, 1956.

Nguyen, Élisabeth. *La famille asiatique, dépassée ou prophétique?* Une mission extraordinaire 18. Versailles: Éd. Amis de Van, 2014.

Nichols, Michael R. "Pham Van Đông". In Tucker, *Encyclopedia of the Vietnam War.*

———. "Tôn Thất Đính". In Tucker, *Encyclopedia of the Vietnam War.*

Nolting, Frederick. *From Trust to Tragedy: The Political Memoirs of Frederick Nolting, Kennedy's Ambassador to Diem's Vietnam.* New York: Praeger Publishers, 1988.

Power, Charlotte A. "Thích Trí Quang". In Tucker, *Encyclopedia of the Vietnam War.*

Rignac, Paul. *Ngo Dinh Diem: Une tragédie vietnamienne.* La chaussée d'Yvry: Éd. Atelier Fol'fer, 2018.

Ross, Rodney J., "Hòa Hao". In Tucker, *Encyclopedia of the Vietnam War.*

———. "Phan Bôi Châu". In Tucker, *Encyclopedia of the Vietnam War.*

Shaw, Geoffrey D.T. *The Lost Mandate of Heaven: The American Betrayal of Ngo Dinh Diem, President of Vietnam*. San Francisco: Ignatius Press, 2015.

Tana, Li. *Nguyễn Cochinchina: Southern Vietnam in the Seventeenth and Eighteenth Centuries*. Ithaca, N.Y.: Southeast Asia Program Publications, 1998.

Thao, Trinh Van. *L'école française en Indochine*. Hommes et Sociétés. Paris: Éd. Karthala, 1995.

Thi, Kim Phuc Phan. *Fire Road: The Napalm Girl's Journey through the Horrors of War to Faith, Forgiveness, and Peace*. Carol Stream, Ill.: Tyndale, 2017.

Trung, Ngo Ngoc. "Ngô Đình Khôi". In Tucker, *Encyclopedia of the Vietnam War*.

———. "Ngô Đình Luyện". In Tucker, *Encyclopedia of the Vietnam War*.

———. "Ngô Đình Thục". In Tucker, *Encyclopedia of the Vietnam War*.

Tucker, Spencer C., ed. *The Encyclopedia of the Vietnam War. A Political, Social, and Military History*. Oxford: Oxford University Press, 1988.

Viet, Nguyen Thi. *Việt Nam: Histoire d'une nation*. Paris: Éd. du Jubilé/Hachette, 2017.

Vo, Nghia M. *The Vietnamese Boat People, 1954 and 1975–1992*. Jefferson, N.C.: McFarland, 2006.

The History of Missions in Vietnam

Beckmann, Joachim. "La Congrégation de la Propagation de la Foi face à la politique internationale". In *Neue Zeitschrift für Missionswissenschaft* 19, no. 4 (1963): 241–71.

Buzelin, Françoise. *Des Instructions aux vicaires apostoliques (1659) à l'encyclique Maximum Illud (1919): Permanence et inflexions de la stratégie missionnaire du Saint-Siège.* Paris: Missions Étrangères, 2019.

Comby, Jean. *Deux mille ans d'évangélisation: Histoire de l'expansion chrétienne.* Bibliothèque d'histoire du christianisme 29. Paris: Éd. Desclée, 1992.

Deville, Raymond. *L'école française de spiritualité.* Bibliothèque d'histoire du christianisme 11. Paris: Éd. Desclée, 1987.

Fauconnet-Buzelin, Françoise. *Le père inconnu de la mission moderne: Pierre Lambert de la Motte, premier vicaire apostolique de Cochinchine (1624–1679).* Paris: Archives des Missions Étrangères, 2006.

Forest, Alain. *Les missionnaires français au Tonkin et au Siam (XVIIᵉ-XVIIIᵉ siècle): Analyse comparée d'un relatif succès et d'un échec total.* Vol. 1, *Histoires du Siam.* Vol. 2, *Histoires du Tonkin.* Vol. 3, *Organiser une Église, Convertir les infidèles.* Recherches asiatiques. Paris: Éd. L'Harmattan, 1998.

Fouques Duparc, Antoine. *Pierre Poncet, missionnaire au Vietnam (1932–1968): Lettres à sa Famille (1956–1968).* Églises d'Asie 19. Paris: Archives des Missions Étrangères, 2004.

Garcia, Luc. *Quand les missionnaires rencontraient les Vietnamiens (1920–1960).* Paris: Éd. Karthala, 2008.

Guennou, Jean. *Les Missions Étrangères de Paris.* Des chrétiens. Paris: Éd. Le Sarment-Fayard, 1986.

Keith, Charles. *Catholic Vietnam: A Church from Empire to Nation.* Berkeley: University of California Press, 2012.

Launay, Marcel, and Gérard Moussay. *Les Missions Étrangères. Trois siècles et demi d'histoire et d'aventure en Asie.* Paris: Éd. Perrin, 2008.

Lecleir, Stefaan. *Siméon-François Berneux (1814–1866): Missionsbischof und Märtyrer in Korea.* Cologne: Böhlau, 2000.

Mantienne, Frédéric. *Mgr Pierre Pigneaux: Évêque d'Adran; Dignitaire de Cochinchine.* Études et documents 8. Paris: Archives des Missions Étrangères, 1999.

Marmy, Émile. *Les grandes encycliques missionnaires, de Benoît XV à Jean XXIII.* Paris: Éd. Saint-Paul, 1964.

Moussay, Gérard, and Brigitte Appavou. *Répertoire des membres de la Société des Missions Étrangères (1659–2004): Ordre alphabétique suivi de l'ordre chronologique.* Paris: Archives des Missions Étrangères, 2004.

Oury, Guy-Mari. *Le Vietnam des Martyrs et des Saints.* Paris: Éd. Le Sarment-Fayard, 1988.

Pallu, François, and Pierre Lambert de la Motte, *Monita ad Missionarios: Instructions aux Missionnaires de la S. Congrégation de la Propagande, rédigées à Ayuthaya, Siam, en 1665.* Paris: Archives des Missions Étrangères, 2000.

Ramsay, Jacob. *Mandarins and Martyrs: The Church and the Nguyen Dynasty in Early Nineteenth-Century Vietnam.* Stanford, Cal.: Stanford University Press, 2008.

Tallon, Alain. *La Compagnie du Saint-Sacrement (1629–1667): Spiritualité et société.* Paris: Éd. du Cerf, 1990.

Thuan, Cao Huy. *Les Missionnaires et la politique coloniale française au Vietnam* (1857–1914). New Haven, Conn.: Yale Center for International and Area Studies, 1990.

Wei Tsing-sing, Louis. *La politique missionnaire de la France en Chine (1842–1856): L'ouverture des cinq ports chinois au commerce étranger et la liberté religieuse.* Paris: Nouvelles Éditions Latines, 1960.

The Paris Foreign Missions Society is a good source of information on the work of its missionaries in Asia (https://missionsetrangeres.com/?lang=en).

The Institut de recherche France-Asie (IRFA) includes the MEP archives, an Asian library, and a map library (https://www.irfa.paris/en/).

INDEX

Regular font: persons
*Italic: congregations, buildings,
institutions, titles of works,
and so forth*
Bold: places

Allys, Eugène-Marie-Joseph
  (1852–1936)
  Bishop of Hue (1908),
  239–40, 264
Am. *See* Nguyen Van Am
Amantes de la Croix
  The first native Vietnamese
  congregation, 22–23, 233, 290
An Ninh
  Formerly a minor seminary,
  situated in the modern-day
  village of Cua Tung, 25–31

Bach Mai
  Hospital in Hanoi, 102n37,
  143, 270
Bai. *See* Nguyen Huu Bai
Bao Dai (1913–1997)
  The last emperor, 198, 201,
  202n, 206, 208, 230, 242,
  243, 267
Binh. *See* Nguyen Van Binh
Binh Dinh
  Coastal province in the
  south-central area of the
  country where Khoi was
  governor, 187

Binh Thuan
  A major province in the
  southeast of the country
  where Diem was governor,
  55, 198
Binh Tuy
  Province in the South, 55
Bui Quang Tich (André,
  1895–1978)
  Vietnamese priest and
  teacher at An Ninh Minor
  Seminary, 30, 120
Buu Te (Jean-Baptiste)
  Member of the paternal side
  of the family, 98, 281

Can. *See* Ngo Dinh Can
Caodaism
  Main Vietnamese religion,
  101, 200n, 243n16
*Catholic Organization for the
  Reconstruction of Vietnam
  (COREV)*, 58, 85, 86
Cay Vong
  Parish west of Nha Trang
  and place of house arrest for
  Bishop Thuan (1975), 65n2,
  87–90, 109n, 128, 288, 298
Cellitinnen sisters
  Cellitinnen zur hl. Maria:
  congregation of sisters in the
  Diocese of Cologne whose
  convent maintains archives